Solitary Survivor

Also by Ron Martz:

Disposable Patriot: Revelations of a Soldier in America's Secret Wars (1993) with Jack Terrell

White Tigers: My Secret War in North Korea (1995) with Col. Ben S. Malcom, USA (Ret.)

SOLITARY SURVIVOR
The First American POW
in Southeast Asia

Col. Lawrence R. Bailey, Jr., USA (Ret.)

with Ron Martz

BRASSEY'S
Washington • London

Library of Congress Cataloging-in-Publication Data

Bailey, Lawrence R.
    Solitary survivor: the first American POW in Southeast Asia/
Lawrence R. Bailey, Jr., with Ron Martz.
        p.   cm.
    ISBN 1-57488-004-7
    1. Laos—Politics and government. 2. Bailey, Lawrence R.
3. Prisoners—Laos. 4. Prisons—Laos. 5. United States. Army—
Officers—Biography. I. Martz, Ron, 1947–   . II. Title.
DS555.8.B33   1995
959.704'37'092—dc20
[B]   95-19973

10 9 8 7 6 5 4 3 2 1

Printed in the United States of America

Dedications

To my family, for their prayers and love that helped carry me through my captivity, and to the men of Rose Bowl and their families, especially Ralph Magee, who saved my life without ever knowing it.

For my parents, Louis and Beatrice Martz, for their love and the courage to let me find my own way.

The purpose for separating us was quite evident, as the individual becomes a single animal fighting for survival, losing the ability to identify or associate with anything other than himself and basing his actions on his immediate needs.

—James N. Rowe
Five Years to Freedom

As prisoners of war, we knew full well that we could not withstand the ordeal of imprisonment by ourselves. Our instinct to identify with fellow Americans, our familiarity with the military chain of command and discipline, and our knowledge that we could have strength in numbers motivated us to unify. Alone we had no counsel, no power. Alone we despaired.

—Charlie Plumb
as told to Glen DeWerff
I'm No Hero

 **An AUSA Book**

The Association of the United States Army (AUSA) was founded in 1950 as a not-for-profit organization dedicated to education concerning the role of the U.S. Army, to providing material for military professional development, and to the promotion of proper recognition and appreciation of the profession of arms. Its constituencies include those who serve in the Army today, including Army National Guard, Army Reserve, and Army civilians, the retirees and veterans who have served in the past, and all their families. A large number of public-minded citizens and business leaders are also an important constituency. The association seeks to educate the public, elected and appointed officials, and leaders of the defense industry on crucial issues involving the adequacy of our national defense, particularly those issues affecting land warfare.

In 1988 the AUSA established within its existing organization a new entity known as the Institute of Land Warfare. Its purpose is to extend the educational work of the AUSA by sponsoring scholarly publications, to include books, monographs, and essays on key defense issues, as well as workshops and symposia. Among the volumes chosen for designation as "An AUSA Institute of Land Warfare Book" are both new texts and reprints of titles of enduring value that are no longer in print. Topics include history, policy issues, strategy, and tactics. Publication as an AUSA book does not necessarily indicate that the Association of the United States Army and the publisher agree with everything in the book, but does suggest that the AUSA and the publisher believe it will stimulate the thinking of AUSA members and others concerned about important issues.

Contents

Acknowledgments

Far too many people have encouraged me and supported me in writing this book for me to thank them individually, but I must single out a few for their special contributions.

First, I would like to thank my family and many friends, who waited and prayed and worried and hoped and never gave up their belief that I would survive the ordeal of my capture and imprisonment in a distant, unfriendly country and return home.

I would like to thank Bob Freeland for his friendship and guidance when I arrived in Laos in December 1960 and for kindly allowing me to use his photographs of those early events of the war in Southeast Asia, about which so few people in this country paid any attention.

I will never forget or be able to repay the wonderful treatment I received from the other POWs—Roger Ballenger, Lorenzo Frigilano, John McMorrow, Ed Shore, and Grant Wolfkill—when I arrived at Lat Huang after seventeen months in solitary confinement. Their humane and caring attention to my plight made a difficult adjustment much easier.

Special thanks go to my good friend Bill Lnenicka for his support and especially for his practical wisdom during our 1992 trip to Laos, which proved to be for me an intensely personal and emotional experience.

I would also like to thank my good friend and co-author, Ron Martz, who has been so loyal, patient, and encouraging during the research and writing of this book. While it is my story, Ron's writing skill, knowledge, persistence, and dedication have brought this story to life.

And I would especially like to thank my dear wife, Jean, without whose love and patient encouragement the writing of this book would not have been possible.

I pray that this book may answer some questions about the past and serve a useful purpose for all who read it.

Foreword

What makes a person a hero? Sacrifice? Bravery? Physical prowess? Courage? Certainly all of these play a part. But the most important attribute of every hero is strength—strength of character and strength of will. Bob Bailey has that strength. Bob Bailey is a hero.

In this book you'll read about Bob's distinguished record in three wars, about his struggle to survive despite crippling injuries as the first American prisoner of war in Southeast Asia, about his seventeen months in solitary confinement in a small, unlit Pathet Lao prison cell, and about his difficulties adjusting to life after captivity. You will also read about the triumph of the human spirit—his spirit—under incredibly adverse and dehumanizing conditions. You will read how this man, through his strength of character and will, through his belief in his God and his country, rose above the grim and primitive circumstances into which he was suddenly thrust.

Yet the fact is Bob Bailey was already a hero before going off to war. He was a hero to his parents, to his wife and family, because he had faced adversity—in school, in military training, in living life itself—and overcome it to succeed, just as he would later do as a POW.

Heroism isn't just "Horatio at the bridge." In a free society, heroism is every man and every woman every day doing the best they can. There is heroism in raising a child, in earning a living, and in doing the right thing for the community. All require personal strength and personal commitment. In our American civilization, personal strength is vital.

Personal strength can be defined as seven key aspects: integrity, courage, hard work, perseverance, discipline, responsibility, and respect for others. Integrity means behaving with honesty in the way you wish others would behave. It is at the core of a free society. To be free, you have to have courage. To listen to yourself and do what your inner self tells you to do, sometimes takes great courage. Perseverance is a result of discipline. Without the discipline to make the perseverance possible to do the hard work, it just doesn't happen. All of this grows out of a sense of responsibility. The Declaration of Independence notes that we are endowed with the right to pursue happiness. But that means you have the responsibility to exercise that right. Finally, you can't have a healthy society unless you have respect for others.

Integrity, courage, hard work, perseverance—and all the other factors that go into developing personal strength—are evident as Bob Bailey tells his story of growing up, going to war three times, and surviving the horror of being a prisoner of war in Southeast Asia. Bob Bailey was able to survive and triumph over his captors through a strength of will and character that was developed through a lifetime of building up a sense of personal strength that is still very evident today. In civilian life he has created a successful career and life for himself and his family, again demonstrating how personal strength can prevail over adverse circumstances.

I first met Bob through my political activities years ago. I was impressed then by his quiet strength and humility despite his military accomplishments. For years Bob has been there with his support, his integrity, his honesty, and his strength of character. When I began having town hall meetings in my new congressional district to listen to the concerns of the constituents the crowds were sometimes sparse. But invariably I would look up, and there would be Bob and his wife, Jean.

I have known for years that Bob was a POW in Southeast Asia. However, until I read this account of his captivity, I did not realize what he went through during those seventeen long, lonely months. Nor did I realize the uncertainty and fear his family went through during his captivity. *Solitary Survivor* also taught me a great deal about this period in America's history when Laos was such a serious foreign policy concern.

As a young man growing up in a military family, I know the sacrifices men like Bob are asked to make for their country. I know, too, the sacrifices their families make. In times of war, those sacrifices are even greater. Bob is a soldier of another era, a soldier of my father's era, when it was common for belief in country to be stronger than personal wants and needs. Like so many military men of this era, Bob volunteered to do his duty without complaint. And when he was captured, he relied on his belief in God, his faith in the United States and what it stands for, and on his personal strength of character developed as a young boy growing up in southern Georgia to see him through the dark days of his captivity.

Bob Bailey is a reminder to all of us of the kind of men this nation has produced through the years who freely give of themselves and their families when their country calls. All of America owes a debt of gratitude to its men and women in uniform. It owes an even greater debt to those who through no fault of their own have found themselves captives of the enemy but have kept the faith with their God, their country, and themselves. These men are heroes.

Solitary Survivor is a story about uncommon valor, unparalleled courage, and untiring personal strength. It is a story that teaches us to love life, love freedom, and love our country. It is a story about a true American hero, who, in the words of a great son, "more than self his country loved, and mercy more than life."

It is a story you will never forget.

—Newt Gingrich
Speaker
U.S. House of Representatives

Prologue

I close my eyes and see the cell. It rises slowly out of the blackness, gray and indistinct at first, as it was all those mornings so many years ago. The cell sits there behind my eyes, waiting to emerge, triggered by a smell or a sound or a random thought.

The cell is small, twelve feet east to west, fifteen feet north to south. The ceiling is no more than ten feet high. The walls are plaster, once white but now gray with grime. The floor is made of red tiles, each tile eight inches square. There are seventeen tiles east to west, twenty-three north to south.

In the southeast corner is a small fireplace. The door in the north wall is wired shut from the outside. In the east wall is a double window, with the glass knocked out and tin nailed over the frame. The tin flaps loose in the upper left corner, allowing thin streaks of gray light into the cell when there is sun. But from late afternoon to early morning I am shrouded in blackness so thick I can feel it pressing in on me.

For more than one year I lived in that dark, bleak cell in north-eastern Laos in a mountain village called Sam Neua, a prisoner of the Communist Pathet Lao. Now, the cell lives within me.

My cell was a vacuum, a place without light or life or hope. I was allowed no reading material, nothing with which to write, no way to occupy my mind. There were no other prisoners with whom I could communicate and no one to lean on for support, comfort, or guidance. I was alone, the only American held in that cell in that village at a time when few people at home knew a war had started in

Southeast Asia. I was a prisoner in a war that had not yet acquired form or substance or a name.

I was cut off from all outside stimuli. I could see little and was told nothing, and what I could hear and smell was an indistinct jumble of barking dogs, cackling chickens, and a singsong Lao language of which I knew just a few words.

I was treated with resigned indifference by young soldiers who knew as little about me as I knew about them. I suffered no beatings or physical torture, few overt threats, and no efforts to use me as a propaganda tool. There was nothing. I was stripped of everything I knew and held in total isolation for more than a year.

In that cold, dark void that was my cell, time was more than a burden. It became the enemy. I fought with time each day, trying not to be overwhelmed by its enormity and praying for something to happen that would speed its passage, that would make the seconds turn into minutes, the minutes into hours.

How long is forever? No longer than a day spent in that dark vacuum of a cell. How slowly does time move? Never more slowly than a minute spent in that cell waiting for something to happen.

When I received a telephone call in the fall of 1991 from a reporter for a small newspaper in Massachusetts, I saw the cell again and felt the slow, steady, unsympathetic tread of time that weighs so heavily on every prisoner of war.

"Are you the Lawrence R. Bailey Jr. who was on a C-47 shot down in Laos on March 23, 1961?" the reporter asked.

"Yes," I replied, curious that someone else would understand the significance of that date.

"Do you know they found the remains of the other men?"

I was stunned into silence. Eight of us had been on the C-47 on 23 March 1961 when it was hit by antiaircraft fire over the Plain of Jars in north-central Laos and crashed. I was the only one on board wearing a parachute, the only one who could make it to the door and jump before the plane began to break up. A wing burned away and fell off, and the plane dived straight into the ground, carrying seven good men to their deaths as I tumbled out the side door and survived. Now, thirty years after we were shot down, someone had located the bodies of the crew members and was bringing them home.

"How many did they find?" I asked.

"Four, but they only identified three."

"Who were they?"

"Ralph Magee, Leslie Sampson, and Frederick Garside. I'm interested in Garside. He was from Plymouth. Did you know him?"

Garside? I tried to think. Which one was he? The engineer? His assistant? The radio operator? I remembered Magee, the pilot, who had inadvertently saved my life by giving me, the senior officer on board, a choice of parachutes. I chose the least comfortable chute, one that had to be strapped on and worn at all times and the only one of its type on the plane.

I couldn't remember the others, crewmen on a plane on which I was a passenger, whose names and faces had long since been relegated to history's mists. I had had no reason to remember them until it was too late. The flight should have been like so many thousands of other flights I had taken in my career as an army aviator, the crew like so many other crews—seasoned, dependable, trustworthy young men doing the jobs their country asked them to do. Then we became a target of the Pathet Lao, and I became an unwilling and uncooperative guest of the Communists for seventeen months, the first American prisoner of war in Southeast Asia.

When I began researching this book, the Defense Intelligence Agency (DIA) confirmed what I had long suspected, that I was one of the first American POWs in Southeast Asia. The DIA uses a seven-digit numbering system (sometimes reduced to four digits) to keep track of the cases of Americans missing in Southeast Asia.

Case No. 0001 is that of Richard Fecteau and John T. Downey, the Central Intelligence Agency agents captured in China and held more than twenty years. Case No. 0002 was Charles Duffy, a State Department employee with the U.S. Overseas Mission in Vientiane, who disappeared in January 1961 while out hunting and was never seen again.

My case is No. 0003, specifically 0003-1-01. Those with me on the C-47 the day it was shot down are listed as No. 0004-1-01 through 0004-1-07. The names of those seven men—Alfons Bankowski, Frederick Garside, Ralph Magee, Glenn Matteson, Leslie Sampson, Edgar Weitkamp, and Oscar Weston—are on the first two lines of the first panel of the Vietnam Veterans Memorial in Washington. Only through the grace of God is my name not there with them.

The news of the discovery of the remains of the seven men gave me a sense of relief. For years their bodies lay in unmarked graves in a grassy field in north-central Laos near where the aircraft went down. Those men deserved to be buried at home, under their own flag, not in anonymous graves far from everything they held dear and everyone who loved them.

The news also set me on edge. The cell came back more vividly that night as I lay in bed. When I closed my eyes, I could see it more clearly than I had for years, almost as if I were there again, inside, trapped and hopeless and alone.

The idea of returning to Laos and trying to find the cell again began to gnaw at me. For the families of the crew members on the plane, the war was finally over, but as long as I carried that vision of the cell around in my head, I would never be rid of it. My war would never end. I realized I had to see the cell again, to open the windows and doors to the cell and let light flood the room to flush it clean of the memories that hold me there. Perhaps in the clear light of peace I could escape that cell's dark hold on me.

I also needed to see the country again and talk to the people. I spent twenty months in Laos from December 1960 to August 1962, long before most Americans knew where it was or how to say its name, but seventeen of those months had been as a prisoner of war, locked in that cell in the Pathet Lao headquarters of Sam Neua. I knew little about the country, the people, or what had happened in Laos since we gave up on the secret war and came home. I felt compelled to go back and complete the circle started more than thirty years earlier.

To understand how I was captured and why I was treated as I was requires knowledge of the political and military situation in Vientiane when I arrived in December 1960 to begin a year-long tour as assistant army attaché.

At the time, Vietnam was little more than a vague premonition to most military planners, and Cambodia had not yet emerged on their map of immediate concerns. Laos was the true flash point of Southeast Asia, ground zero of the long-awaited superpower confrontation. It was being squeezed from two sides, Vietnam and the Soviet Union from the east, Thailand and the United States from the west. With three factions vying for power in Laos in the late 1950s and early 1960s, the country has been described by Americans assigned there as the Land of Oz, Disneyland East, and Wonderland. It was even more bizarre than that.

Unfortunately, when the story of American involvement in Southeast Asia is told, the sacrifices of those who fought in the early stages of the war and the hardships suffered by those of us who became prisoners are often overlooked. It is almost as if what happened from 1960 to 1963 in Laos had no relevance to the wider war that emerged later in Vietnam and that those who died in Laos were mere victims of circumstance. My purpose here is not only to remember those men and, based on my own experiences, provide some historical perspective to the early days of the war in Southeast Asia, but also to give some sense of the uncertainty regarding American involvement there.

Nevertheless, the significance of my story is not what happened to me but rather what did not happen. My story is not one of dramatic escapes and rescues, of firefights and battles, of great armies surging at one another to gain control of territory. Mine is a story of loneliness, fear, and uncertainty, a story of my struggle against myself to maintain my sanity when suicide or madness sometimes seemed such easy and comfortable alternatives to what I was forced to endure in solitary confinement.

The mental torture of being left alone in a dark room may have been worse than any physical torture. Making time pass was such a constant, overwhelming struggle that at times it seemed not worth the effort. During those dark, lonely months, I realized how truly insignificant I was, a speck whose life or death would have little impact outside the circle of family and friends. With that realization, I became more comfortable with myself and with whatever fate might hold for me. Death would prove no burden for me. I could accept my own mortality. It was life with which I struggled.

Although writing this book has helped me better understand the political and military forces that contributed to my capture and confinement, it did not answer the question that lingers, the one question I cannot answer: "Why were you the only one who survived?"

Over the years I've asked myself that question many times, and over the years I've found no answer. In the end, though, I feel no guilt that I lived. For whatever reason, God's intent was that I not die that day, and God continued to smile on me for those seventeen long, dark, terrifying months of captivity in Sam Neua.

Now, not a day passes that I don't think of my captivity in that cell. Nor does a day pass that I do not cherish my freedom from it.

Solitary Survivor

LAOS

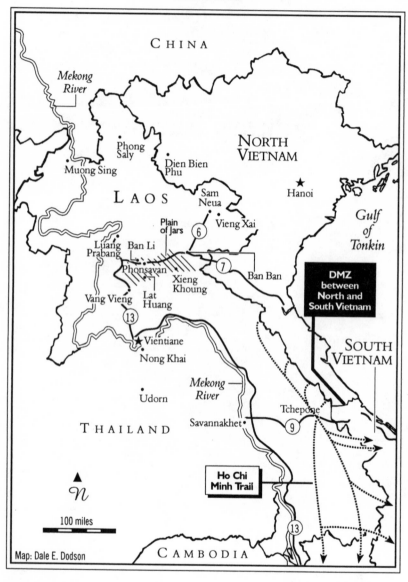

Map: Dale E. Dodson

1

Rose Bowl

Squinting into the crystalline brightness of a Southeast Asian morning, Ralph Magee emerged from the darkened interior of the C-47's cargo hold. The young air force lieutenant held a parachute in each hand. "Major," he said, smiling slightly, "we wear parachutes on these flights. You have a choice. Do you want a backpack or a chest pack?"

I hesitated for a moment. It had been some time since I had flown with a parachute. My own plane, a twin-engine Beechcraft L-23D assigned to the army attaché's office in Vientiane, where I was an assistant attaché, did not have parachutes and I had gotten out of the habit of wearing one. Besides, this flight from the Laotian capital to Saigon, with a slight detour over north-central Laos and the Plain of Jars, would be a milk run. A parachute seemed an unnecessary and uncomfortable precaution, even though Laos was embroiled in a messy and confusing civil war.

That morning, 23 March 1961, the war was in a period of ill-defined and inconsequential skirmishes far removed from those of us who worked in the capital. We had developed a false sense of security about the war and our roles in it. Still, "I'll take a backpack," I said with a shrug.

Magee, the aircraft commander, chuckled and handed me the rig. "I only have one of those on board and you're welcome to it," he said, as he disappeared back inside the C-47 and continued going through his preflight checks.

I took the bulky backpack chute with its confusing assortment of buckles, straps, and harnesses and began adjusting them to fit me. I pulled the straps tight around my legs to keep the chute from bouncing as I walked. I tightened the harness over my shoulders and squatted to check if it would be comfortable while I sat. Then I stood outside the plane in the morning sun, waiting for Magee to tell me to board.

The remainder of the chutes available on the C-47 that day were two-piece chest packs. I could sense the crew members were relieved that I had chosen the lone backpack. Chest packs were more comfortable. They required crew members to wear only the harness; the canopy was stowed where, in case of an emergency, it could be quickly grabbed and hooked onto the harness. None of the crew wanted to spend the next eight hours with that bulky backpack rig strapped to his butt, as I would do.

To this day my reasons for choosing that particular parachute remain a mystery to me, but the moment is forever etched in my memory. I think of it frequently and reexamine the moment for some explanation, which has never been forthcoming, or some understanding, which also has eluded me. That moment of decision is as clear now as it was then, only now there is an eternity between each of what seemed then to be a few inconsequential words between Magee and me. Now, during the moment of decision, I am suspended between life and death. I watch and listen again to my own words and Magee's and wait to hear myself make the wrong decision, waiting to hear myself choose death over life.

I hear Magee offering me a choice of parachutes, his face bright and cheerful and innocent. I feel my hesitancy over which one to pick, this seemingly inconsequential decision, with the morning sun warm on my back. Then, as always, I hear myself choosing life, telling Magee, "I'll take the backpack."

Perhaps I chose the backpack chute because I had used them on my B-29 missions during World War II, but perhaps that chute was chosen for me. I have never ruled out divine intervention. I know only that within a few hours my choice had become the most important single decision in my life. That simple, seemingly insignificant choice of a backpack parachute over a chest pack saved my life, and I am forever indebted to Magee for giving me the choice.

I glanced at my watch as Magee motioned us to board. It was shortly before ten. We would be in Saigon by 6:00 P.M., with any luck. The C-47's engines kicked to life with a throaty rattle, shaking the plane and sending out thick plumes of exhaust. Magee finished his instrument checks, and within minutes the plane with its six crew members and two passengers was rattling across the pierced steel planking that made up Wattay Airport's landing strip and hardstands.

I settled into a seat on the left side of the plane, just in front of the door but behind the trailing edge of the left wing, so I would have a good view of the countryside below. I had seen this part of Laos from the air numerous times over the previous three months, but the scenery, so beautiful and yet so potentially deadly, mesmerized me every time I flew over it.

I was an army artillery officer and pilot by training. My job as assistant attaché required both skills. One of my duties was to fly the American ambassador, Winthrop Brown, and members of the embassy staff throughout Laos, Thailand, and Vietnam to inspect military facilities. They, in turn, were to give Pentagon officials some sense of what was happening in the region. My most frequent passengers were my boss, Col. Joel Hollis, the army attaché for Laos, and his assistant, Maj. Robert Freeland.

The sturdy little L-23D assigned to our office was needed to travel around a country that had no railroads, very few passable roads, and a nineteenth-century communications system. Without that airplane, we were virtual prisoners in Vientiane. On this morning I was on my way to Saigon to retrieve the plane, where it was being fitted with a new engine and undergoing its hundred-hour inspection.

Across the aisle from me was the plane's other passenger, army WO Edgar Weitkamp, an administrative assistant in the attaché's office. Weitkamp, thirty-one, from York, Pennsylvania, was accompanying me to Saigon for several days of much-needed rest and relaxation.

Magee, a soft-spoken twenty-nine-year-old first lieutenant from Port Sulphur, Louisiana, was the pilot of the C-47; 1st Lt. Oscar Weston of Norfolk, Virginia, a big, square-jawed, thirty-year-old father of three, was the copilot. The navigator was 2d Lt. Glenn Matteson, a boyish-looking twenty-three-year-old from Dallas, Texas.

The remainder of the six-man air force crew included S.Sgt. Alfons Bankowski, thirty-one, of Stamford, Connecticut, the engineer; S.Sgt. Frederick Garside, twenty-four, of Plymouth, Massachusetts, the assistant engineer; and S.Sgt. Leslie Sampson, twenty-four, of Richey, Montana, the radio operator.[1]

Their faces are little more than a blur now; I had no reason to take notice of this crew on this morning. They were simply crew members doing their jobs, one crew among the thousands with whom I flew over the years. They smiled and went about their jobs quietly and professionally. Magee pushed the throttles forward, and the C-47 lumbered into the thick morning air. It skimmed the emerald rice paddies at the end of the runway before slowly gaining altitude and turning north for the Plain of Jars.

The morning was unusually clear and bright for late March in Laos. The sky was cloudless, and the usual dense clouds of choking gray smoke—a part of the spring ritual of premonsoon slashing and burning of vegetation to ready the fields for planting—were curiously absent. The spring smoke and haze in the skies over Laos often made navigation difficult, even in the best of weather, but this morning was different.

When the plane was airborne, two crew members lifted the cargo door behind me off its hinges and set up a large camera for aerial reconnaissance. This was no ordinary cargo plane, I had learned. This particular C-47 assigned to the air force attaché's office in Saigon was specially configured for aerial reconnaissance and communication intercepts. In addition to the special photographic equipment, the plane had radio direction-finding gear and extra fuel tanks. Its code name was Rose Bowl.

Rose Bowl had been flying over Laos for the previous two months, trying to get a fix on the civil war. It carried a camera known as a K-17 that photographed troop positions and equipment. The photos were passed to air force intelligence in Saigon for a preliminary assessment before they were sent on to the Pentagon.

The war was not going well for what remained of the Royal Lao government. It was being besieged internally by the Pathet Lao and a group of rebel paratroopers under the command of a short, feisty captain named Kong Le, who had occupied Vientiane for four months in late 1960. External pressures were coming from Vietnam, the Soviet Union, the United States, and Thailand.

We were making every effort to learn just how much outside assistance the combatants were actually receiving, but we were having great difficulty getting a good handle on it. We had sources in the field, but their information was often outdated by the time we received it. We also could count the Soviet cargo aircraft coming into Wattay Airport and the number of boxes they were unloading. We were never permitted close enough to find out exactly what was in those boxes, although obviously they contained weapons and ammunition.

Fighting was desultory and had settled into the Plain of Jars around Xieng Khoung, where two of the three factions—the Pathet Lao and the Neutralists—had formed an alliance backed by the Soviets and the North Vietnamese. The Pathet Lao were nominally under control of Prince Souphanouvong, a member of the royal family, but they were influenced greatly by the Viet Minh and Communist Chinese. What made the situation so confusing was that

Prince Souphanouvong's half-brother, Prince Souvanna Phouma, sided with Kong Le and the Neutralists, while enjoying the backing of some elements within the U.S. State Department. The Royal Lao, meanwhile, under Prince Boun Oum and Gen. Phoumi Nosavan, had CIA support, and the ambassador was feuding with other State Department officials and the CIA over which faction to back.

Rose Bowl had been sent in to supplement our human intelligence-gathering efforts. Crew members also were using the plane's sophisticated electronics equipment to try to locate a radio beacon that had been set up on the Plain of Jars to guide resupply aircraft into the airport at Xieng Khoung. The Soviets had openly brought in tons of arms and ammunition to the Neutralists through Wattay Airport in December, and we could do little but watch. This Soviet version of Air America (the CIA's proprietary airline that later in the war became the major cargo carrier for pro-Western forces) continued after the Neutralists took control of the Plain of Jars. Ilyushin-14s were making regular runs into the airstrip at Xieng Khoung, no matter what the weather. Even in the worst smoke and clouds, the IL-14s were able to locate the airport and drop through for a safe landing.

By the fourth week in March, the beacon still had not been pinpointed. Rose Bowl's crew needed some rest, and the plane needed maintenance not available at Wattay. The crew planned to make one last flight over the Plain of Jars on 23 March to search for the beacon and then head for Saigon and a party to be given that night for some members of the air attaché's office who were rotating home.

Our flight plan took us north from Vientiane, past the embattled village of Vang Vieng, before turning slightly east to the province of Xieng Khoung and the strategic Plain of Jars. From there we would turn south and fly along the border with Vietnam into Saigon.

All of us knew this region of Laos could be dangerous. We realized that being shot at somewhere along the line was a possibility. Americans were not yet considered combatants, however, and neither Kong Le's gunners nor those of the Pathet Lao had demonstrated proficiency in hitting aircraft with their heavy machine guns, the largest weapon available to them at the time. After the heavy flak I had flown through over Tokyo near the end of World War II, a few poorly aimed machine-gun rounds weren't going to bother me.

The only real threat to our C-47 was from radar-controlled antiaircraft weapons, but we believed neither side had any at that time. Unknown to us, the Vietnamese had begun moving antiaircraft weapons into the Plain of Jars shortly after the Neutralists and Pathet Lao joined forces.

We had been in the air little more than thirty minutes when I got out of my seat and waddled forward to the cockpit, the parachute clinging to my back like an uncomfortable growth. My pilot's eyes looked immediately to the fuel gauges and altimeter. The fuel looked fine, and we were cruising comfortably at eight thousand feet, an altitude we would maintain for the rest of the morning.[2]

"There's Vang Vieng," Magee shouted over the roar of the engines, pointing out the left side of the plane. I looked down and saw the familiar T-shaped landing strip and taxiway I had recently flown into in the L-23D.

As I stood between Magee and Weston, Magee motioned to someone and was handed two cups of water. Magee took one for himself and gave the other to Weston. The two looked at one another, smiled slightly, clinked their cups together, and took a sip. It was their salute to one another, as if to say, "Here's to you kid; let's get to work."

I felt as if I was intruding on this private ritual that they weren't even sharing with the rest of the crew. I quietly turned and walked back to my seat, allowing them their moment of privacy.

The plane droned on steadily and easily, moving to the northeast as the K-17 camera behind me clicked away. Below, the sparkling emerald rice paddies of the Mekong Valley gave way to the deeper, darker greens of old-growth trackless jungle and the stark, gray-white karst cliffs that separate the valley from the highlands. Finally, the rolling, scrub-covered hills told us we were over the Plain of Jars.

I glanced again at my watch. It was shortly before 11:00 A.M. I had eaten breakfast nearly five hours ago, and I was hungry. I had brought a sack lunch, prepared for me that morning by our Chinese cook, Ho, and stashed it at my feet. Although eleven was a bit early for lunch, I decided I was too hungry to wait.

I reached down for the sack and looked out the window. Below us a small grass airstrip marked the village of Phonsavan. Next to the runway was a metal building with a large red cross on top. I was puzzled by the marking. "Who has need for an aid station at the airport?" I asked myself. I had flown into that airport in a C-47 back in December with Lt. Col. Butler B. Toland, the air force attaché for Southeast Asia. I remembered the metal building, but not the red cross. The airstrip was still in friendly hands then. Now, it belonged to Kong Le's Neutralists and the Pathet Lao.

Just as I reached again for the brown paper sack at my feet I heard two loud explosions in rapid succession: Bam! Bam! The plane wobbled slightly, then righted itself. I looked over at Ed Weitkamp. He had a strange, puzzled look on his face. "They're shooting at us," he said, as if he couldn't believe anyone would do that.

"Are we hit?" I shouted.

One of the crew members passed us heading for the cockpit. "Yeah, right side, pretty bad," he said calmly.

I immediately got out of my seat and went to the right side of the plane, stooping to see out the small window. A hole about four feet in diameter showed in the outer wing panel. The metal was shredded and the U.S. Air Force star obliterated. Something large had hit us, possibly 37mm or 40mm antiaircraft fire.

The realization that we were under fire came as a shock. We had no intelligence, no indication, and no reason to believe that the forces in this area had large antiaircraft weapons or, if they did, that they knew how to use them.

That particular round had not caused any structural damage to the aircraft. Knowing the plane could still fly, I felt a wave of relief sweep over me. Magee was an experienced pilot in that aircraft and could easily nurse it back to Wattay.

I moved closer to the window to look at the number two engine, and my sense of relief vanished instantly. There was a second large hole in the wing, this one in the fuel cell directly behind the engine. Bright orange flames and black smoke were bubbling out of the hole, and molten metal was streaming past the window.

As a pilot I knew intuitively that that C-47 wasn't going to fly much longer. The fire was burning through the spar. When it did, the right wing would fold up and tear off, and the plane would roll over on its back and spin straight down into the ground. Rose Bowl was doomed.

I stared at the smoke and flames, fascinated and unable to take my eyes off the sight of our plane coming apart, even though in the back of my mind I knew that in only seconds the plane would begin its death spiral. Yet something held me there. The whole scene was so incomprehensible—the idea of being shot down in the middle of a war in which we weren't even combatants.

Finally, I pulled myself away. I turned and saw Weston, the copilot, coming out of the cockpit. He looked at me as if to say, "What's going on?"

"We're on fire! We've got to jump!" I shouted over the noise of the engines and the rush of wind through the cargo bay.

The crew members quickly scrambled forward for the parachute canopies stacked against the forward bulkhead. The interior of the C-47 became a maelstrom of shouts and hands clutching at the stack of canopies that were their only hope of survival. "Get me a chute!" one crew member yelled.

"Get me one too!" shouted another.

They clawed at the canopies, trying desperately to hook them onto the harnesses. There was nothing I could do to help them. One more set of hands, one more body added to the congestion, would only make matters worse. I knew what I had to do.

I dashed across the empty cargo bay and threw myself out the open door. The instant I stepped into space I felt the C-47 break into a violent spin to the right. The fire had burned through the spar and the right wing had come off. I didn't need to see it—I could feel it.

Had I hesitated even a second longer, I would have been thrown back inside and trapped there by the centrifugal force of the airplane spinning suddenly and violently out of control.

Something hit me hard on my left side. The acrid smell of flaming fuel and molten metal engulfed me. I was spinning, tumbling, falling through flame and smoke, as if I had jumped straight into the middle of hell. I had no sense of fear or death. It all happened too quickly. It was beyond my control. I gave myself over to gravity and fate.

Then, just as suddenly as I had fallen into the mass of fiery metal, I was falling through clear, clean air, free of the inferno.

Despite being battered by the airplane, I was still thinking clearly. My immediate concern was to open the parachute, which I had to do quickly or become a bloody blob on the green fields below. I reached for the D-ring. I couldn't find it. An instantaneous surge of fear and panic swept through me.

I reached again and felt the fingers of my right hand curl around the ring. I pulled, nothing happened. I pulled harder. Finally, the chute popped out. There was a merciful jolt as the canopy filled with air and my descent slowed. I looked up and saw a marvelous white halo blossoming above me with rustles and pops. I had a good chute.

As soon as the chute opened, I began to assess my situation. My left arm was flopping around uncontrollably. I tried to pull it in but couldn't. It was dancing around up in the risers as if it had a mind of its own. I realized the arm was broken. Although I felt no pain, I couldn't control the arm. I didn't know what other injuries I might have suffered when the airplane rolled over on me, but I knew I had been knocked around pretty good.

I turned my attention to the C-47, which was making a terrible howling sound as it fell. I could hear it, but I couldn't see it. I looked above me and around me, but I couldn't see the plane or any other chutes. Finally, I looked almost straight down and saw the plane beneath me in a wild, corkscrew spin heading into the ground, with its engines still running at cruise power.

I was so low by then that I didn't actually see the plane hit because it dropped behind some low, scrub-covered hills, but I heard the impact and immediately saw a plume of black smoke. I scanned the skies again and still saw no other chutes. The other seven men on the plane, I knew, were dead. No one else could have escaped that out-of-control inferno.

I turned my attention to my own predicament. I could not steer the chute because of my broken left arm. For a moment I thought I might come down right in the middle of the burning C-47. But a slight breeze carried me east into an area of low, rolling hills.

Directly beneath me were about ten water buffalo grazing contentedly on the lush green grass. When I was just a few feet off the ground, one of them apparently heard the rustling of my parachute, looked up, and was startled by what he saw. He ran off, and the others followed in a slow, lumbering stampede.

I hit the ground hard, feet first, and toppled onto my back. I lay stunned for a moment, gasping for air with the wind knocked out of me. When I regained my breath, I sat up and looked around. I was in a flat, grassy field, surrounded by low hills studded with clumps of pine trees. There were no signs of civilization—no houses, no roads, no people.

My mind was a jumble. The shock of the shootdown had left me dazed. Only a few minutes earlier, I had been flying comfortably at eight thousand feet, contemplating lunch, and thinking of dinner that night in Saigon. Now I was alone, the only survivor from the aircraft. The plane was a burning hulk over a hill to the west, beyond my sight.

I closed my eyes and tried to shut out the pain in my legs. What was I to do? I needed to get organized. Think, Bailey; stay in control of yourself. I breathed deeply, trying to regroup.

I decided to shed the parachute so the wind wouldn't drag me, even though it was light and the canopy lay on the ground like a large discarded handkerchief. I had a great deal of difficulty unhooking the harness because I had only my right hand to work with. The left was useless.

Once out of the parachute, I scanned the horizon for smoke from the crash. I could see it rising from behind a low hill about a mile to the west. I wanted to get closer. The plane was my only contact with the outside world, and I knew the closer I was to the plane, the better my chances of being rescued.

I was having great difficulty moving, however. Not only was my arm broken but my lower legs, ankles, and feet were badly bruised and cut. I struggled awkwardly to my feet and took a few steps. A current of pain shot up through each leg, merging and exploding behind my eyes in a white-hot flash.

Gasping and sweating, I fell back to the ground, my face twisted with pain. I couldn't walk, and I was hurt much worse than I thought. Still, I refused to accept the realization that I was incapacitated. I needed to get out of there. I needed to be anywhere other than where I was. Suddenly, getting to that burning airplane seemed the most important thing in the world. If I couldn't walk, I thought I might be able to crawl to the plane. It would take a while, but I was determined to get there.

I scanned the terrain and tried to find the easiest route. If I crawled south, I would eventually come to a low ridgeline that I could follow around to the west by keeping the smoke in sight until I came to the wreckage. But crawling proved as futile as walking. I couldn't use my legs for leverage, and my one good arm couldn't drag me that distance.

I lay back in the grass in frustration and disgust, trying to organize my thoughts. I had always been precise in my planning and meticulous in my preparation. Previous combat situations had taught me to expect the unexpected and to be prepared for anything, but getting shot down was the last thing I expected when we took off that morning. I was not ready for what had happened, and my mind was a blur as I tried to sort out the possibilities and come up with a plan.

In addition to the pain, I now had a raw, grating frustration that I had not been able to do more, either for myself or for the other men on the plane. I was trapped by my injuries, isolated by the circumstances, and unable to defend myself or escape.

I desperately wanted a cigarette. I searched my pockets and found a pack of Camels that somehow had survived my exit from the C-47. But my lighter had parted company with me somewhere on the way down, and I had no matches. I gave up on the cigarettes and did a quick inventory of my belongings. I had been carrying my passport, a fountain pen, and some cards in my shirt pocket, in addition to the cigarettes. Everything but the cigarettes had disappeared.

I glanced down to check my watch and found it also was gone. Without time, there was no structure to the day; without time, there was no order to things. That watch, taken for granted minutes earlier, suddenly seemed the most important thing in the world.

I glumly continued my inventory. I still had my wallet, a handkerchief, and a pocketknife given to me as an early Christmas present by my youngest daughter, Elaine, just before I left for Laos. With the pocketknife I could cut some of the parachute's shroud lines and fashion a crude splint for my arm. I knew I needed to immobilize the arm to reduce the chances of additional injury to it.

I slowly inched my way back to the parachute and cut away several of the shroud lines. I wrapped the lines around my left arm, pulled the arm against my body, and then wrapped the lines around my body. The longer I worked, the more frustrated I became. I was already angry and frustrated—angry that seven good men had died suddenly and violently in a strange war so far from home, and frustrated that I had no control over the situation.

This shouldn't have happened, I kept telling myself. The military forces in this area were not supposed to have sophisticated antiaircraft weapons, but antiaircraft artillery, most likely radar-guided, had downed us. Someone had upped the ante in this war, and we had become the first victims of the escalation.

With only one good hand, fashioning the crude splint was a long, slow process. When I finished, I was nearly exhausted. However sloppy the job, the splint would serve to keep what seemed to be a simple fracture in my left arm from becoming much worse.

I lay back in the grass, trying to figure out what to do next. I couldn't walk, I couldn't crawl, and I had only one good arm. My survival gear consisted of a pack of Camels, a handkerchief, and a pocketknife. To survive, I would have to be found and helped because I couldn't help myself.

I was terribly thirsty and the pain in my arm and legs was getting worse. Despite that, I couldn't help but think how warm and pleasant it was lying there in the grass, the blue sky now suddenly so peaceful. A few water buffalo grazed nearby. A light wind ruffled the grass.

I don't know how long I lay there before I heard the unmistakable sound of a low-flying airplane. It was flying a search pattern, looking for the wreckage of the C-47 or for me. When it came into view just above the tops of the low hills, I could see it was a DeHavilland L-20 Beaver, a single-engine, high-wing aircraft. I had spent many hours flying Beavers. At that moment I would have given anything to change places with that pilot.

The plane stayed low to the ground to the west, and there was no indication that the pilot saw me or my chute. After a few minutes, the comforting sound of that engine faded away, and I was alone again. All I could hear was the wind rustling in the grass. I felt more alone and helpless than I'd ever felt before.

Within a few minutes of the airplane's departure, I heard what sounded like gunshots from the direction of the crash site. I couldn't tell if someone was shooting or if rounds from the two M-1 carbines and the flare pistol stored on board were cooking off. The shooting stopped as quickly as it started, and the quiet returned.

I continued to watch the top of the hill between me and the crash site, hoping to see someone coming over the top. Surely the pilot of that search plane must have seen the smoke and the wreckage, and someone must have seen my parachute as I came down.

But there was nothing except the plume of black smoke and the long grass swaying in the breeze. The minutes passed slowly, the shadows of the pine trees on the hills around me beginning to lengthen. I glanced down again, looking for the watch that was not there, searching for some structure in a day that had exploded in uncertainty around me. Time slowed to an agonizing crawl as the pain increased.

It was midafternoon before I finally heard voices. People were shouting at one another. I couldn't tell what language they were speaking or what direction they were coming from. I sat up and looked to the south. About a dozen soldiers were advancing over the ridgeline, moving quickly, searching for something, shouting to one another, and firing their weapons at random. As they reached the ridgeline, they paused, looked around, and moved on. They were too far away to tell if they were friendly, but they appeared quite excited about something. I figured they were looking for me.

I didn't want to prolong my situation. I couldn't run with my injured legs and broken arm. I couldn't hide in this open country. I couldn't defend myself with a pocketknife. Escape and resistance were out of the question, and a futile gesture made no sense. I knew I needed medical attention, and these people, whoever they were, were my only chance. I didn't know—and at that point didn't care—if they were friendly. If I lay in that field without medical attention, I would die. My only hope was to give myself up.

When the search party got within about a quarter-mile, I yelled as loudly as I could, "Hey, you!" The soldiers froze in place, startled at the sound of my voice. They looked at one another and then came rushing toward me, their rifles ready. When they got within fifty or sixty feet, they stopped again.

My heart sank when I saw their uniforms. The soldiers wore American-issue olive drab fatigues, and most carried American-made M-1 carbines and .45-caliber pistols. They were soldiers of the Neutralist forces of Capt. Kong Le. Despite being armed and supplied by the United States, they had cast their lot with the Pathet Lao. I had parachuted right into the middle of enemy territory.

One soldier, who appeared to be the patrol leader, held up his hands, indicating I should surrender. I pointed at my left arm and shouted, "It's broke! It's broke!" My limited knowledge of the Lao language did not include that particular phrase.

He motioned again, this time more emphatically, for me to surrender. Again I held up my right arm, pointed to my left, and shouted, "It's broke! It's broke!"

The patrol did not move. Slowly, the leader raised his M-1 carbine and pointed it in my direction. How strange, I thought, as I stared down the barrel of that weapon, to be killed by an American weapon in a civil war that few people in the United States knew anything about.

The soldier fired once, the round cracking over my head. Lao soldiers were notorious for their poor marksmanship, but nobody was this bad. I figured his intention was not to hit me, just to scare me into raising my hands and surrendering, but I couldn't raise my left arm. In frustration I said to myself, "The hell with this" and collapsed on the ground. "You guys come get me," I muttered under my breath.

The patrol moved forward, slowly and cautiously, weapons pointed in my direction. The soldiers were young, probably in their late teens or early twenties. They appeared more frightened of me than I was of them. I felt no fear, only anger, frustration, and pain. The leader jabbed his rifle toward me and shouted excitedly in English, "Can kill! Can kill!"

I pointed to my arm again and said, "It's broken."

"Can kill!" he said, his voice shrill and his eyes wide. I said nothing and pointed to my arm again. Finally, he realized I had tied my left arm to my body and was no threat. The patrol members relaxed slightly and moved closer. The leader said something, and instantly a dozen hands were rifling through my pockets and pulling off my shoes. They talked excitedly among themselves in Lao, giggled and showed off their treasures to one another. They took my wallet, my cigarettes, my pocketknife, and my shoes. I was left with only my clothes and the handkerchief.

Their looting finished, the soldiers stepped back from me and raised their rifles again. The leader motioned for me to get up and go with them. I was their prisoner.[3]

2

Prisoner of War or Prisoner of Politics?

I swam slowly out of a drug-induced daze, my mouth dry, my lips cracked. I desperately needed a drink of water. I was lying on a military cot in a small building made of corrugated metal. The building smelled vaguely of medicinal alcohol and antiseptic and appeared to be a clinic. The pain in my legs and broken left arm had been knocked down to a dull throb by medication, but I found myself unable to move.

My left arm and upper torso were locked in a cast, the arm at a forty-five-degree angle from my body, held there by a brace and a strap over the shoulder. I could move only my head and right arm. My legs had been washed, and some type of salve had been applied to the wounds, but they were raw, deeply bruised, and unable to support me.

My clothing had been removed, and I was wearing a pair of pajamas with a blue top and white bottoms. Someone had thrown a blanket over me to ward off the night chill, a simple gesture that touched me. But I was truly helpless now, at the mercy of my captors.

The treatment at the clinic was the first measure of compassion I had received since the shootdown the previous day. The soldiers in the patrol who had found me had no concern for my injuries. They were upset that I was unable to walk and argued among themselves about how to transport me. The patrol leader finally ordered one soldier to carry me on his back. I was five-foot-nine and 185 pounds, a full nine inches taller and eighty-five pounds heavier than this soldier, and I knew this method of transport would not work as soon as he hoisted me onto his back. We had gone only a few meters before the pain became too great and I tripped him, both of us falling by the trail in a gasping, sweaty heap.

I saved the patrol a great deal of exertion and myself untold pain by convincing the soldiers to make a stretcher out of my parachute. I had to demonstrate this simple solution by pantomime because my knowledge of Lao was as limited as the soldiers' knowledge of English. I took out my handkerchief, placed it on my chest, and folded it into a rectangle. The soldiers watched, almost hypnotized, as if I were performing a magic trick. When I placed two sticks along each side of the handkerchief and pointed back to the parachute, the soldiers immediately recognized what I was trying to tell them. Within minutes they had gathered up the canopy and chopped down two stout saplings to serve as poles.

Several grueling, tortuous hours later, during which I was first carried by members of the patrol, then transferred to the back of a jeep, and later moved to an ambulance, I was taken to the medical clinic. It was the metal building emblazoned with a large red cross at the Phonsavan airport that I had seen from the air shortly before the shootdown.

My injuries were not life-threatening, but they were serious enough to warrant the full attention of the medical personnel who attended me, all of whom claimed to be Vietnamese doctors. They gathered around me when I arrived, as curious about me as I was frightened of them. My apprehension over being treated by them, coupled with the pain, made me somewhat belligerent.

"Can you fix this broken arm? Can you fix?" I demanded loudly, almost shouting, as I pointed at the arm. It was the voice of fear speaking in the face of great odds, not courage.

"Yes, we can fix," one of the Vietnamese said soothingly in excellent English. His voice calmed me. The Vietnamese continued talking, as a good doctor does to soothe a nervous, frightened patient. He said he and several others had been sent to establish this clinic and provide medical aid for soldiers and wounded civilians in the region. He gave no indication that I was anything other than a patient. To him, I was not a prisoner of war, hostage, or criminal. I was simply a man in need of medical attention.

"We are International Red Cross," he said quietly. The Vietnamese carried me to a cot and lifted me onto it. Suddenly, the shock and stress of what had happened caught up with me. Waves of nausea swept over me. I tried to suppress them but could not. I vomited violently, spraying the Vietnamese and the clean sheets with the pungent remains of my breakfast.

I was so exhausted and so racked with pain that I was unable to feel any embarrassment. The Vietnamese seemed unfazed by my sudden loss of control; he quickly and quietly cleaned me and the bed and began tending to my injuries. A drip bottle with a clear solution I assumed was saline was inserted into my left ankle. A box of plaster of paris was held up for my inspection before one of the Vietnamese began mixing it with water in a large bowl. Someone gave me a shot, and I fell into a blessed, painless void for the rest of the night.

Now, in the cold, dim light of morning, the gravity of my situation began to sink in. I was a prisoner, but a prisoner of what? A prisoner of war? A prisoner of politics? A hostage? And just which group was it that held me prisoner? The Neutralists, who had captured me? The Pathet Lao, who controlled the Plain of Jars and the Neutralists? The Vietnamese, who controlled them both? The answers were not readily apparent.

As I made some effort to clarify the situation and find some order in the chaos, the English-speaking Vietnamese doctor returned to check on the cast and the wounds on my legs. He was a pleasant-looking young man whose face bore no traces of animosity. He performed his duties with a thoroughness that impressed me and made me feel more at ease with my condition. "My country has been at war here for a long time," he said wistfully as he worked, a faraway look in his eyes. "I wish it would end. I want to go home."

I looked at him and nodded. I wanted to reach out and shake his hand, for there was an instant bond between us, an understanding between two soldiers far from home caught up in a war not of our making. "Yes," I said quietly, unable to say more.

I wanted to ask him who was running the show here, who was in charge, but his demeanor gave me the impression that the Vietnamese medical personnel had no control over their own destinies and certainly would have little knowledge of the military and political factors that would govern the fate of this lone American who had fallen into their hands.

The situation became even more muddled later in the morning when three military men came into the clinic. They began clearing it of all medical personnel and rearranging furniture for the first of what would be a series of formal interrogations. It was an elaborate demonstration designed to impress me. I was interested, but hardly impressed.

Two of the men were small and hard-looking. They wore the tan uniforms of the Pathet Lao. As was customary with the Pathet Lao, their uniforms had no insignia to indicate their ranks, although I guessed these two were high-ranking officers by the looks on their faces and the deference with which the other soldier treated them.

The third soldier was dressed in the American green fatigues favored by the Neutralist forces. He wore the insignia of a first lieutenant, and I recognized him as the officer I encountered after the shootdown, just before the search party loaded me on a jeep. He interrogated me briefly at that time, in reasonably good English, as he examined the contents of my wallet and took a long, hard look at my military identification card.

I learned later that his name was 1st Lt. Sabab Bounyavong. A former member of the Royal Lao Army, he had worked in government intelligence before siding with Kong Le and the Neutralists. He had served as a liaison officer to American military advisers and seemed to know as much about the U.S. embassy and the other assistant army attaché, Bob Freeland, as I did. For that first interrogation, he served as an interpreter for the two Pathet Lao officers, who obviously controlled the interrogation and my fate.

"Who are you?" Lieutenant Sabab asked.

"Major Lawrence R. Bailey Jr., United States Army," I said, feeling somewhat foolish because they already knew that from my identification card.

"Why have you come here?"

"I was on the airplane you people shot down yesterday," I replied.

"Where were you going?"

"The airplane belongs to the air attaché's office. We were returning it to him."

"How many Americans are in Laos?"

"I don't know."

"What are their jobs?"

"I don't know."

"What are their ranks?"

"I don't know."

"Where are the Royal Lao Army forces of General Phoumi Nosavan?"

"I don't know."

"When do Phoumi's forces plan to attack?"

"I don't know."

The answer seemed to anger the two Pathet Lao interrogators. They spoke to one another, shuffled the papers in front of them, and then spoke in Lao to Lieutenant Sabab.

"You know well these things," he said, a touch of frustration in his voice. "You are an attaché. It is your job to know these things."

At last they had recognized my status as a diplomat. That gave me an opening. I was wearing civilian clothes at the time of my capture, as did most American military personnel in Laos at the time, and I thought if I could convince them I was a diplomat, I would have a better chance of a quick repatriation.

I wanted to believe that technically I was not a prisoner of war. As a POW, my captors were likely to be far less lenient than they would be with a diplomat. The Pathet Lao knew the problems they might encounter with the United States by provoking an international incident involving a diplomat. Negotiations over the future of their country were at a delicate stage, and I did not think they would do anything to jeopardize their position in the bargaining.

Still, the question remained, Did anyone other than these people know I was still alive? By that time the plane was nearly a full day overdue in Saigon. Message traffic between the embassy there and Vientiane would be thick and fast, inquiring about the fate of the C-47 and its crew and passengers.

If it was known that I was alive, the Pathet Lao could have major diplomatic problems on their hands, but if there was uncertainty as to the fate of the passengers and crew, as there was, my captors would hold the upper hand and I would have to fend for myself. There would be no outside pressure to free me. I could easily slip unnoticed into the black hole of captivity and never be seen again.

Claiming to be a diplomat and invoking diplomatic immunity seemed to be the most prudent course at that point, but in doing so, I would have to forgo the standard "name, rank, and serial number" restrictions of the POW Code of Conduct. I would have to appear to be going beyond those restrictions without really doing so. I had to adopt an attitude that asked, How can I be a prisoner of war when my country isn't at war with these people?

I was concerned that I might divulge classified information about the extent of American involvement in Laos at the time because I did not know how adept my interrogators were. I did not know whether they had the expertise the North Koreans and Chinese had demonstrated during the Korean War. If they did, I could be in for trouble because I had had no formal training on how to handle myself as a POW in World War II, Korea, or since then. There were definite shortcomings in training for that possibility, and I made a mental note to tell someone if I ever got out of there. At that point, however, the chances of a quick release seemed remote.

Thankfully for me, my interrogators were not particularly adept. They obviously had not done this job before and had no real sense of what they were doing. That made it easier for me to dance around their questions, which often were so ludicrous that I nearly laughed.

One of their favorite questions concerned the number of ships in the U.S. Seventh Fleet. They kept insisting I was in a position to know not only where the fleet was but also how many ships were in it.

"Where is the Seventh Fleet?" Lieutenant Sabab asked.

"I don't know," I said.

"Where will Phoumi's forces attack from?" he asked again.

"When there are military operations, the only way we can get information is from the foreign office," I said. "They put out releases which go in the newsreels. This is the only source of information we have on military operations."

The two Lao officers muttered among themselves and then spoke to Lieutenant Sabab. He turned to me and, with a look that spoke more of frustration than of malice, said, "If you do not cooperate, we will kill you."

The prospect did not particularly frighten me at that point. I was already trussed up like a hog ready for slaughter and still woozy from the painkillers and shock of the shootdown. I figured I had cheated fate once already by escaping the plane before it crashed. Death at that moment seemed little more than destiny catching up with me.

"Listen," I replied with some exasperation. "I have diplomatic immunity. I am a major in the United States Army assigned to the American embassy as an assistant attaché by the invitation of your government. I don't know the answers to those questions."

The interrogation developed into a cat-and-mouse game. I was not belligerent, but neither was I cooperative. I was argumentative and elusive, which confused and frustrated the interrogators, amateurs that they were. Had I been subjected to more professional interrogations, I'm not sure how well I would have handled it.

These guys were new at the job, however, and confusing them was relatively easy. If they asked me one question, I'd answer another. If they strayed into areas I didn't want to talk about, I'd try to lead them in another direction. I was trying to avoid more detailed questioning that touched on classified information, something I was determined to keep from them at all costs.

Finally, after more conferring with the Pathet Lao, Lieutenant Sabab turned to me and said, "Now, I'm going to see your friend, Lieutenant Magee, and I will compare your answers to his."

I was stunned for a moment. Had Magee survived the crash? I waited impatiently, hoping to see him alive again, hoping that it was true, and hoping that I was not alone in this. There had been a similar flicker of hope shortly after the shootdown, when Lieutenant Sabab was inspecting my wallet. Another soldier walked up and handed him a second wallet. When he opened it, I could clearly see Ed Weitkamp's military ID card. Neither the card nor the wallet appeared to have been burned.

Had Weitkamp gotten out the plane? Had he somehow survived, even though I saw no other parachutes on the way down? I wanted desperately to believe I was not the only survivor and that I would have someone else to lean on during my captivity.

Weeks later, after I had been transferred to a prison cell, an English-speaking Pathet Lao soldier told me he had been in Xieng Khoung at the time of the crash and that one other person had managed to get out of the aircraft before it crashed. That person had been too close to the ground, however, and his chute failed to open in time to save him. I surmised it was Weitkamp, if the guard's story was true. The crew's training would have dictated preparing the passengers to jump before they did. Because I was the first out of the plane, Weitkamp would have been second. If he had, in fact, gotten to the door and been able to jump before the plane hit, then his wallet would not have burned.

There was never any evidence that anyone else survived the crash. At one point during my stay at the clinic in Phonsavan, Lieutenant Sabab told me what I believed to be the truth. "You are very lucky," he said. "All your friends are dead. I have seen. I am truly sorry."

At the end of that first day, Lieutenant Sabab handed me a neatly typed document in Lao and English. The English version stated I had been operated on and the bodies of the other seven Americans were being taken care of. There was nothing incriminating in the document, and I thought it might be an opportunity, if it got into hands on the other side, to let my government and my family know that I was still alive. I signed without hesitation.

Over the next six days, a semblance of routine evolved. I was given a mixture of water and Russian condensed milk to drink several times a day, but there was no solid food, not even rice. Once or twice I was offered some sort of soup, but I had difficulty choking it down. The meager ration of milk was taken away at one point for what the interrogators said was punishment for not cooperating, but it was resumed the next day.

I was allowed to sleep at night. I was given medical treatment when needed and medicine to ease the pain. Except for the daily interrogations, I continued to be treated more like a medical patient than a prisoner of war or a political prisoner.

Still, it was clear my captors considered me a special trophy. They were intent on keeping me alive because I was important to them and their propaganda machine. I was, in their eyes, the first evidence of American involvement in their civil war.

To document my captivity and to demonstrate the beneficence of the socialist soldiers to their enemies, I was photographed and filmed several times during those first few days. Twice on the day of the shootdown, the ambulance transporting me to the clinic stopped in villages, the back doors were opened, and photographers, still and video, crowded around to get pictures of the captured American.[1]

A more elaborate photo session was held on 26 March, the third day of captivity. Several people came into the clinic and began cleaning up. Fresh sheets were thrown over one crude table, and I was placed on top of it. A female nurse came into the room with one of the Vietnamese who had set my arm. Both wore fresh hospital gowns, and the man also wore a surgical mask.

Once the stage was set, about a half-dozen photographers with still and movie cameras were ushered in. The medical people went through the motions of examining me, taking my temperature and pulse, and using the stethoscope to check my heartbeat as the cameras clicked away. It was a blatant propaganda show, intended to demonstrate to the world how well the Pathet Lao treated their enemies. The Viet Cong did the same thing with its first few prisoners in an effort to convince the world they were the good guys and we were not.

One of those 26 March 1961 photos taken in the clinic eventually found its way into the DIA files. It became known as photo No. 109 among the thousands of photos of prisoners and missing Americans that emerged from Southeast Asia over the next fourteen years. The grainy black-and-white photo shows me lying on my back, with my left arm in a cast, and looking dazed and badly in need of a shave.

The daily interrogations helped me establish a routine and provided some order in the chaotic surroundings. I always knew when the interrogations were about to begin because the two Pathet Lao officers and Lieutenant Sabab would stride officiously into the clinic and begin rearranging furniture.

One day, the routine changed abruptly. They came storming into the clinic and dispensed with the usual formalities. "Was your airplane armed?" Lieutenant Sabab loudly demanded.

"We were an unarmed transport," I said, surprised at the sudden change in tactics. "We had no weapons."

Lieutenant Sabab motioned to another soldier, who was carrying a piece of tarpaulin. He unwrapped it and dumped on the floor several pieces of burned, twisted metal, which appeared to be the remains of the two M-1 carbines, the flare pistol, and some cameras from the C-47. "You lie!" Lieutenant Sabab screamed. "Here is proof! Here are the arms that were on your airplane!"

"That does not constitute an armed airplane," I said hotly. "That was for protection in case we went down in the jungle."

"You lie!" Lieutenant Sabab's voice became a screech, the

heavily accented English almost indecipherable in his rage. He continued to insist that Rose Bowl was an armed aircraft. I continued to deny it without losing my composure.

"You lie!" he screamed again.

"I am not lying. It is the truth," I said evenly. The calmer I became, the more incensed Lieutenant Sabab and the two Pathet Lao officers became. I was firm without being bellicose or frightened, which seemed to annoy them even more. When it became apparent that none of the shouts or threats was going to have an effect on me, the soldiers were ordered to gather up the charred pieces of metal, and the group stomped out of the clinic.

The hostile confrontation had failed, so they tried a subtler approach. One night, five people were ushered into the clinic and set up chairs in a semicircle around my bed. Their spokesman and interpreter was a young, smiling Chinese man who said he was from the New China News Agency. He pointed to several of the others and said they belonged to a Chinese youth group. I assumed the spokesman was a journalist and the others members of some Communist youth group. "We have come to interview you," the interpreter said. I smiled and nodded at them. "We would like to know what you were doing in this area. Would you tell us?" said the interpreter.

"Well, I was aboard the air attaché's airplane," I began. "The air attaché has certain things to perform in the country to keep its own country informed of what's going on. We were just looking to see what's going on."

After my response had been translated, I sensed a degree of dissatisfaction with the answer. "Didn't you know you'd be shot down if you flew over free Laos?" the interpreter said.

"No."

"What is your opinion of Laos?"

"Well, all I know is that I came to Laos as the assistant attaché and I'd been in Vientiane for four days when the civil war broke out."

"What do you think about American intervention?"

"I don't look at it as intervention. My country has given support to Laos for a number of years. They have recognized each government in turn. In every case everything the U.S. has done out here was intended to help the Lao people."

The issue of American aid to Laos was batted around for a while before the discussion turned to the Southeast Asia Treaty Organization (SEATO), which was scheduled to meet soon in Bangkok. I told the group that if there was intervention in Laos by other countries, "You could have World War III right here."

Then the group leader said he wanted some of the others to give me their opinion. "I'd like to hear your opinion," I said.

"We blame the whole problem on America," said the interpreter. "We think the Americans should pull out of Laos altogether and then there wouldn't be any problem."

"Well," I replied, "you have your opinion and I have mine."

At that point, one member of the group who had been relatively quiet jumped up and began screaming in perfect English, "You and your attaché talk—all lies!"

He ranted and raved about American imperialism, but I refused to argue with him. In fact, I refused to say anything more. His tirade effectively ended the interview or interrogation or whatever it was, and the group left without getting an apology or an admission of guilt.

After six days of fruitless questioning, my captors apparently decided they had gotten out of me what they could. I felt a certain sense of relief when I realized the interrogations were behind me for the time being, but I also felt a growing anxiety about what the future held. My captors seemed to have no idea what to do with me, their first American POW.

On the night of 29 March, I was finishing my sixth day in captivity. I had fallen into a comfortable routine, despite the interrogations, and was looking forward to a long sleep and a restful night. I dropped off to sleep earlier than usual with a halfway good feeling, even though I could hear Soviet resupply aircraft taking off and landing at nearby Xieng Khoung Airport.

Suddenly, five Neutralist soldiers came storming into the clinic, tossing furniture aside. They jerked me out of bed and threw me onto a military stretcher. They said nothing as they carried me out, roughly tossed the stretcher into the back of a jeep, and drove off into the darkness.

The jeep stopped after only a few minutes. The stretcher was lifted out, and I was carried through a wooded area to a small clearing. The soldiers set the stretcher on the ground and walked off, leaving me alone. It was cloudy and had started to rain lightly. I couldn't figure out what was going on. I had not been physically abused while in captivity, and most of the threats to that point had been implied.

As I lay there pondering the possibilities, I saw the dark form of a man approaching from the tree line. I couldn't see his face and couldn't tell who he was until he spoke. Then I recognized the voice of Lieutenant Sabab. "You have one last chance to talk," he said slowly, his words menacing. "If you do not tell us what we want to know, we will kill you."

I swallowed hard. The flow of events was out of my control, and I could do nothing to influence them at this point. I told Lieutenant Sabab wearily, with a peace I believed was a prelude to death, that I didn't know any more. "I have told you all I am going to tell you," I said.

"I am sorry for you," he said and stomped off. The rain came down harder. I was alone in the darkness. I looked up into the sky, water streaming down my face, and began to think of how my maternal grandfather, the man who had raised me and the man I most admired, would deal with imminent death. Robert Carter was a quiet man with a strong belief in God, the sanctity of man, and the power of prayer. I knew he would handle this time as he lived his life—with grace, with dignity, and with a great strength of character that was derived from his belief that God would take care of him and those he loved.

And so I prayed what I thought would be my last prayer on earth. "Dear God," I said to myself, "please take care of my family." I knew my fate truly was in the hands of God at that moment. I was convinced I was going to die there in that muddy clearing. Unable to move, unable to defend myself, I accepted my own death with a calmness that surprised me. I felt a great sense of relief that I no longer had to bear the burden of deciding my own fate.

As I prayed, the faces of my wife, Betty, and my teenage children, Barbara, Larry, and Elaine, swam before my eyes. I had thought of them constantly since the shootdown. I wondered how they would deal with the news of my disappearance. I wanted them to know what had become of me, that I had survived, even though at that moment my chances of surviving the night seemed slim. I wanted them to know that I loved them and was sorry I was not there all the times they needed me. Nevertheless, I knew they were strong. Although they did not always like it, they had come to accept, and learned to live with, the numerous separations during my military career. I knew they would survive and go on with their lives.

My prayer finished, I closed my eyes and lay there in the rain, waiting for the inevitable. I began to shiver in the chilling rain. The wait for death was becoming lengthy and uncomfortable. I wished the soldiers would get on with whatever they were going to do. Kill me or get me out of the rain, one or the other—just do something.

How would they kill me? A single pistol shot to the head? Most likely that's how I would be killed. It would be fast and painless—a sudden flash of light and then blackness. I would simply be an eighth body added to the seven from the downed C-47.

Finally, I heard distant voices coming my way. They were returning to kill me. I braced myself. Then, unexpectedly, I felt the stretcher being lifted. The soldiers began carrying me back through the woods. "They must be taking me somewhere else to kill me," I thought, but if they were going to kill me, why take me somewhere else? A sliver of hope intruded on the blackness and despair of the night. I started to think I might live to see another day.

In a few minutes, we came to a small stream. The soldiers were mumbling and grunting as they struggled to carry me. One of them stumbled and the stretcher tipped, dumping me into the water. I was soaked, muddy, and miserable, but at least I was alive to complain.

The soldiers dragged me out of the water, put me back on the stretcher, and carried me to a nearby tent. About a dozen Lao soldiers were lounging around inside. The soldiers who had carried me there set down the stretcher in one corner of the tent and left. The others wanted nothing to do with me. No one said anything. They looked at me briefly, then turned away. Their complete lack of curiosity puzzled me. I wondered if they had been told to ignore me.

I was wet, dirty, and hungry, with no idea what was to become of me, but I wanted to shout out that I was alive, that I was here. I began to have some hope that maybe I wasn't going to die after all, at least not this night.

I slept fitfully, waking the morning of 30 March to find a thick, wet fog covering the ground. During the night, the soldiers had moved out, leaving me alone in the tent. I had no food, no water, no toilet facilities, and no one to tell me what was to become of me.

I lay in the tent for some time before several soldiers came in, picked up my stretcher, and carried me outside to a Soviet jeep. The blue civilian shirt I had been wearing when I was shot down was wrapped around my head, covering my eyes. Every time I tried to lift it, someone reached out and pushed it back into place.

The jeep took off and bounced along for fifteen or twenty minutes before I began to hear the roar of another engine. It sounded like a truck engine without a muffler. When the jeep stopped, the engine noise got louder. I didn't hear any voices, so I lifted the makeshift blindfold and peeked out. In the distance was Xieng Khoung airstrip and a tan, single-engine Soviet biplane, an Antonov-2 (An-2) Colt, with its engine running. I slipped the blindfold back in place and waited.

I would not allow myself to consider even the possibility that I might be released. More than likely, I would be sent deeper into the Communist prison system, away from the fighting around the Plain of Jars, until there was some resolution. Hanoi loomed as a distinct possibility, as did Peking and Moscow. They were all inextricably bound, and my destination all depended on who had the most need for an American POW.

Hanoi would be a mixed blessing. Medical treatment was likely to be better, but there was also the possibility of long-term imprisonment and harsher interrogations. Peking and Moscow offered much the same. My ploy of claiming diplomatic immunity had failed, and my prospects for a quick release seemed dim.

Finally, the jeep pulled close to the plane and I was loaded aboard, still on the stretcher. Someone whose face I never saw went along to ensure I didn't remove the blindfold during the trip. Every time I reached up to move the blindfold, a hand reached out and gently moved mine away.

We flew for about an hour before the An-2 Colt descended and bumped to a stop. From the landing, I could tell we had come down on a rough grass strip, but I didn't know if I was in North Vietnam, China, or a Kansas wheat field.

I was taken out of the airplane and set down on the stretcher in a field of tall grass. The airplane taxied away and quickly took off, severing my last tie with anything I had been able to relate to over the last seven days. I had no sense of place or time. Once again I was lost and alone in the middle of a grassy field, just as I had been after the shootdown.

I pulled the shirt back from my eyes and looked around. There was not much to see because the grass was too tall and the cast kept me from lifting myself off the stretcher. I could neither see nor hear anything that spoke of civilization. The sun broke through the low clouds to shine down on me white and hot. I had no water and had not eaten in more than two days. I was hungry and thirsty, and pain was once more gnawing at my legs.

Lying in that field as I pondered the uncertainty of what was to become of me was the most frightening aspect of my captivity to that point. The uncertainty made it more frightening than the prospect of death the night before. I could accept death, but I had difficulty dealing with uncertainty. I would rather be told I was going to die than be told nothing. At least I could prepare myself for death, but I could not prepare for this uncertainty.

The first indication that I was near a village came when a tinny squeal of Oriental music erupted through a loudspeaker somewhere off to my left. The music startled me. "What the hell is this?" I muttered aloud.

The music played for a few minutes, then stopped. Still, no one came. The minutes passed slowly as I lay staring at the sky. How long was I there? Thirty minutes? Sixty? Two hours? I couldn't tell. I had no sense of time passing.

The sun had begun its descent by the time a jeep full of Pathet Lao soldiers came to retrieve me. I slipped the blindfold back in place as I was lifted, still on the stretcher, into the back of the jeep.

The new guards were not as conscientious about my blindfold as my previous captors, and as the jeep drove along I lifted the shirt to get some sense of my new surroundings.

I was in a small village somewhere in the mountains. It had the usual split-bamboo houses with thatched roofs, wandering water buffalo, mongrel dogs, and scrawny chickens scratching in the dirt, but I could tell little more about where I was. It could be Vietnam, it could be China, or it could be Laos; it most certainly was not Kansas.

Then, the jeep swept past a small Buddhist monument. Like a moment of divine revelation, I instantly recognized the monument from photographs of Laos I had studied in a course for country attachés given by the State Department prior to my posting. That monument, I knew, was in the village of Sam Neua, the Pathet Lao headquarters and military stronghold in northeast Laos, just a few miles from the Vietnam border.

I was elated. Now I knew where I was and could pinpoint my location on the planet, which at that moment seemed the most important thing in the world. I wasn't nowhere; I was in Sam Neua. I knew where I was, even if no one else I cared about did.

The jeep drove into the center of the village and came to a stop in front of a two-story stucco house that appeared to be of French design. I was lifted out of the jeep, still on the stretcher, and carried inside. A narrow central hallway ran the length of the house, with doorways on either side leading to rooms. The hallway was too narrow to maneuver the stretcher so the guards took me off it and half-dragged and half-carried me into the first room on the left. They put me down on a fiber mat and placed a pillow under my head.

The guards talked among themselves in Lao but said nothing to me. I got the impression none spoke English. They did not manhandle or abuse me, but they also did not treat me with any of the gentleness that someone in my condition might expect. To them I was little more than another object to be moved about, another sack of rice.

The stretcher was set in a corner of the room, and the guards put two bedpans sent from the clinic down beside it. Then they left, locking the door from the outside and taking the light with them. Darkness enveloped the room. At midafternoon, my cell had become a black hole.

Despair engulfed me. The ballgame had changed, and the players had changed. I was now a prisoner of the Pathet Lao, not the Neutralists. My chances for repatriation were now nonexistent. I had been sent so far into the Pathet Lao prison system that I had nearly ceased to exist. There was no future. There was no tomorrow. There was only now.

3

Love at First Flight

The old biplane smelled of an intoxicating mixture of leather and oil as it bounced along the grassy field with its engine coughing out a thick exhaust. Unable to speak, barely able to breathe in my excitement and anticipation, I peered over the edge of the front cockpit. Prentiss Taylor, one of my cousins, was squeezed into the cockpit next to me. Our mothers had pooled their Depression-era pennies to pay $1.50 for our first airplane ride. Behind us was the pilot, his eyes masked by goggles, the leather helmet snapped firmly under his chin, his mouth set in a confident, determined line.

The biplane moved slowly to the far end of the field and turned into the wind. The chugging of the engine became a steady, throaty roar. The plane quickly gained speed, the wind grabbing at our faces, our shirt collars flapping in the breeze, the breath sucked out of us. We were surrounded by noise and wind as the sweet, rich smell of the engine washed over us.

Then, the earth seemed to fall away, and we were suspended in midair. The takeoff had been so smooth and effortless that I thought the pilot had kept the plane level and somehow the earth had tilted away from us. There I was, above the earth, flying for the first time. We soared on the updrafts, effortlessly reaching into the clouds. We glided in the clear air, the pilot tilting the plane so we could see the landscape of southeastern Georgia beneath us.

The faces in the crowd at little Waycross–Ware County Airport turned skyward, the people shading their eyes against the bright

November sun. They shrank rapidly until they were little more than specks on the ground, miniature people next to a miniature hangar. Waycross became a toy town, its streets and buildings familiar yet so different from this perspective.

To the south the great Okefenokee Swamp, with its tranquil tangle of cypress stands, coffee-colored streams, and profusion of bird and animal life, stretched to the horizon, but none of the swamp's sounds or smells was evident to us up here. We were flying above it all in air that was clean and clear. We were in another world.

There below us was Hebardville, the little community north of Waycross. I could see U.S. Route 1, the railroad running along its eastern side, and the yellow house on State Street a few yards farther east, where I lived with my maternal grandparents, Robert and Idelphia Carter.

I looked for them in the big garden behind the house, but they were not there. I wanted to shout to them that I was flying, but I knew they could not hear me. As we flew, I seemed to be alone in the bright, blue November sky. No one could touch me. I was floating effortlessly beyond all my troubles, all my worries. I was free.

I had been in love with airplanes ever since I could remember. Although my father was an aviator, his influence had not produced my interest. He had left home when I was two years old, and in my early years he was only a vague presence, someone I knew was my father but who lived elsewhere. He went to New Mexico in 1925 after being told he had tuberculosis. The dry air, his doctor reasoned, would clear up the congestion in his lungs. The humid summers and cold, damp winters of southeastern Georgia would only do him harm. My mother, Marguerite, remained in Waycross with me, her only child by that marriage, at the urging of her family. A divorce soon followed, and my father slipped out of my life for the next few years.

My father was a thin, quiet man who was extremely gifted with his hands. He was a skilled carpenter and a mechanical wizard who could tear apart and rebuild any piece of machinery put in front of him. His passion in his younger years was motorcycles, and in later years his interest turned to airplanes. He occasionally sent me photographs of the airplanes he owned because he knew I also had developed an interest in aviation. I wasn't trying to follow in his footsteps. I took my own path in life that just happened to parallel my father's.

I never thought it strange or unusual that my father was not there. He was never like a stranger, although it was years between his visits to Waycross. Family members talked about him regularly, and he was a constant presence. He was my father, but he just didn't live with us. There was nothing unusual in that, I thought at the time.

Still, with the divorce of my parents, I went to live with my mother's parents in their yellow frame house on State Street. My mother remarried and remained in Waycross and I saw her almost daily. I spent numerous weekends with her, my stepfather, Joel Lott, and my half sister, Glenda, after she was born in 1934.

The Carters were quite clannish and the family members close, tied to one another by love of family that extended to me and kept me secure and cared for. I had no feeling of abandonment and no sense of estrangement from my mother or father. It was more like living in an extended family. My room just happened to be in a different house. During those early years of my life, I developed a sense of independence and self-sufficiency because of the circumstances in which I lived that helped me when I became a POW. I knew I could survive on my own. I did not need other prisoners around me. I could reason and rationalize the situations that confronted me on my own, just as I had as a boy.

My grandfather was the biggest influence on me in those early years. His sense of fairness, his work ethic, and his devotion to his family and his faith became the models by which I gauged myself and measured my own conduct. My grandparents were deeply religious and devout Southern Baptists. My grandfather, who served as treasurer of the Hebardville Baptist Church, lived his religion. He never felt it necessary to demonstrate to others how religious he was. He simply lived as he thought the Bible instructed him to: working hard, being faithful to his family, being honest and trustworthy to his friends, and depending on God to carry him through the tough times. That sort of simple, honest faith was instilled in me as a youngster and became a part of my life that helped carry me through the dark days of my captivity. If I lived up to my grandfather's standards, I believed I would do right by myself and my family.

I thought often of my grandfather in those early days in Sam Neua. What would he do in this situation? He would, I knew, confront the task at hand, ask God for help, and then do what had to be done. He would finish each job with careful attention to detail before moving on to the next. He would break down a large, complex job into smaller, simple jobs; he was never fazed by the enormity of a task because he saw it merely as an assemblage of smaller jobs.

By the time I was eleven years old, I knew I wanted nothing more in life than to be an aviator. I made frequent visits to the Waycross–Ware County Airport just to look at the few planes housed there. The airport itself was little more than three buildings set on the edge of a grassy field that served as the airstrip. It had a small hangar with a wind sock on top, an office building, and a house for the airport manager. A rotating beacon on a tower added an air of authenticity to the complex. Without it, a passerby might mistake it for a farm.

When there weren't any planes at the airport, I'd browse through the aviation magazines and catalogs that were always lying around the office. By doing odd jobs at the machine shop owned by my uncle, Charles Carter, I was able to save money to buy books, magazines, models, and other aviation-related paraphernalia.

My most memorable purchase was an aviator's leather helmet with goggles and a white silk scarf. I ordered them from a company in York, Pennsylvania, for about $7.50. Even if I couldn't fly, I could at least look like an aviator. I would put on the helmet and goggles, wrap the silk scarf around my neck, take my bicycle out on U.S. Route 1, and pretend to fly, swerving from one side of the empty road to the other.

The helmet and goggles got me my next airplane ride. I was about eleven years old when a barnstorming pilot came to town on Armistice Day. The barnstormers usually came in November because the air was clear and cool and it was easier to see them perform their stunts. The air show was secondary, though. Selling rides was the pilot's major function. As long as people wanted rides, the air show would wait.

That day, I didn't have the money for a ride, but I went to the airport to watch and be close to the plane and the pilot. As usual, I wore my helmet, goggles, and scarf. For some reason, the pilot had flown in without his and, when he saw me in the crowd, motioned me over. "Say, young man," he said. "I don't have a helmet and goggles and I've got to go up and do an air show. Could I borrow yours?"

"Yes, sir," I said. "But on one condition. When the day is over, you give me an airplane ride."

"You've got yourself a deal," he said. The plane took off, and the pilot put it through a series of loops and spins. Knowing my helmet and goggles were in that plane was almost as good as being up there myself. I knew that when I put them on again the magic of that flight would be transferred to me.

It was near dark when the pilot landed and taxied the plane close to the crowd. He kept the engine running, and I could smell the exhaust and see the little puffs of vapor shooting out the sides.

"Okay," the pilot shouted over the noise of the engine, "I'm going to give you your ride. Who do you want to go with you?"

I grabbed two of my buddies, and we clambered up into the front cockpit and squeezed ourselves in as the pilot revved the engine and headed for the opposite end of the field. Within seconds we were airborne, looking down on our little town that was bathed in the soft orange light of the setting sun. The ride lasted no more than ten minutes, but it once again confirmed my determination to someday fly on my own. One way or another, I was going to be an aviator.

In June 1940, with war threatening in Europe and the Pacific, I graduated from Wacona School in a class of forty. I knew college was not in my future because my family could not afford it. To become an aviator, I would have to do so on my own with just a high school education. The prospects were not bright, but I had made up my mind to be a pilot.

That summer my father invited me to visit him in Albuquerque, New Mexico, where he was teaching a class in aviation mechanics at a local high school. I decided to live with him for a while and got a job delivering groceries to pay for my first flying lessons, which cost all of six dollars an hour. Those first lessons were in a Luscombe model 8A, a high-wing two-seater with a sixty-five-horsepower engine. Although the plane was relatively simple to fly, it was obvious early on that I would be an average student. I was not a born aviator. One of my flight instructors later wrote: "Fairly slow to learn, but once learned, it's never forgotten."

Learning to fly seemed a daunting undertaking when I considered it in its entirety, but broken down, it could be handled: takeoff, climbing turns, gliding turns, stalls, the crosswind leg, the downwind leg, the base leg, and the final approach and the controlled stall that is the landing. I learned each individually, a separate entity unto itself. When I put them all together, I had learned to fly. Prison in Sam Neua would be much the same: Break down the captivity into minute segments, take care of each of those segments as it presented itself, and eventually the whole could be conquered. Otherwise, the enormity and uncertainty of what I faced could overwhelm me.

By November 1940 I had returned to Waycross, a seventeen-year-old in search of myself and my future. I had a series of jobs during that time, none of which offered much of a future and all of which were little more than a means to make enough money to take flying lessons, which I did whenever I could afford them.

By late 1941, at the age of eighteen, I had accumulated about eight hours of flight instruction and was ready to solo. That December day was bright and sunny as I taxied the yellow J-3 Piper Cub we called the Yellow Peril to the far end of the field for the first of three takeoffs.

Frank Ward, who was the only qualified flight instructor at the Waycross–Ware County Airport, had my friend Chub Barefoot guide me through the solo flight. Although Chub had soloed before me, he was still considered a student pilot and technically did not have the authority to solo me. This was 1941, however, and federal controls on aviation were not as tight as they would become in later years. Chub loved motorcycles and airplanes and could not only work on both but also handle them with ease. Although he rode motorcycles with abandon, he was a no-nonsense pilot who later became a flight instructor and taught many fledgling pilots the finer points of being an aviator.

Chub stood and watched as I took off, flew the airport traffic pattern three times, and did two touch-and-go landings before bringing the plane in for a final time. Chub met me partway down the field. I stopped the plane and opened the door for him.

"Good solo, Bailey," he said with a smile as he shook my hand.

I was a pilot. I had learned to fly. Now, I told myself, there was nothing I could not do if I just set my mind to it. I taxied to a tie-down spot and shut down the engine. It was a ritual at the airport that those who solo for the first time buy everyone on hand a soft drink. There were twelve people there that day and I gladly fished around in my pants pockets for the twelve nickels I needed for the drinks.

I was sipping my Coca-Cola and still drinking in the congratulations of my friends and the thrill of having soloed, when a black Chevrolet coupe pulled up to the hangar. Dr. H. M. Pafford and his son, Little Doc, got out of the car, concern evident in their faces. "Have y'all heard about Pearl Harbor?" Dr. Pafford asked.

We looked at one another. Pearl Harbor? The name meant nothing to us. Where was Pearl Harbor? "No," I said. "What about Pearl Harbor?"

"The Japanese attacked Pearl Harbor this morning," the doctor said solemnly.

We pondered the news for a minute, not sure what it would mean to us or the country. We had heard rumblings of war in the Pacific but had no idea of what was to come. After a moment of silence, Chub Barefoot smiled and looked around the crowd of serious faces. "Well, what do you know?" he said. "We solo ol' Bailey and the Japanese declare war on us."

Several months after I soloed, I received a civil service appointment to the Alabama School of Trades in Gadsden, Alabama, for a course in aircraft and aircraft engine mechanics. Following graduation I was transferred to Brookley Army Air Field in Mobile, Alabama, where I went to work in the aircraft overhaul depot. The operation ran virtually nonstop, requiring three eight-hour shifts per day. Although the work was grease, grime, and sweat and not really glamorous, we were contributing to the war effort.

My specialty was the Wright R-1820 engine. It was a nine-cylinder radial engine with 1,820-cubic-inch displacement that generated twelve hundred horsepower. Four of those engines powered the Boeing B-17 Flying Fortress, which then was carrying the bulk of the bombing load in Europe. I came to know that engine better than I knew my friends. I could tear it down and put it back together in my sleep.

Two boyhood friends from Waycross, Philip DeLegal and Wallace Lewis, also worked at Brookley and lived with me in a one-story, brown boardinghouse at 113 Bienville Avenue, just a few blocks from downtown Mobile. We shared the house with a teacher named Q. D. Urquhart; the landlady, Eunice Waybright; and her daughter, Betty.

Mrs. Waybright was a tall, slender woman with black hair going to gray. She had been widowed several years earlier and left with little but Betty (who was in high school), the house, a black 1937 Buick, and her own common sense and determination.

Betty and I were attracted to one another from the moment we met. Like her mother, Betty was tall and thin with black hair and blue eyes. We exchanged glances over the dinner table for some weeks before I got up the courage to ask her to go to the movies.

Life seemed good that summer of 1942. There was Betty and our growing romance and steady work that I enjoyed. The war was a constant topic of conversation, but it somehow seemed remote from our comfortable existence. We saw it not so much a threat as a great adventure waiting for us.

Philip was the first to leave our little group, joining the navy. Wallace, like me, was intent on becoming a pilot. I knew my chances of getting into the military as a pilot were slim because I had no college degree. Instead, Wallace and I applied for the Civilian Pilot Training (CPT) program. In CPT, civilians were trained as flight instructors for military aviators.

The process was tricky. In order to be accepted for CPT, prospective pilots first had to apply for the army's aviation cadet program. They had to fail the basic entrance exam but make a minimum score on it to meet CPT standards.

Wallace and I took the test and, as expected, failed, but our scores were high enough to qualify for CPT. Wallace decided to go that route. I was not content with the idea of being a civilian instructor, however, and wanted to be a military aviator. I took the test again and this time passed. On 14 December 1942, I enlisted in the army and was on my way to becoming an army aviator. I couldn't wait to start flying again. I had done little flying since soloing in Waycross a year earlier, and I was eager to get back into the cockpit, this time for my country.

Basic training was in Miami Beach, not exactly a hardship post. We learned to march, how to salute, and how to wear our uniforms, but not much else. Concentrating on the training was often difficult because of where the training was taking place. We could see the beach from the drill field. When we were off duty, we'd lie on the sand, look out over the blue-green waters at the navy blimps patrolling for German submarines, and talk about flying. Our "barracks" was a luxury high-rise hotel, the Croyden Arms, that had been taken over by the army and converted for our use. The furniture had been taken out, the elevators were shut down, and we slept four to a room on army cots, but it was still a hotel on the beach.

After three months of basic training, we were loaded on a train and sent north to Erskine College in Due West, South Carolina, the first contingent of prospective pilots in what was known as the College Training Detachment. The purpose of the program was to bring prospective pilots who had no formal college education, such as myself, up to a more advanced level of mathematics and science. We were segregated from the general college population, although our courses were taught by civilians.

The one significant change in our lives was that we no longer were "privates." We had become "aviation students" and now were called "mister." We still had no rank, but at least we were elevated from what we had been in Miami Beach.

The next two months were filled with classes in advanced science and mathematics and the requisite military drills. Much to my surprise, I was made a flight lieutenant and given the responsibility of making sure my flight got to and from class in respectable military order. I was quite pleased with myself for having achieved this status, considering that several members of my flight had college degrees and others had previous military training in college.

Our view of the war was rather limited because our little group was insulated. News filtered in only occasionally. Besides, we were much more concerned with day-to-day events that affected our lives. Getting through each class, each drill, each program, and each day was the limit of our horizons.

I was also operating at an educational disadvantage and knew if I did not concentrate on the classroom work I would suffer later. I narrowed my focus to specific details of my own training and let the big picture take care of itself. It was exactly what I needed to carry me through the difficult and demanding classroom work. Twenty years later, this trait helped me endure the helplessness of solitary confinement.

I had been in the army five months, two of them at Erskine College, before I ever saw the inside of an airplane. The program called for us to receive ten hours of dual flight instruction in a J-3 Piper Cub, the same high-wing single-engine plane in which I had soloed little more than eighteen months earlier. My civilian instructor was not overly impressed to learn that I had soloed. He quickly let me know that I had a great deal to learn about flying, despite my familiarity with the J-3. I simply accepted his assessment and pressed on.

Many of my classmates were sitting at the controls of an airplane for the first time in their lives, and the experience was more than a little overwhelming. Of course, I felt much the same way about portions of our academic training.

While I was at Erskine, Betty and I decided to get married. She and her mother rode the bus from Mobile to Greenwood, South Carolina, where we were married in a simple ceremony. Betty lived in a rooming house in Due West for a while so we could spend weekends together and then returned to Mobile when I shipped out to Nashville.

The classification center at Nashville was the make-or-break point for would-be pilots. We were given a series of physical and psychological tests to determine our suitability to become pilots. Four things could happen to us, only one of which we considered good: Reclassification to pilot training was the ultimate goal of all of us. Classification to bombardier or navigator training was not quite what we wanted, but it was still flying in airplanes and could be tolerated. The worst of all possible fates, we thought, was to wash out and be reassigned to the infantry.

Lists were posted on the barracks wall to let us know who had won and who had lost. When I saw my name on the list for pilot training, there was a great deal of handshaking and backslapping. To celebrate, a friend and I went to a hotel in downtown Nashville, where we saluted our success with bourbon and Cokes while listening to Francis Craig play the piano and sing "Near You."

By the summer of 1943, I was at Maxwell Field in Montgomery, Alabama, for preflight training. My status, along with thousands of others, was elevated from aviation student to aviation cadet. Our uniforms changed to identify us as cadets. We were allowed to wear soft aviators' caps with bills and propeller insignia. The uniforms made us stand taller, run faster, and work harder. We also paid more attention in class because we knew we were going to be pilots if we did not wash out.

The pace of the physical training picked up, as did the academic demands. We had classes in navigation, meteorology, the theory of flight, Morse code, aircraft, and aircraft engines. I had an edge on a lot of the students because I knew aircraft engines and aircraft nomenclature—an aileron from a flap and a rudder from an elevator. But it was most satisfying to learn the dynamics of flight and what kept me up in the air when I was flying.

Although I outpaced my classmates in knowledge of airplanes, they were way ahead of me in other academic areas. Mathematics was the most difficult. I could do little but take one class at a time and not allow myself to be overwhelmed by the enormity or the complexity of what confronted me. I was so intent on becoming a pilot that I would not let a few mathematics courses deter me.

In addition to the physical and academic demands, our integrity was being shaped. The one thing our instructors kept pounding into us was honor, honor, honor. Cheating was not tolerated, nor was anyone who cheated on anything for any reason. We were being molded not only as pilots but also as gentlemen.

When someone was caught cheating, we would be roused from our barracks for late-night formations. The cadet commander would call us to attention in his deep Southern drawl and then intone with a seriousness in his voice that spoke of defeat and dishonor as only a Southerner could: "Attention to awders. Aviation cadet Joe Smith has been found guilty of cheating. His name will be removed from the roster of aviation cadets and will never again be mentioned at Maxwell Field. Dismissed." That voice and the finality of the dismissal stayed with us for a long time. We slept fitfully, if at all, the rest of the night as we wondered if the same thing could befall us and pray it wouldn't.

At Maxwell we had some exposure to pilots who had actually flown in the war. Whenever they came around, we eagerly pressed them for information about what it was like. Telling someone about flying in combat, I discovered, was a bit like trying to explain sex to someone who has never experienced it. You could talk about it for days and never really understand the feeling.

Besides, our worst fear at that time had nothing to do with death. We were young, healthy and, we thought, invincible. Death was an abstraction not many of us could grasp. Our worst fear was washing out, being told we weren't good enough to be pilots. We saw that as the ultimate dishonor, worse than death itself, because it would be more difficult to live with the knowledge we didn't measure up than to die doing something we loved. Death we could accept; dishonor we could not.

From preflight training, I moved on to primary flight training at Helena, Arkansas, where I was assigned to class 44-C, scheduled to graduate in March 1944. Once again my focus was almost entirely on my training, not on what was going on in the world. This first of three stages of flight training called for sixty-five hours in a PT-23, a low-wing, fabric-covered two-seater with a 220-horsepower Continental radial engine. The instructor sat in front and the student in back. Primary training introduced us to navigation, aerobatics, and solo flying.

From there we moved on to Walnut Ridge, Arkansas, for basic flight training. At Walnut Ridge we shed the civilian instructors and put ourselves in the hands of the military. We also graduated to the Vultee BT-13 Valiant, a dual-seat, low-wing monoplane with a greenhouse canopy and a 450-horsepower engine. We quickly nicknamed it the Vultee Vibrator because of the way it shook in a spin.

At Walnut Ridge we were introduced to radios, night flying, formation flying, cross-country flying, and instrument flying. I learned early I had a knack for formation flying and began to entertain thoughts of going into multiengine transport aircraft or bombers. I had no real desire to be a fighter pilot, as many of my classmates did. I knew I could fly an airplane with one engine. I was more intrigued by larger, multiengine aircraft.

Learning to fly the twin-engine Beechcraft AT-10 Wichita in advanced flight training at Stuttgart, Arkansas, only strengthened my commitment to multiengine aircraft. The AT-10 was a plywood airplane with two 295-horsepower Lycoming R-680 engines with constant speed propellers and retractable landing gear. Its sole mission was to train those of us who wanted to be pilots of larger aircraft.

Had I been interested merely in the sheer fun of flying, I would have stayed with the single-engine planes, but I considered it a challenge to be one of three AT-10s in formation, jockeying two throttles instead of one to maintain the power balance necessary to keep up with the lead plane. It was equally as challenging to use the differential power, aileron, and rudder controls to take off into a choppy crosswind and then land in it.

In late February 1944, Class 44-C got word that we were due an additional $350 to buy our officers' uniforms. Those were the magic words we had been waiting for. They meant we had passed flight training and were about to officially become aviators and second lieutenants in the army air forces.

When the money came through, we rushed down to the local tailor to purchase our "pinks and greens," the officer's uniform of tan trousers, shirt, tie, brown shoes, green jacket, and aviator's cap. We made the tailor rich, but we didn't care. After almost a year of training, during which we endured innumerable classroom lectures and dozens of hours of flight time with cranky instructors, we were about to become commissioned officers.

When the members of Class 44-C assembled for graduation exercises in March 1944, resplendent in our pinks and greens, we were so full of spit and vinegar we could have taken on anyone. I was immensely proud of myself when my pilot's wings and second lieutenant's bars were pinned on me. I had done what I had set out to do, despite a formal education that had been only eleven years long and despite having to compete against others with college educations.

However impressed I might have been with myself and my accomplishments, my daughter, Barbara, quickly brought me back to earth when I went to Mobile to see her and Betty. Barbara had been born while I was in basic flight training at Walnut Ridge. I had gotten a four-day pass to be there when she was born but had not seen her since. Her first reaction to my new pinks and greens was to throw up all over them as soon as I picked her up.

My request for assignment to multiengine aircraft had come through, and, after a brief leave in Mobile with my family, I moved on to Hendricks Army Airfield in Sebring, Florida, for transition training for the B-17 Flying Fortress, a major step going from two engines to four.

Coming out of an AT-10 and crawling into the cockpit of a B-17, with its multitude of dials and gauges and its six-page preflight checklist, was an overwhelming experience. It was almost like learning to fly all over again, with dozens of new things to learn. Not only did I have to learn to control four engines at a time but also I had to learn to fly with a bomb load, how and when to use oxygen at higher altitudes, and how to use the sophisticated radio navigation system. I welcomed the challenge because flying the B-17 was what I wanted to do. I set about the task of learning to fly the B-17 as I learned everything else: step by step, piece by piece, detail upon detail.

Once I got acquainted with the B-17, it was like flying a big Piper Cub. It was a perfectly designed airplane and incredibly forgiving. Controlling the four engines was much simpler than I had anticipated. The throttles were designed so that all four could be held in one hand. They became like one throttle, and simply by swiveling my wrist from right to left or back again, I could adjust the power differential.

The B-17 course at Hendricks was designed to produce aircraft commanders. Those who were graduated from the course were fully qualified to have their own aircraft and crew assigned to them, and then it was off to Europe for a combat assignment. Most of the new guys like me were thrown straight into combat. The transport spots were being filled by combat veterans who had survived their twenty-five missions and were being rewarded with something less dangerous.

At the end of two months of B-17 training I was faced with

another decision. I was offered the opportunity either to have my own B-17 and crew or to become a copilot on a new airplane, the B-29 Super Fortress.

The decision was relatively easy. The B-29 was newer, larger, and much more sophisticated than any other aircraft in the fleet at that time and presented a challenge I could not pass up. I knew I could fly a B-17. Now, I wanted to see if I could fly a B-29. I also knew if I went into B-17s I would go to Europe. If I went B-29, I would be assigned to the Pacific. Ever since I was a kid, I had wanted to go to the romantic, mysterious Orient. Little did I realize then the influence that the Far East and its wars would have on the remainder of my life.

4

Where in the World Is Laos?

For many of us who fought against Japan in World War II, dying and surviving were the only two options available. Being taken prisoner did not enter into the combat equation because of the nature of what we did. It was not something we thought about or talked about. Not until after the war, when we learned of the horrors to which many American prisoners had been subjected, did we begin to grasp the full meaning of being a prisoner of war. Then, in retrospect, it seemed at times a fate worse than death.

At the time we were flying, however, the POW experience was beyond the scope of our understanding. We were Americans, tough, strong, and in control of ourselves and the free world. Nothing anyone could do would crack our resolve, sap our strength, or force us to grovel in the face of the enemy. The invincibility of the American fighting man was a given in the ranks of the military and the minds of the American public. We had God and the right of free-world might on our side. We were richer, bigger, stronger, and tougher, mentally and physically, than our adversaries.

The 504th Bomb Group, of which I was a member, lost twenty-six B-29s and 260 crew members in combat operations against Japan during the war. No one is sure how many crew members were captured, but our group records indicate that only eighteen survived Japanese POW camps. Of the more than five thousand crew members from the Twentieth Air Force shot down during the war, fewer than two hundred were liberated at the end of the war.

Some were killed by irate Japanese civilians. Others were killed by the Kempei Tai Secret Police, who considered B-29 pilots to be war criminals.

From February through April 1945, I flew fifteen combat missions as a B-29 copilot with the 504th off the island of Tinian. Most of those missions were over the mainland of Japan. The most significant, the most dangerous, and the most memorable were the low-level firebomb raids on Tokyo, the first of which was on 9 March 1945.

The high-altitude precision bombing for which the B-29 was designed was not working in Japan because of frequent bad weather and the presence of the jet stream, both of which made target acquisition extremely difficult. For this mission the altitude would be 5,000 to 8,000 feet, practically treetop level for the B-29. Tactically, the mission orders made sense. The lower altitudes would improve vision and bomb accuracy. Flying low would also enable us to carry a heavier bomb load because we wouldn't need all the fuel necessary to climb to 26,000 feet.

Our target was Zone 1, a heavily populated, heavily industrialized section of Tokyo divided by the Sumida River. Railroad yards, storage areas, and the Hattori Company, which made fuses for artillery shells, were our primary targets. Clustered around these facilities were thousands of homes housing tens of thousands of Japanese who contributed to the war effort by making small parts for aircraft and other war matériel. The area was one of the most densely populated in Tokyo. An estimated 1.1 million people lived in Zone 1, about 135,000 people per square mile.[1]

There were to be no formations this night, no solace or protection in togetherness. We had precious little ammunition for our guns to do any damage to Japanese fighters anyway. Our plane was to come in at six thousand feet, flying north along the Chiba peninsula east of Tokyo before turning northwest to the initial point. The docks at the mouth of the Sumida River were our aiming point. The more realistic advice was to simply find a dark spot and aim for it. The inside of our B-29 was filled with five-hundred-pound clusters of M-69 incendiary bombs. More than 250 B-29s from the Twentieth Air Force were scheduled for the mission, including twenty from the 504th.

We took off from Tinian as scheduled and flew at one thousand feet much of the way to conserve fuel. First Lieutenant Art Tomes, a lanky Minnesotan, was our aircraft commander. We were still far southeast of the city, flying through layers of clouds, when we began to see a glow in the sky. "That must be Tokyo," somebody said nervously over the intercom.

"No, it's not," said our navigator. "We're too far out."

The first man was right. The glow from the fires started by the Pathfinder aircraft that went in ahead of the main body of planes was diffusing through the cloud layers and spreading many miles from Tokyo.

We continued heading northwest. Suddenly, a large black shadow passed beneath us, heading northeast, so quickly that no one had any time to react. It was another B-29, already on its bombing run. It missed us by no more than one hundred feet.

The closer we got to Tokyo, the brighter the sky became and the more turbulence we experienced. It got so rough that Tomes and I both grabbed our wheels and flew the plane in unison. Then came the smells, wafting up to us on thermals created by the fires. We could smell burning pine and bamboo, molten metal, and flesh.

When we got over Tokyo, there was a stunned silence throughout the aircraft. None of us could believe what we were seeing. Beneath us was a roiling mass of flames that stretched to the horizon. It was like looking straight into the middle of hell.

The plane was bucking and pitching from the severe turbulence, and it was all Tomes and I could do to control it. He set climb power and hung onto the heading, and the bombardier jettisoned our incendiaries as soon as he saw a dark spot beneath us. Free of the bombs and riding on thermals, the plane shot up through ten thousand feet like a jet fighter, bucking and bouncing all the way. At fourteen thousand feet, we leveled out and turned for home.

No one on the airplane said anything about what we had seen or what we had done. The sights and the smells were overwhelming. We all went quietly about our jobs of getting the aircraft back over the water and home to Tinian. None of us had ever seen anything like that before, nor would we ever again.

That raid on Tokyo proved to be the single most devastating bombing raid in history. Later reports showed that more than 83,000 Japanese were killed and 41,000 injured. The fires destroyed more than 267,000 buildings, made more than one million people homeless (about 25 percent of whom were part of the work force), and badly damaged the Hattori Company and many other small manufacturing facilities in the area.[2]

Over the next ten days I flew three of the four additional missions in that specially planned firebomb blitz of Japan. On 13 March we hit Osaka, Japan's second-largest city and a major shipbuilder. On 16 March we attacked Kobe, and on 18 March Nagoya was the target. In none of these did we experience the firestorm that we had seen in Tokyo.

The raids were having their effect on the morale of the Japanese people, though. Once secure in their homeland, they began to question their military leaders' effectiveness and their efforts to protect them. The civilians were running out of food. Many were homeless. Their will to fight was being sapped, as well as their means to fight.

In early May 1945, I got an urgent message from the Red Cross. My mother back home in Waycross was seriously ill. Her doctor had put in a special request that her only son be allowed to come home. Not only was I shocked to learn my mother was ill but I was also shocked that I could pick up and leave in the middle of the war. I reluctantly said my good-byes to my crew. I was eager to get home but had the feeling that I hadn't quite finished the mission.

It took me several days to get home, and by the time I arrived my mother had improved considerably. The army reassigned me stateside for the remainder of the war, and I spent much of my time at Muroc Army Air Field in California in a squadron testing bomb shapes.

In the chaotic drawdown of the army following World War II, I decided to return to civilian life. There seemed to me no more wars to fight, and I could not see myself flying a desk for the next dozen years. I accepted a reserve commission in lieu of my regular commission because I thought it would get me out of the service and home faster, but I never really got out of the army. I moved my family to Albuquerque, New Mexico, where I did some flight instruction and joined the New Mexico Army National Guard, serving for a time with an antiaircraft battery.

In April 1951 our unit was recalled to active duty because of the Korean War, but I had no intention of spending this war pumping shells into 90mm guns. My heart was still in the air, in airplanes and flying, and I applied for the army's aviation program.

The bulk of the army aircraft at that time consisted of helicopters and L-19 light observation aircraft. The L-19, later redesignated O1-G Bird Dogs, were nothing more than high-wing, single-engine Cessna 170s adapted for military use. They weren't fast, they weren't powerful, and they weren't sleek. They were a lot of fun to fly, however, and at a cost of only eleven thousand dollars each they were the perfect airplane for the low, slow flying necessary for artillery spotting.

I was sent back to aviation schools at San Marcos, Texas, and Fort Sill, Oklahoma, to relearn airplanes and flying. The only new twist came at Fort Sill, where I had to learn how to adjust artillery fire from the air. That was to be my job—an artillery officer who just happened to fly airplanes—although I knew far more about the workings of the L-19 than I did about the 105mm howitzer.

By the time I graduated in July 1952 and earned my second set of aviator's wings, there was no question where I would be going or what I would be doing. The stalemate in Korea was beginning to settle in along the 38th Parallel. It had become a war of position, of small-unit raids, of artillery, and of protracted peace talks.

I arrived in Korea in October 1952 and was assigned to the 90th Field Artillery Battalion of the 25th Infantry Division. At the time the 25th occupied a sector northeast of Seoul near the Imjin River.

My first view of the battlefield was a shock. As I flew in low over friendly forces, I could see thousands of troops moving around, vehicles choking the roads and throwing up clouds of dust, and bright green fields of rice tucked into the valleys between the mountains. Then came the artillery positions, followed closely by no-man's-land—a deserted, brown, chewed-up piece of real estate. North of that was the other side of the moon.

The enemy side of no-man's-land was worse. It looked as if someone had taken a huge bulldozer and removed every piece of vegetation, every vestige of life and human habitation. There were no houses, no trees, no roads, no nothing. The landscape had been laid bare by constant bombing and artillery fire. How anyone could survive in that was beyond me. The Chinese and North Korean troops had all but vanished underground. They lived like rats in a maze of caves, tunnels, and elaborately constructed bunkers.

"I'm supposed to find targets of opportunity in that?" I asked. I was, but I rarely did. Seldom did I find anything moving on that barren, lifeless ground. For six months I flew artillery spotting missions, and not once did I call in artillery fire on what I considered a worthwhile target. If I saw anything moving around, it usually was no more than three or four Chinese or North Korean troops. I'd dutifully call in fire on them, but by the time it got there our "targets" had scurried underground to the safety of their reinforced bunkers.

Never once during those six months did I get shot at by enemy troops, even though I usually flew as low as fifteen hundred feet. The Chinese and North Korean soldiers were reluctant to show themselves in the daylight and even more reluctant to shoot at an observation plane. They knew that calling in a fire mission took only a few seconds.

There were targets to shoot at on the enemy side, of course, but they were out of bounds. Political considerations forbid us from dropping bombs on them or calling in artillery. The rules of engagement were as incomprehensible as the politics that produced them. We could bomb and shoot up an insignificant target but not a militarily important one because it was out-of-bounds. It was a policy I never understood and, philosophically, never accepted.

The 25th Division later moved west to a sector adjacent to the restricted corridor the peace negotiators used to move back and forth to Panmunjom. I would fly combat missions searching for targets in enemy territory while watching the negotiators from both sides driving into Panmunjom to hold their never-ending talks.

I knew going in that this war was far different than World War II. This was a war, to be sure, but it was a war without clear-cut goals, a war without missions, and a war in search of a political solution, not a military victory. There was no commitment to victory in Korea.

My reasoning, however antiquated, was that if we were going to commit troops to an armed conflict, the military reality of the situation called for us to commit enough to fight the battles, win the war, and go home. The idea of sitting there stalemated while peace negotiations dragged on and people on both sides died every day was ludicrous, if not criminal. This piecemeal approach to the war was not going to win anything. It was only going to cost lives.

This same shortsighted policy of limited warfare—an oxymoron—was later pursued in Southeast Asia, but there is nothing limited about warfare. Limited warfare implies defeat. Mere usage of the phraseology robs the military psyche of the will, strength, and moral courage necessary for victory. It denies the military the philosophical high ground necessary for victory.

Limited warfare didn't work in Korea, and it didn't work in Southeast Asia. In Vietnam, Laos, and Cambodia, the concept produced even more catastrophic results for those of us who fought there and for those who tried to implement this no-win policy of political expediency.

On the night of 26 July 1953, Brig. Gen. Lewis T. Heath, the division artillery commander, called his staff together. I had been reassigned from the 90th Field Artillery to division artillery staff as its aviation officer, although I was still flying spotting missions.

"Gentlemen," General Heath began solemnly, "I've been told this war is ending tomorrow. Frankly, I don't think we can call this a victory." We looked at one another with a curious sense of relief and puzzlement. We were relieved the shooting had stopped and people no longer were dying, but we were puzzled at how we had come to this unsatisfactory conclusion. It went against everything we thought the American soldier believed in and fought for.

General Heath was clearly not happy with the resolution of the war. He advised us to keep a tight rein on our emotions when the cease-fire was announced. He wanted no outward displays of emotion. We had not won anything, he said; the shooting simply stopped. Not many of us felt like celebrating anyway.

After serving a brief stint as Eighth Army Flight Detachment operations officer in Seoul following the cease-fire, I returned to the United States and a future as uncertain as it had been when I left. I had seen enough of Korea and enough of the war, and I was eager to get back to civilian life. Nevertheless, that lure of airplanes and flying that kept drawing me back to the military life was a lure I could not resist.

Following Korea I was sent to Fort Bragg, North Carolina, and eventually was assigned to the XVIII Airborne Corps Aviation Detachment. After Fort Bragg came a two-year stint as the aviation officer at Fort Meade, Maryland, with the Second Region Air Defense Command. In the winter of 1959 I was sitting in my office at Fort Meade when my assignment officer at the Pentagon called. "Hey, Bailey," he said, "I've got an assignment for you."

"What is it?"

"It's an assignment to go to Laos."

"Where in the world is Laos?" I said, puzzled. I had never heard of the place.

The assignment officer laughed. "It's in Southeast Asia," he explained, "next to Thailand. It's the only embassy in the world with an army aircraft assigned to it. They need an artillery officer who's also a pilot to be an assistant attaché and you're the only one I've got who fits the requirements."

"Okay, what do I have to do?"

I would have a year of schooling to learn how to be an attaché prior to my departure, he explained. I would have a French language course, as well as intelligence school at Fort Holabird, Maryland. Laos would be a hardship tour, with no families permitted. I had just purchased a house in Laurel, Maryland, and my family would remain there while I went to Asia again.

For the next year I was pumped and primed for my assignment to Laos. I attended the strategic intelligence school, where I learned some French, some basic intelligence-gathering techniques, and the protocol of conducting oneself as a military attaché in a foreign country.

Of course, I never thought I would need to acquire such knowledge. What I knew of Laos indicated I was going to a country troubled by a minor guerrilla insurgency that surely could be cured with massive infusions of American aid and dollars. I certainly did not anticipate walking into the middle of my third war when I arrived in Bangkok 8 December 1960 on my way to Vientiane. But the next morning, when I went to the airport in search of a ride across the Mekong, I was given some inkling of what I would face at my new post.

"Where are you going?" an Air America pilot in a C-45 asked me.

"Vientiane," I said.

The pilot smiled ruefully and shook his head. "Watch yourself there," he said. "They're thinking of closing down the airport."

"Why? What's going on?"

"Strange things," he said. "Strange things." He said it twice, as if to magnify how just strange the situation on the east bank of the Mekong had become. *Strange* was not the word for what was happening in Laos; at times it was downright bizarre.

5

A Very Uncivil War

Northeast of Bangkok the Khorat Plateau stretches out flat and fertile for more than three hundred miles before encountering the wide, muddy Mekong River and the border with Laos. During the dry season, this land of rice paddies bounded by dikes and spotted with an occasional thatched bamboo hut is a dun-colored wasteland. The air is dry, dusty, and inhospitable, filled with haze and choking gray smoke, as farmers burn their fields to prepare for the summer rains. When the rains come, the plateau shimmers with incandescent greens of freshly planted rice stalks.

December is a month of reprieve. The rains have stopped, but the land retains its rich, vibrant greenery. That December 1960 I watched in amazement as mile after mile of bright green fields unrolled beneath the twin-engine C-45 carrying me to Vientiane. The landscape was spectacular, unlike anything I had ever seen, even in Korea. Still, the excitement of this new land and my posting as assistant army attaché to the embassy in Vientiane was tempered by the uncertainty of the political and military situation into which I was stepping.

Laos had become the flash point of Southeast Asia. Long before Vietnam traumatized and polarized the American public, this landlocked country of about two million people was at ground zero for the long-awaited superpower confrontation between the United States and the Soviet Union. The situation had developed following the French defeat in Indochina in 1954. Under terms of the

Geneva Convention, Laos was to be a buffer between its more ambitious neighbors: Vietnam and its Soviet backers to the east versus Thailand and its supporters to the west. Laos was to be neutral, as was Cambodia, and Vietnam was divided at the 17th parallel. Neither Laos nor Cambodia could enter into any military alliances or have any foreign bases or foreign troops on their soil, and the Pathet Lao, the Communist insurgency in Laos, would eventually be integrated into the government and armed forces of Laos. An international control commission (ICC) with observers from India, Poland, and Canada would oversee implementation of the treaty.

The man given the unenviable task of making some sense of the confusion in Laos, of integrating the Pathet Lao into the coalition government, and of fending off advances of both North Vietnam and the United States was Prince Souvanna Phouma, a short, pudgy, cigar-smoking member of the royal house of Luang Prabang. A French-trained civil engineer, Souvanna Phouma tended to lean to the West. He wore expensive three-piece suits with a flower in the lapel, a stylish homburg, and carried a cane.

Among his opponents was his half brother, Prince Souphanouvong, the so-called Red Prince because of his leadership role with the Communist Pathet Lao. Souphanouvong had spent much of World War II working on public works projects in central Vietnam after earning a degree in civil engineering in France. While in Vietnam he came under the influence of Vietnamese nationalists, including Ho Chi Minh.

Although the Pathet Lao (which means "land of Lao") received support from Ho Chi Minh and his Viet Minh cadres, they had little military success and eventually were confined to the provinces of Sam Neua and Phong Saly in extreme northeastern Laos. It is an area of rugged mountains and impenetrable jungles, whose people have more in common with their Vietnamese neighbors to the east than with the lowland Lao of the Mekong River Valley.

The Viet Minh had encouraged development of the Pathet Lao to divert French attention and resources from the fight in Vietnam. The support, which continued after the defeat of the French, was not intended to help the Lao as much as it was part of a plan to reunify Vietnam. Laos provided the perfect pathway to South Vietnam. With the 17th parallel to become a demilitarized zone, heavily defended first by U.S.-backed South Vietnamese troops and then by American forces, the infiltration routes through Laos into South Vietnam were needed to implement the master plan for the reunification of Vietnam and eventual conquest of Southeast Asia.

While the North Vietnamese saw "neutral" Laos as part of their overall strategy for unification, the United States saw it as a separate problem, one that could be postponed until the situation in South Vietnam was resolved. As a result, Laos failed miserably as a buffer state. The success of any such state depends on its own strength, resilience, and sense of national identity, none of which Laos had. Its gentle and caring people were easily influenced by outside forces. Its government, never stable in the best of days, was fraught with corruption and uncertainty, as Communist and Western forces vied for control of the real estate between the mountains and the Mekong.

The government of Laos went through a number of changes after 1954, most of which moved it to the Right and made it increasingly dependent on Western aid. That direction was not popular with many members of the military, among the most outspoken of whom was a diminutive, twenty-six-year-old paratroop captain named Kong Le.

Kong Le was commander of the six-hundred-man 2nd Paratroop Battalion, unquestionably the best of a rather motley assemblage of twenty-five thousand Royal Lao Army troops. Kong Le's battalion had participated in much of the fighting against the Pathet Lao guerrillas in Sam Neua province, but Kong Le was a nationalist who wanted the government free of all outside influences, be they American, French, Soviet, or Vietnamese.

On 9 August 1960, as I was studying to become an assistant attaché in Laos, resentment against the government exploded. At 3:00 A.M. Capt. Kong Le's paratroopers rolled out of their barracks, got into their jeeps, and drove into the streets of Vientiane. They took over the power station, surrounded government offices, and commandeered the radio station. They blocked access to the airport by parking jeeps in the middle of the runway and took control of Camp Chinaimo, the large army base south of town. When dawn broke, the residents of Vientiane awoke to find the streets filled with Kong Le's paratroopers clad in camouflage uniforms and distinctive maroon berets. Captain Kong Le and his troops held the capital and the government for the next four months, but by December 1960 the situation was rapidly deteriorating.

As the Air America Beechcraft C-45 ferrying me to Laos approached the border on 9 December 1960, the pilot got on the radio and requested weather and news about the situation in Vientiane. A voice quickly crackled back with a warning: "You want to be careful going in there," the voice said, "and better get out before dark. Things are happening."

Major Robert Freeland, the number-two man in the attaché office, met me at Wattay Airport and confirmed the warnings.

"You're the last flight in," Freeland said as he shook my hand and directed me toward an embassy car. "They've closed down the airport."

Colonel Joel Hollis, the army attaché, had remained at the embassy instead of meeting me at the airport, as he tried to get a grasp on the changing situation. But getting a grasp on anything in Laos at that time was next to impossible. I was amazed by the bizarre complexity of the situation that was changing almost hourly. Our intelligence network was running nonstop trying to figure out not only who was siding with whom among the Lao but also which agency of the United States government was supporting which anti–Pathet Lao faction.

Over the next few days Hollis provided some background briefings while Freeland did his best, through more informal chats, to bring me up to speed on the chaos in the country, which by then was teetering on the brink of an all-out civil war.

The struggle over Laos was among three factions: Prince Souphanouvong led the Pathet Lao, with backing from the North Vietnamese; Capt. Kong Le was the leader of the antiforeign military faction, the Neutralists; the third group, the Royalists, was headed by Prince Boun Oum, a descendant of the royal house of Champassak in southern Laos, and Gen. Phoumi Nosavan, a reformed socialist turned right-winger.

Boun Oum had also led a Lao rebellion against the Japanese in the south during World War II and was, like many southerners, suspicious of the royal family of Luang Prabang, fearing a union of Laos under its rule. He also was opposed to trusting the future of Laos with anyone who advocated closer ties to the Vietnamese.

General Phoumi was a large, round-faced man whose easy smile belied his quick temper and pugnacious manner. A former boxer, he had quickly risen in the ranks after joining the Royal Lao Army and in 1954 was sent to the Geneva Conference as a military adviser. Despite his checkered past, Phoumi became a favorite son of the CIA. His control of the military represented one of the few relatively stable institutions in a country that lacked decent roads, communications, railroads, and any government agency that appeared able to rise above the confusion and petty politics of the moment.

Prince Souvanna Phouma, because of his predilection for compromises, negotiated settlements, and being willing to include the Pathet Lao in a coalition government, was not a favorite of either the CIA or hard-liners within the State Department.

Kong Le made it clear he wanted nothing to do with any foreign power. He simply wanted to prevent what he believed was another attempt at colonization. He equated the United States with France.

The CIA's support of General Phoumi was strengthened following Kong Le's coup, but the CIA's decision to back Phoumi was unilateral and contradicted official U.S. government policy.

That particular situation was perhaps the most bizarre of all those that greeted me on my arrival. Here was one branch of the United States government (the CIA) freely and openly giving aid to a rebel faction (General Phoumi's Royalists) that was in direct conflict with a government (Souvanna Phouma's coalition) with which we had diplomatic relations and that was being supported by another branch of the United States government (the State Department).

If it seems absurd from a distance, it was sheer madness up close. I sometimes got the feeling that no one in the U.S. government was monitoring Laos. In this foreign policy without direction or purpose, no one seemed to know what to do, how to do it, or with whom to do it.

The troops General Phoumi controlled hardly constituted a crack fighting force. The $300 million the United States had given Laos to create a national army had created instead a twenty-five-thousand-man police force that was ineffective, inefficient, susceptible to bribes and blackmail, and lacking even rudimentary combat skills. By no stretch of the imagination could it defend the country against invasions from either Communist China or North Vietnam or conduct effective antiguerrilla campaigns in the mountains.

The army was a conventional force trying to fight an unconventional war. It had little experienced leadership, among either its officer corps or its noncommissioned officer ranks, because the French had generally held most of those positions in the past. It had twelve infantry battalions, an artillery battalion, an armored reconnaissance battalion, two paratroop battalions, a transportation corps, a quartermaster corps, and a small air force including AT-6 Harvard trainers that eventually were equipped with bombs and cannons. However, it was an army with little mobility, dependent on trucks and jeeps to move equipment and heavy artillery in a country with few roads.

The ranks were filled almost entirely with lowland Lao. The Lao living in the border regions and the mountains, who would have been most effective fighting the Viet Minh incursions, were never recruited. In their oversized GI helmets and carrying too-large M-1 Garand rifles, the soldiers of the Royal Lao Army looked like children playing at war. It was difficult to take them seriously, and few Americans did. "Your chief of staff couldn't lead a platoon around the corner to buy a newspaper," one American told General Phoumi.[1]

An American adviser, remarking on the qualities of the Lao soldier, said, "Only a few months ago, the Laotians used to retreat without their weapons; now they take their weapons with them when they run away."[2]

Although harsh, these assessments were not far from the truth. General Phoumi's soldiers did nothing to distinguish themselves in combat or endear themselves to their advisers in the aftermath of the Kong Le coup. The United States did try to provide some order. The Programs Evaluation Office (PEO), the supposedly surreptitious Military Assistance Advisory Group (MAAG), was to do that with its soldiers in civilian clothes.

Under the terms of the 1954 Geneva Convention, only the French were allowed to have military trainers in Laos. The Americans tried to get around the prohibition by creating the PEO as part of the U.S. operations mission and staffing it with "technicians."

These strapping, well-muscled "technicians" showed up in Laos aboard Air America planes in 1959 wearing slacks, sport shirts, and tattoos on their arms with such endearments as "Third Infantry Forever." Their nonmilitary dress was as much a uniform as the greens they left behind, and their presence in Laos was one of the worst-kept secrets of those early stages of the war. The average Lao probably knew more about the PEO than those of us assigned to the embassy.

Everyone who worked in the PEO was "mister," even though many were senior officers in the United States Army who seemed to have dropped off the face of the earth when they were assigned to Laos. Typical was the first head of the PEO, U.S. Army Gen. John A. Heintges, a career officer with a distinguished combat record during World War II. In 1959 he disappeared from army rolls after being assigned to U.S. Eighth Army in Korea. His assignment was not Korea, though; he was the boss of Special Forces soldiers sent to Laos.

The PEO operated out of what was known as the Green House, a separate facility within the CIA compound several miles from the embassy. It was as large as the embassy compound itself and much better defended. It was surrounded by barbed wire and had its own fleet of vehicles and mechanics to maintain them.

Access to the Green House was tightly controlled, in part because of the group's secrecy and in part because of the amount of money that flowed through it. That money, paid to the Royal Lao Army, was the only reason the country had any semblance of an economy, even though much of the money was siphoned off through graft and corruption before it reached the soldiers in the field. Marine guards often were recruited to assist in unloading the bundles of *kip*, the Lao currency, at the Green House before it was passed on to Lao army officers.

One particularly strange event, which had occurred in the hours prior to my arrival, contributed even more to the unfathomable nature of the conflict that I was about to enter.

At 4:00 A.M. on 8 December Col. Kouprasith Abhay, commander of the Vientiane military region, staged a countercoup, ostensibly to protect Prince Souvanna Phouma from the influences of Kong Le. Colonel Kouprasith's troops adorned their uniforms with strips of white cloth to set them apart from Kong Le's, who wore red. The two sides set up barricades on the road leading to Camp Chinaimo south of town, often within a few yards of each other, but many of the soldiers, close friends and devout Buddhists whose religion forbade them to take lives, agreed that if there was any shooting they would point their weapons in the air and not shoot at one another. That peaceful compromise was to have disastrous results for the citizens of Vientiane in the coming days.

The next afternoon, 9 December, General Phoumi's troops began to move on the capital. They had waited until the end of the rainy season to begin their offensive and now had Colonel Kouprasith's troops at work for them within the city. Prince Souvanna Phouma, unable to find a solution or a compromise, fled to Cambodia.

With the airport closed I could not fly Hollis, Freeland, and other embassy officials around the country to monitor the military situation. We did not really need to go far, in that Vientiane was the focus of most military activity in the country at that time, but while Wattay was closed to our flights it was open to Soviet supply planes. The Neutralists had come under the influence of the Soviets, who began pouring military aid into the country for Kong Le because he controlled the airport.

The day after I arrived in Vientiane, Hollis told me to go to the airport and keep track of incoming flights. My job was simply to count the Soviet airplanes and determine as best I could what weapons were coming in. Kong Le's men did not appreciate my presence at the airport but never made any move to bar me or keep me from observing the flights.

The Soviets were using Ilyushin-14s, their version of the C-47, for the supply flights. The flow of aircraft landing, unloading, and taking off was nonstop—fourteen an hour at one point. Often three aircraft were in sight—one unloading, another taking off, and the third setting up in the landing pattern.

I watched with grudging admiration at the assembly line efficiency of the operation. The planes would come in low, cut the power, land, and pull off to the side of the runway, where they would be swarmed by Lao. If they had fought half as well as they handled those shipments, the war would have been much bloodier.

Although the unloading was done on the far side of the runway and I could not use binoculars to determine the cargo, weapons constituted the bulk of the shipments. There were some howitzers, some 82mm mortars (one of which we later liberated and I boxed it up and shipped it to Aberdeen Proving Grounds in Maryland), and plenty of ammunition. Although we did not know it at the time, North Vietnamese gunners were being brought in to man these weapons. None of Kong Le's paratroopers knew how to use Soviet artillery.

The Soviets were violating the Geneva accords with the shipments, and the United States officially protested. However, the Soviets were doing the same thing as the CIA, supplying the Neutralists while the CIA supplied General Phoumi.

The situation deteriorated even more over the next few days. Vientiane was palpably tense, especially during those times Freeland and I drove around the city to check troop movements. Guards were nervous and bleary-eyed, having gone too long without sleep or proper food.

One morning we were driving through downtown Vientiane when Freeland abruptly stopped the car near a group of soldiers. "There's Kong Le," he said. "I want to introduce you to him."

Freeland had dealt with Kong Le in the past and knew him well. Normally a friendly, charismatic man, Kong Le on this day was anything but. He looked like a cornered man, ready for all hell to break loose. He nodded at me and shook my hand, and that was it. We never met again, although in the coming months my fate would rest in his hands.

Slight, short (five-foot-two), and lacking in command presence, Kong Le nevertheless had earned the fierce loyalty of his troops. He made it clear he was not one of the elite, and he was able to converse easily with his soldiers. The 2nd Paratroop Battalion he commanded was considered the most disciplined and effective of Lao units, and eventually an aura of invincibility arose around Kong Le. He became a man of myths, who often told of his nightly battles with the *phis,* or spirits, which he invariably defeated. His wrists were festooned with the white strings the Lao use as tokens of blessing, giving him the appearance of being heavily bandaged.

Kong Le was not so much anti-American as antiforeigner. At one point he had ten American advisers assigned to his battalion, but he saw their influence as dangerous and as degrading as that of the Viet Minh. He was convinced that the Lao really didn't want to fight and that outside forces were pushing them into war.

By mid-December 1960 the diminutive paratroop captain was being squeezed by the Viet Minh and the Soviets on one side and the Royalists and their Thai and American benefactors on the other. His vision of a Laos free of foreign intervention was unrealistic, given the international political climate of the time.

With Prince Souvanna Phouma in Cambodia, the government of Laos was dissolved by royal decree on 12 December, and a new body, headed by Prince Boun Oum, was installed. The United States and Thailand rushed to recognize the new government. Kong Le and his Neutralist rebels stood firm in Vientiane, waiting for the Royal Lao Army attack they knew would come any day.

On 13 December Hollis, Freeland, and I were driving along the dirt road on the east bank of the Mekong River on our way to a quick lunch at a restaurant near the airport north of town. Freeland was behind the wheel, Hollis to his right, and I sat in the back, still trying to orient myself in the city under siege.

The Mekong had fallen quickly with the end of the monsoons, exposing huge expanses of mud flats stretching from the banks on the Lao side to the channel. When it got even drier, residents of Vientiane used these flats to plant temporary vegetable gardens. Suddenly, I heard what sounded like muffled explosions to our left.

"Uh-oh, look at that," Freeland said.

"Where?" I said. Freeland pointed out to the flats, where great gray and brown geysers of mud and water were blossoming. They were 105mm howitzer explosions. The three of us stared at the explosions for a few seconds before Hollis, without the slightest hint of emotion or concern in his voice, said, "Well, the war has started."

The explosions we saw apparently were long rounds fired by Royal Lao Army troops aimed at Kong Le's airport headquarters. When Lao troops fired their artillery, only God knew where the rounds would land. The civilians eventually paid the consequences for that poor marksmanship.

Freeland immediately turned the car around and took us back to the embassy. Hollis hustled off to the ambassador's office to check on the situation while I remained in the attaché's office. We still were not sure who was fighting whom or whether this was the attack on Vientiane we had been expecting. Hollis returned a few minutes later, his face grim. "Let's burn all the classified documents," he said.

No sooner had he said that than mortar rounds began exploding just beyond the motor pool compound across the street from our office. We tried to ignore the explosions and began rifling through the safes and file cabinets for classified documents.

I began pulling files, tearing them in half, and tossing them into a large container. When one container got full, it was carried outside, its contents were dumped in holes dug along a low wall, and magnesium grenades were tossed into the holes.

The attaché's office in the embassy compound was in a building separate from the embassy building itself. The front of our office faced northeast across what is now Thanon Bartolini. At the end of the street, just a few yards to our left, was the famous That Dam, the Black Stupa that Lao legend says is the home of a dormant seven-headed dragon that protects the city from Thai invaders.

Within a few minutes, Royal Lao Army troops were moving slowly and nervously along the street, heading north. They stopped frequently, crouching by the low wall in front of the attaché's office, but never bothered us.

As I continued to pull and burn documents, Hollis and Freeland decided to show the colors. Hollis wanted to make it clear to the troops in the area that the Americans were not cowering in the embassy. The two left the office and walked down to the Black Stupa as casually as if they were out for an afternoon stroll. When they returned a few minutes later, Hollis was smiling.

"What's going on?" I asked.

"Over there in the grease pit is one of Phoumi's soldiers," Hollis said, pointing to the motor pool compound. "He doesn't want any part of this war. He's going to stay there until it's over."

I looked out the window and saw a soldier cowering in the grease pit, unwilling to move any farther. I kept burning documents.

Off-duty personnel began making their way to the embassy for whatever protection it afforded. The second floor of the embassy was sealed off by the Marines, who hastily destroyed radio codes and other documents—so many that the Marines simply tossed documents into the walk-in safe, threw in some thermite grenades, and shut the door. The documents and everything else in the safe were destroyed, including uniforms the PEO personnel had put there for safekeeping. When several PEO men tried to get to the second floor to rescue their uniforms, the Marines turned them back at gunpoint.

The intensity of the shooting, although not necessarily the fighting, continued to increase throughout the day. The PEO had several advisers with General Phoumi's forces, but the embassy never received any information from them about the severity of the situation. By late afternoon a decision had to be made: Should we abandon the embassy and take the flag to Bangkok or merely evacuate all nonessential personnel and try to weather the firestorm?

Ambassador Winthrop Brown decided to stay with Hollis, Freeland, and the Marine guards. I was ordered to take charge of the evacuation. Hollis told me to round up all the nonessential personnel and take them downriver to the ferry that crossed over to Nong Khai, Thailand. All dependents, including the wives of Hollis and Freeland, had been evacuated to Thailand in August following Kong Le's coup. Only embassy employees, cooks, and housekeepers remained.

I organized a small convoy and left immediately for the compound south of town where Hollis, Freeland, and I lived. Things had quieted down somewhat, with most of the fighting moving north. I policed up the Chinese cooks and housekeepers, most of whom did not have passports; in the confusion, I couldn't find my passport either.

On the road out of town, we passed numerous shot-up military vehicles, but what armed stragglers we saw ignored us, and we were able to cross into Thailand without incident. The Thais at first were leery of letting me or the Chinese in without passports, but eventually I was able to convince them to let us enter the country.

Thai army trucks were sent for us and, near dark, finally delivered us to the air base at Udorn. Waiting there were Air America C-46 cargo planes, which flew us to Bangkok. When we arrived, I went to the embassy and provided a brief report on the fighting.

Vientiane was a shambles by midafternoon on 14 December. Hundreds of buildings had been destroyed by shell fire or burned to the ground. The U.S. embassy was shredded by mortar fire, a large hole had been blown in the back of Ambassador Brown's chair, and several buildings had been set on fire by incendiary rounds. Neither side had targeted the embassy; it just got caught in the cross fire.

There were far more civilian casualties than military. Civilian dead were estimated at six hundred, while Kong Le reportedly lost only about twenty-two men and Kouprasith fourteen. In this battle, only the innocents suffered, and the combatants escaped nearly unscathed.

By 16 December, little more than seventy-six hours after the fighting began, Kong Le's outnumbered and outgunned paratroopers began retreating from the airport, heading north, away from the Royal Lao Army and directly into the arms of the Pathet Lao. Satisfied that it had retaken Vientiane at relatively little cost, the Royal Lao Army decided not to pursue the defeated rebels. Kong Le's men were allowed to move north at their own pace.

I returned to Vientiane from Bangkok on 17 December, the day after General Phoumi's troops regained control of the capital. One of the casualties of the fighting, I learned, was the L-23 aircraft assigned to the embassy. It had been caught in the cross fire around the airport and riddled with shrapnel. It would need major repairs before it could fly again. As a result, we were without one of our major intelligence-gathering resources, yet we needed to get north to get a fix on Kong Le's troops.

On 19 December, Hollis learned that Lt. Col. Butler B. Toland, the Saigon-based air attaché for Southeast Asia, would be arriving the next day to assess the situation in north-central Laos by air. Toland had his own C-47, which had sufficient room for Freeland and me to tag along.

Kong Le's troops were still on the move somewhere between

Vang Vieng and the Plain of Jars. The Plain of Jars, so named because of the dozens of huge, ancient stone urns scattered about the upland plateau, was militarily critical because whoever controlled it controlled the only transportation routes in northern Laos. Route 7, the primary east-west route in the north, ran through the plain and connected other key roads leading to Vietnam, Sam Neua, and Luang Prabang.

We suspected Kong Le was headed for the Plain of Jars because it had airfields of sufficient size for the IL-14s supplying him to take off and land. Among those was the grass strip at Phonsavan, several miles east of the main field at Xieng Khoung, the same Phonsavan airstrip where I was later taken and kept in an infirmary for several days following the shootdown in March.

Toland flew the C-47 into Phonsavan and was appalled by what he found there and by what he saw later at Xieng Khoung. The defenses were terribly inadequate for the importance we placed on the region.

Although our inspection was disheartening, the return trip proved an intelligence windfall. The Soviets still denied they were furnishing arms and ammunition to Kong Le's troops, but we all knew it was being done. I had watched for several days as dozens of Il-14s disgorged supplies onto the runway at Wattay Airport. The problem was that we had no proof to offer the world, and there was no small amount of international skepticism regarding our claims about the flights.

Somewhere north of Vientiane, Toland brought the C-47 down through the clouds and leveled off at about four thousand feet. As he did, he noticed a plane off to his left, flying low and dispensing something out of the side of it. Because seeing more than one airplane in the sky over Laos at any one time was rare, Toland dropped down to take a look. "Man, I've got something here," Toland said to the rest of us.[3]

We rushed to the windows. No more than one hundred feet below was a Soviet Il-14 clearly marked "CCCP 61796."[4] The pilot was flying a racetrack pattern, trying to find the drop zone. I was jumping from window to window to keep the plane in sight. Freeland looked at me as if I were crazy, but I found it difficult to contain my excitement. We seldom got to share air space with the enemy.

Toland called for a camera and began taking photographs of the Il-14. We shadowed it for quite some time, the camera clicking away, before Toland turned and headed for Vientiane.

After dropping off Freeland and me and refueling the C-47, Toland and his crew rushed on to Bangkok with the precious film. It was quickly developed, and several sets of prints were made to send to various commands up the line on their way to the Pentagon. Within a week, publications ranging from *Life* magazine to *Stars and Stripes* ran Toland's photos of the Soviet resupply plane. The photographs bolstered our claims concerning Soviet involvement in Laos and lent credence to official reports of 180 Soviet airdrops made between 15 December and 2 January.[5]

Nevertheless, that intelligence coup was a rarity in Laos. Most of the time our intelligence sources were woefully inadequate, which made it particularly difficult to deal with the dozens of rumors that spread daily through Vientiane, a city on the verge of panic. Even the slightest hint of trouble could produce a barrage of gunfire.

One tense evening Hollis and I were driving downtown when shooting started all over the city. It sounded as if we were coming under attack. "Let's go to General Phoumi's house and find out what's going on," Hollis said.

In only a few minutes, we got there. I stopped the car in front of Phoumi's house and Hollis jumped out. "Wait here," he ordered, slamming the door and rushing up the steps. I waited impatiently, listening to the gunfire, not knowing what to expect. Hollis returned a few minutes later, relaxed and casual, although the gunfire was still raging.

"What's going on?" I asked, my voice tense.

"The frog's trying to eat the moon," Hollis said with a laugh. I thought the man had lost his mind. Then he explained that a lunar eclipse was taking place. The Lao believe that during an eclipse a frog is trying to eat the moon. The gunfire was to scare away the frog.

By 31 December, Kong Le and his Neutralist forces had reached the Plain of Jars. To this point the Pathet Lao had offered Kong Le neither weapons nor troops to fight the Royalists, but once the paratroopers reached the Plain of Jars the two former adversaries came to an uneasy truce. The paratroopers with their maroon berets, Western-style uniforms and rank structure, and American weapons would join forces with the Pathet Lao, who eschewed the accoutrements of military rank and depended on the Viet Minh for their weapons and resolve.

They were an odd couple, to be sure. The Pathet Lao did not like Kong Le's troops because of what they believed to be corrupt Western influence. Kong Le's soldiers frequently referred to the Pathet Lao as *kap kap*, or toads. Still, at that moment in the history of Laos, each needed the other for survival.

The Neutralists gave new life to a movement that had survived only through the insistence of the North Vietnamese. Without realizing it, Kong Le and the Neutralists turned the Pathet Lao from a not-too-serious threat into a significant military power.

Prince Souphanouvong's troops received an immeasurable boost in military capabilities as a result of Kong Le's presence on the Plain of Jars. The alliance also was aided by an infusion of North Vietnamese troops, who brought with them heavy artillery and antiaircraft guns, which until then had been absent from the battlefield.

Not until the middle of January 1961 was I able to get a replacement for the damaged L-23 and resume flying. No sooner had I taken delivery of the plane than I was given a mission to return to the Plain of Jars. The most prevalent rumor in the aftermath of Kong Le's departure was that his troops were massing for a counterattack somewhere north of the city. Our intelligence continued to be terrible, and Hollis wanted to find out if there was any merit to this rumor. "Bob, I hate to do this, but I've got to send you up to Xieng Khoung to find out what's going on," Hollis said.

The area was not as safe as it had been just a few weeks earlier. Flying low and slow over the Plain of Jars could attract a lot of .50-caliber machine-gun fire from Kong Le's rebels. The air attaché's plane had taken a .50-caliber slug through one of its engines on a recent flight. As a result, a minimum altitude of ten thousand feet was set for all aircraft flying over the area. That altitude would give us some protection against rounds from heavy machine guns. We had no reason to believe antiaircraft weapons were in their arsenal. Henri Dericourt, a French pilot who knew the area well, flew with me, acting as observer and photographer. We were looking for tanks, massed formations, and any other indication of a military buildup or threat to Vientiane.

We went in at the required ten thousand feet, Dericourt taking photographs with a handheld camera. Visibility was good, and the cloud formations were such that we could maneuver around them and still maintain a clear view of the ground. We saw nothing that would indicate an attack on Vientiane and, on our return, reported the news to Hollis, who was greatly relieved.

Over the next two months, I flew regularly throughout Laos, frequently taking Freeland with me so he could inspect military installations or talk to planters or government officials about any inroads the Pathet Lao might be making in a particular region.

Flying in Laos was risky, at best, but not because of any threat from the Pathet Lao. The weather played more havoc with flight operations than any other place I've ever flown. Visibility was always limited. If it wasn't a solid wall of clouds, it was thick gray smoke from fields or patches of jungle being burned to prepare them for planting. With few navigational aids in the country, air travel was done primarily by dead reckoning. What few maps existed had large blank areas that had not been surveyed. Villages often had different names on different maps and yet another name once you got into the village.

Every flight had some degree of hazard. Some days I would take off from Wattay and almost immediately find myself in the soup. I would turn on the radio and tap into the informal air traffic control system American pilots ran in Laos. The country had no air traffic control, not even at Wattay. There was no need for it. Except for Air America flights, there was virtually no air traffic. "This is Army four-eight-five-four-seven," I'd say. "I'm climbing through fifteen hundred feet on a heading of zero-seven-five."

Invariably someone would come back: "Army four-eight-five-four-seven, this is Air America. I'm at two thousand feet on a heading of two-six-five. You anywhere near that?"

Without radar or air traffic control, we had to work out our safety cushions by ourselves. Running into another airplane in the skies over Laos was never a major concern, however, because not enough airplanes were flying for that to happen. Running into mountains was another matter. North of Vang Vieng the mountains jump up quickly. The closer to the Chinese border, the thicker and higher the mountains, the more dense and forbidding the jungles that cover them, and the less predictable the weather.

Flying in northern Laos was no fun. It was easy to get lost. It was even easier to get killed. A simple lapse of concentration could bury you on the side of a mountain you didn't even know was there until it was too late. Thick fogs, tricky winds, and low clouds made the place a pilot's nightmare. And that was during the day. Flying after dark was simply out of the question.

On one trip to northern Laos in early February, bad weather nearly caused me to deliver two-thirds of the army attaché staff into the hands of the People's Liberation Army of China.

Hollis and I were flying to the small village of Muong Sai near the China border to check on problems with the Pathet Lao. We stopped in Luang Prabang to pick up an interpreter and were back in the air within minutes. As soon as we left the ground we hit bad weather. I immediately went to my instruments. I had plotted my course out of Luang Prabang, calculated the distance, and knew about how long it would take me to get Muong Sai. Yet, flying by dead reckoning in Laos can be hazardous to your health.

I was in the clouds much longer than expected. I was continually climbing to get on top, and it seemed like forever until I broke clear. Even then I was bouncing in and out of cloud tops. I flew for the planned amount of time on the course I had chosen and decided it was time to start letting down. I was anything but confident.

When we eased out of the clouds, I didn't see anything I recognized. I started circling, enlarging my circles with each pass to find something on which I could get a bearing. On one of the passes, we went directly over what appeared to be a military base. We circled that a couple of times, and I went lower until we could see people on the ground. They showed no excitement over being buzzed by an airplane, but something did not feel quite right.

The village looked cleaner than most Lao villages I had flown into, and the structures were more substantial. They were made out of wood, not bamboo. And the people appeared taller with fairer skin than the Thai and Lao mountain people we normally saw in this region. "Colonel," I finally said to Hollis, "I don't know where we're at, but I don't think we're in Laos anymore."

"I think we're over China," Hollis said.

No sooner did we come to that realization than I pulled back the throttle and we went rocketing up through the clouds. I kept expecting to see tracers whizzing past us and hear the clunks of rounds hitting the aircraft at any minute. I didn't relax until I was back on top of the clouds and we were headed south again. We forgot about finding Muong Sai that day, dropped the interpreter off in Luang Prabang, and returned to Vientiane.

The situation in the north was even more confusing than in the rest of the country because of the inclusion of several other military factions that few people knew about. One of those factions was the Kuomintang (KMT), the remnants of Chiang Kai-shek's defeated Chinese Nationalist Army. It had been chased out of China into Burma, Thailand, and Laos, where it entertained delusions of grandeur about reclaiming the homeland while firmly establishing itself in the opium trade of the notorious Golden Triangle.

By early 1961 a full battalion of KMT troops had been hired by the CIA to fight the Pathet Lao in northwestern Laos. Existence of this unit was kept secret for a number of years, and little is known about what, if any, success it had, although its achievements seem to have been rather minimal. My own knowledge of KMT involvement came during a trip on which I flew Hollis to the village of Muong Sing, five miles from the Chinese border. We went there to visit a wounded KMT soldier being treated at the small hospital started by Dr. Tom Dooley.

Dooley was the famous *Than Mo America,* or Dr. America, to the Lao. He had set up medical clinics in the remote mountain villages of northern Laos to treat hill tribes. Stricken with cancer after several years in the jungle, Dooley returned to the States in late 1960 and died there on 18 January 1961. Despite his loss and frequent harassment from the Pathet Lao and Chinese Communists, Dooley's staff continued his work, which included treating wounded KMT soldiers. Although Dooley and his staff frequently denied U.S. government involvement in their operations, Hollis's easy access to the soldier demonstrated more than a casual working relationship.

The situation in central and southern Laos was somewhat less confusing. The Viet Minh and Pathet Lao (including the Neutralists) were beginning to make their presence felt by early 1961.

On 15 February Freeland and I flew south to the home of a French planter named Cadoux, who lived with his wife and son on a large ranch on the Bolovens Plateau in central Laos. They had a small airstrip large enough to accommodate my L-23. Cadoux greeted us warmly but was worried about our presence. "You better not stay on the ground too long," he said. "There's Pathet Lao all around this area. They heard your airplane and they know you're here. If you stay too long, they'll come looking for you."

Although the French embassy had urged Cadoux to leave his ranch because of the threat, he refused. He said he had reached an accommodation with the Pathet Lao: They did not bother him, and he did not bother them. We stayed little more than an hour before returning to Vientiane and wished Cadoux and his family luck. Less than a month later we heard reports, never confirmed, that the Pathet Lao attacked the ranch and killed Cadoux's son.

Sporadic attacks in remote areas throughout Laos were beginning to increase through the first few weeks of 1961. The situation was worsening by the day, and no solutions were forthcoming from Washington. John F. Kennedy's victory over Richard Nixon in the November 1960 presidential elections and the impending switch from a Republican administration to a Democratic one allowed the Eisenhower people to put the perplexing problem of Laos on hold. Kennedy saw Laos in a different light than Eisenhower had. To Kennedy, neutralization was the only proper policy. He was determined to obtain a negotiated settlement, even a forced one.

To do that, however, he first had to convince the Soviets to end their resupply missions and then convince the Pathet Lao–Neutralist coalition they could not win militarily, even though every time they took to the field against Phoumi's troops they routed them. "We cannot and will not accept any visible humiliation over Laos," Kennedy said in early 1961.[6]

During the final transition meeting between Eisenhower and Kennedy on 19 January 1961, the incoming president was told that the most pressing international problem was Laos, which seemed to be a problem without a solution. Kennedy asked more questions about Laos than about anything else. Eisenhower openly called the situation a "mess" and told Kennedy, "You might have to go in there and fight it out."[7]

Being handed such a "mess" did not please Kennedy because it demanded immediate and decisive attention. He told his advisers,

"Whatever's going to happen in Laos, an American invasion, a Communist victory, or whatever, I wish it would happen before we take over and get blamed for it."[8]

It was not to be. Kennedy was consumed by Laos during his first two months in office. He spent more time, effort, and administration manpower on it than on any other single problem.[9] Nevertheless, the more energy the Laos problem absorbed, the more the situation deteriorated. By early March the Plain of Jars had become an armed fortress for the Pathet Lao and Neutralists. Unknown to us, sophisticated antiaircraft weapons were being shipped in and crews trained to use them.

On 13 March I flew my L-23 to Saigon for its one-hundred-hour inspection. The inspection discovered a crack in the supercharger housing of one engine. The engine had to be replaced, which would take a week to ten days. I couldn't wait that long in Saigon and returned to Laos on a commercial flight.

I planned to fly back to Saigon the same way until the air force crew from the attaché's office showed up in Vientiane with their C-47. When they offered me and Ed Weitkamp a return trip with a bit of sightseeing over the Plain of Jars, I jumped at the chance. Their mission was to photograph military installations with a special high-speed camera. Toland's previous photographic efforts had been so spectacular that his office wanted to try to duplicate them.

I was in the army attaché's office in Vientiane the afternoon of 22 March 1961 when Ralph Magee, the pilot of the C-47 known as Rose Bowl, stuck his head in the door. "Take a lunch," he said cheerily. "We'll be in the air for some time."

6

Alive But Alone

On 23 March 1961 President John F. Kennedy entered a briefing room at the White House for a nationally televised news conference. The event was timed to coincide with the dinner hour on the East Coast in an era when the nightly news was becoming a staple of the evening meal for many families across the country. The primary focus was Kennedy's most pressing foreign policy problem— Laos.

"My fellow Americans," Kennedy said gravely, "Laos is far away from America, but the world is small. Its two million people live in a country three times the size of Austria. The security of all Southeast Asia will be endangered if Laos loses its neutral independence. Its own safety runs with the safety of us all, in real neutrality observed by all."[1]

Using three large maps showing Communist gains in the country since 7 August 1960, Kennedy attempted to demonstrate to the American public and a skeptical press corps the importance of Laos to Southeast Asia and the rest of the world. He proposed a cease-fire and an international conference to end the fighting and settle the differences. "I want to make it clear to the American people and to all the world that all we want in Laos is peace, not war; a truly neutral government, not a cold war pawn; a settlement concluded at the conference table and not on the battlefield."[2]

While Kennedy was attempting to educate the American public about the country, however, he was in some need of education

69

about it himself. Throughout the news conference he mispronounced its name. He called it "LAY-os," using two syllables rather than the one-syllable correct pronunciation, "louse."[3]

As Kennedy was speaking in Washington, it was twelve hours later in Laos, the morning of 24 March. Rose Bowl had been shot down, carrying its crew and one of its passengers to their deaths. I had been captured and was lying in the North Vietnamese medical clinic on the airstrip at Phonsavan, a prisoner of the Pathet Lao. No one in the U.S. government yet knew exactly what had happened.

The air attaché in Saigon, air force Lt. Col. Butler B. Toland, became concerned about the overdue plane and at 6:00 P.M. on 23 March sent a cable to the embassy in Vientiane inquiring about it. It was eight o'clock on the morning of the twenty-fourth before he got a reply, which said simply that we had left Vientiane as scheduled. There was no additional information. Realizing the plane was down somewhere, Toland began culling information from various sources along our route. Given our tremendous lack of intelligence sources in the region, that proved troublesome.

It was several days before Hmong, or Meo, guerrillas operating in the Plain of Jars reported to my old friend Henri Dericourt, the French pilot, that a C-47 had gone down near the village of Ban Li.[4] Initial reports indicated one injured man had been captured and the other crew members killed.

Three days after the shootdown, the first news of it, including the names of those on board, began filtering out to the public. Two days later press reports were identifying me as the lone survivor.[5] On 30 March the *New York Times* ran my photograph. The same day, the State Department issued appeals to the French and Lao governments for assistance in obtaining my release.[6]

The diplomatic maneuverings were lost on me. I was trussed up in a plaster cast, unable to walk because of the injuries to my legs, and I was being held incommunicado by troops who had little reason to care if I lived or died. I began my struggle for survival without the slightest reason to believe outside help was on the way. I was alive, but alone.

By the time of the shootdown and Kennedy's speech, the United States was coming precipitously close to introducing American combat troops into Laos. The Seventh Fleet had moved to the South China Sea; Task Force 116, about eighteen thousand soldiers and marines, was put on alert on Okinawa; five hundred Marines and helicopters were sent to Udorn, Thailand; and gasoline, weapons, and ammunition were stockpiled at key points along the west bank of the Mekong.

The plans for American military operations in Laos were contained in what was known as Oplan (Operations Plan) 32-59, a top-secret document outlining the forces and conditions under which they would be used. Oplan 32-59 made clear that any military commitment to Laos would be limited.[7] Even so, the military, remembering the piecemeal commitment in Korea and the problems it produced, was reluctant to commit troops to ground combat in Indochina on a basis as limited as that outlined in the operations plan. It wanted authority to use no fewer than sixty thousand troops and tactical nuclear weapons to beat back the Communist aggression.[8]

By early April 1961, with the situation in Laos worsening and America's military leaders increasingly reluctant to get involved, the Pentagon upped its ante yet again. It now wanted at least 140,000 men and tactical nuclear weapons before it would agree to committing ground troops to Laos. It also wanted clearance to bomb Hanoi and Peking if it was deemed necessary.[9] Although the information was not widely known at the time, there were some reports that tactical nuclear weapons had been moved into position in Thailand during the waning days of the Eisenhower administration and loaded aboard F-84 fighter aircraft.

Confusion over Laos was rampant at every level of U.S. policy making. As before, no one knew what to do or how to do it. Typical was the response by the Joint Chiefs of Staff to a suggestion from Vice President Lyndon Johnson that each compose a scenario for solving the Laos problem. The four joint chiefs and three service secretaries wrote seven separate memorandums with seven vastly different solutions.

Although the Soviets continued to supply Kong Le and the Pathet Lao, they did not demonstrate the concern over an East-West confrontation that consumed Pentagon planners. While we planned for an intervention with troops and nuclear weapons, the Soviets sat back and watched.

The reluctance of America's military leaders to commit a sizable contingent of troops to Laos had to do not only with the lingering aftertaste of Korea but also with the reality of the situation. The U.S. forces were not prepared to fight a war in the jungles of Southeast Asia. Divisions were badly undermanned. There were no stockpiles of equipment or ammunition, and production was not geared to fill the gaps. Many units were so equipment-heavy as a result of the focus on a possible land war in Europe that it would have taken months to move a division from the States to Laos.

Kennedy and his advisers were able to put off a decision on committing troops until other events overtook them. Those events became known as the Bay of Pigs.

On Saturday 15 April, a group of Cuban expatriates backed by the CIA and aided by members of the Alabama Air National Guard launched an ill-fated invasion of Cuba. Although the invasion was quickly crushed on the beaches of the Bay of Pigs, the fallout lingered long afterward. Many supporters of American intervention in Laos found their arguments overshadowed by events in Cuba. The Communist threat was not halfway around the world, but less than one hundred miles from the shores of Florida.

The Bay of Pigs, a disaster in its own right, undoubtedly saved the Kennedy administration from a larger disaster in Laos. Kennedy admitted as much to his aides: "Thank God the Bay of Pigs happened when it did, otherwise we'd be in Laos by now and that would be a hundred times worse," he told them.[10]

The fallout from the Bay of Pigs resulted in changes in the foreign policy in Laos almost immediately. On 19 April the facade of the PEO being civilians was officially removed, and all military personnel were ordered into uniform. The PEO soldiers became part of the Military Assistance Advisory Group, Laos (MAAG Laos).

The order to dump the civilian clothes and put on military uniforms left many of the PEO "technicians" scrambling for something to wear. Their uniforms had been destroyed in the embassy safe by the Marine guards during the battle for Vientiane, and no one had bothered to replace them. Lt. Gen. Andrew Jackson Boyle, head of the newly formed MAAG Laos, ordered replacement uniforms shipped in. The only problem was that all the uniforms and insignia were army, so the morning the order to be in uniform took effect, every American military man in Laos, whether he was Marine, air force, or navy, showed up for duty in an army uniform.

At one point shortly after the order was given to go back into uniforms, General Boyle was required to wear army dress whites to an embassy function. He was unable to get a set on short notice and went scrounging through the embassy for some. The only unclaimed dress whites available were mine. I had no need for them where I was in Sam Neua, so Boyle borrowed mine.

From the blackness of my cell, I could not tell if any diplomatic initiatives were being pursued on my behalf. I did not even know if anyone knew I was alive. If no one knew, I had no reason to believe efforts were being made to get me released. I also did not know whether the Pathet Lao were holding other American prisoners. I was in total isolation.

In retrospect, the reasons for that isolation are clear. An individual's will to resist is easier to break down when he is isolated from all he knows and has no one to assist him through the times of despair and self-doubt. However, I am not sure my captors were ever that focused early in my confinement. In fact, there appeared to be some initial confusion over why I was sent to Sam Neua.

Near dark my first day in Sam Neua, I heard someone fumbling with the lock on the door to my cell. The lock was old and balky, and to get the key in the proper position took several minutes. Later, when I regained the use of my feet and legs, that stubborn lock became my early warning system. Whenever I heard the key being worked in the lock, I knew I had a few minutes to stop whatever I was doing and face the guards as they came in the cell. That gave me an edge on them. I never wanted them to know what I was doing. The more I kept from them and the more I kept to myself, the more control I had over my life.

When the door opened a wave of gray light washed into the cell. I lifted my head to see my visitor. The guards ushered in a Lao man dressed in civilian clothes. It was evident by their deference that he was a man of some influence and power. I never learned his name, but over the next seventeen months I saw him numerous times and came to suspect he was the head man of Sam Neua. I began referring to him as Number One.

When the door was shut, the darkness closed in again. I could sense more than I could see, as Number One walked to the east wall of the cell without saying a word and squatted Oriental-style. When my eyes readjusted to the light, I could see he was only about five feet tall. He had a narrow, angular face topped with an unruly shock of bushy black hair. He appeared to be in his late thirties or early forties. "Where did you come from?" he finally asked, speaking in French. The tone of his voice surprised me. There was no malice. He seemed genuinely confused.

"Xieng Khoung," I replied.

"How did you get here?" Number One asked, again in French.

"By airplane," I said in English. My French was terrible, and I doubted any answer I might give would be understood. He nodded his head and looked at the floor, apparently still confused.

Now I was confused. Had the Pathet Lao simply thrust me on the people of this village without informing them I was coming? It appeared from the puzzled expression on Number One's face that that is exactly what happened. The Pathet Lao high command had made a decision and implemented it. Those who would bear the burden of the decision were not informed of it until after the fact.

"Are you hungry?" Number One asked, this time in reasonably good English.

"Yes," I said. I was hungry and terribly thirsty. I had had no solid food since 23 March, existing for the past week on small helpings of watered-down condensed milk.

"Bread," I said. "Do you have any bread?"

Number One shook his head. "No bread. Can you eat Lao food?"

"I don't know."

Number One nodded his head again and looked at the floor as if not quite sure what to say to me or what to do with me.

Finally he arose, knocked on the door, said something in Lao to the guards, and left. A few minutes later, one of the guards brought some warm water and watered-down condensed milk into the cell and put it next to my sleeping pad.

I drank the water and milk, lay back on my sleeping pad, and, looking for hope and help from above, stared at the ceiling. I was alone, frightened, hungry, sore from my injuries, and unable to move more than a few inches at a time because of the bulky cast around my chest.

I closed my eyes and drifted in and out of sleep. There was a sense of unreality to it all. At times I wasn't sure if I was dreaming or awake. When I opened my eyes, there was nothing but the blackness of the inside of the cell, a blackness so thick and complete that I seemed to be suspended in a vacuum. Only the smell of wood smoke and animal dung and the sounds of an occasional dog barking or guard coughing kept me from floating into oblivion. When I closed my eyes, I saw images and faces of people I knew, disjointed and out of sequence. Who knew that I was here? Who knew that I was alive?

Then I thought of the men on the plane, of Weitkamp and Magee and Weston and the others, and I was filled with an ineffable sadness for them. Although I had come down alive, I knew there was no hope for the other seven. I chided myself for lapsing into self-concern. I was still alive, and my mind was still alert. I could still function mentally, if not physically.

This was no time to feel sorry for myself. It certainly was no time to give up, despite the helplessness of my situation. I had faced difficult tasks before and gotten through them, although none so difficult as this, to be sure. I simply needed to approach this as a new level of test, one elevated beyond all that I had encountered before, but a test, nonetheless.

I closed my eyes and looked into my soul. I knew I could not survive this test alone, no matter how much determination or willpower I might have. I thought again of my grandfather and his quiet strength, and I knew I was not alone. I had him with me. I had the love of my family with me. I had God and my faith in him with me. I began to pray: "Our Father, who art in heaven, hallowed be thy name. Thy kingdom come, thy will be done, on earth as it is in heaven. . . ." I finished the prayer and opened my eyes. It was as black inside the cell as it was behind my eyes, but the prayer had calmed me. It had restored the lifelong link I had to my faith and my family. It gave me the courage to make it through the night. The next day I would say the prayer again, asking for my family to be taken care of, asking for courage to bear the burdens of whatever was to come.

In a life that had become devoid of meaningful events, a life shut off from all that I had known and loved, saying the Lord's Prayer each day about dusk became my contact to the outside world, to my life, to my family, and to God. It would provide substance at a time I most needed it and would carry me through the dark, lonely days ahead.

7

The Dawn of Darkness

I came spiraling down out of the blackness and awoke with a start, shivering and reaching for the thin blanket that had slipped down by my feet. My left arm ached. My feet and legs throbbed with a dull pain. I opened my eyes slowly and was greeted by darkness and the frightening confusion of not knowing where I was. I could see nothing. Roosters crowed nearby. People were moving around outside, their voices a jumble of indistinct Oriental words. I could hear the sounds of other men hacking and coughing as they tried to rouse themselves from the fitful, restless sleep of men far from home and the comforts of a warm bed and a warmer wife. I could smell the wood smoke of morning cook fires and the thick, pungent aroma of animal dung and human waste.

I reached out with my right hand and felt the rough plaster cast that trapped my chest. My left arm was immobile and ached from the damp chill that covered me. Then it came back: the C-47, the shootdown, my capture, the six days of interrogations at the clinic in Phonsavan, and now Sam Neua and captivity by the Pathet Lao.

The first morning in the cell was cold and damp. I lay on the floor, looking up at the ceiling of my cell. I was confused and frightened. I began to think, my mind a blur. How would I deal with this? How would I cope?

There must be order, I thought. I must establish some order in my life. I must maintain as much control of myself and the situation as I could. Without some order, without some control, I was lost. My captivity would easily become a free fall into despair and possibly madness if I had no structure.

I also realized that I would have to begin to adapt to whatever regimen and isolation that were to be imposed on me. I would have to adopt a lifestyle that would enable me to survive on the barest minimums of food and hope, a lifestyle in which I would be comfortable with myself and the long periods of darkness and silence I was likely to be forced to endure. I would have to draw on all the inner strength, all the values and beliefs learned years earlier as a young boy in rural southern Georgia to pull me through this.

I could not approach this one day at a time. I would have to live event by event, moment by moment, allowing the days and the weeks and the hours to take care of themselves. As I had done so often throughout my life, I would have to take each event as it presented itself and deal with it on its own terms before moving on to the next. Step by slow, painful, solitary step, I would learn to survive the isolation, the darkness, the loss of all I knew and loved.

To my right, I could see gray fringes of light. What was that? Where was the light coming from? Then I remembered the window. Someone had broken out the glass and nailed tin over the window frames and the transom, but it had been a shoddy job. Several inches of tin flapped loose from the top of the transom, allowing a hint of light to infiltrate my cell.

There was no other indication of light in the room, and I guessed—correctly, as it turned out later—that the window and the front of the house faced east. I was lying in the middle of the floor on a thin pad, my head to the south and my feet to the north.

Now I had some sense of direction. To a pilot, it was always of paramount importance to be properly oriented, even when bound to the ground. At that moment, discovering my position in the universe seemed to be a monumental achievement. I congratulated myself for completing what at any other time was a mundane task, one of those things I did so often and so casually that I took it for granted.

Here, though, in this cell, trapped by the cast, my injuries, and the Pathet Lao, I could take nothing for granted. I had nothing, so everything I gained was of major significance. Every accomplishment would be a major accomplishment, every success a wonderful victory, and every bit of information a treasure to be savored.

I was a man deprived of mobility and thrown into a black hole. I was, in a sense, starting over with my life. I would have to learn how to live again with a new set of rules imposed by my captors. Each piece of information gained would be a step forward, a foothold to assist me out of this place.

Yet each success, each victory, and each piece of information gathered and gained and hoarded for future reference brought a moment of despair. Once achieved, that victory could never again be achieved; once won, that battle could never again be won. I would have to move on to another challenge, another battle, in search of another victory.

Finding east and orienting myself had brought a moment of exultation. It also brought that moment of despair. What next? The day. What day was this? I knew I had to keep track of time. Time brought order, and calendars brought order, but I had nothing to write with and nothing with which to make a calendar. I had to keep the calendar in my mind.

I began to count the days. I was shot down and captured 23 March 1961. I was brought here 30 March. That was only yesterday. It seemed like a week ago, or was it a month ago? The night had passed slowly. Now, as dawn approached, time slowed to a standstill. I was suspended in time, unable to goad it into moving faster and unable to do anything to speed it along its appointed route.

I moved my right hand along the floor next to the mat and felt something cold. It was one of the bedpans sent with me from the clinic at Phonsavan. Of course—I needed to use the toilet, but how? I couldn't stand and could barely move. I pulled the bedpan closer and rolled onto my right side, my jutting left arm an awkward and unwilling participant in this normally routine chore. Nothing, I discovered, would be easy for some time because of the bulky cast.

Only with great difficulty was I able to relieve myself, pull up the bottoms of my pajamas, and push the bedpans away. I lay back on the mat, nearly exhausted. It was to be that way for most of the next month, my morning toilet a difficult and demeaning job that sapped my physical strength and eroded my self-respect.

The sun was beginning to come up now, filling the room with a soft, gray, indistinct light. I was to live in that perpetual twilight for more than a year, straining to see and deprived of the warmth of the sun. Had my captors given me any reading material, I would not have been able to read in that light. Nevertheless, there was enough for me to see the interior of my cell and to examine this place I knew would be my home for a long time.

Because the house faced east, there was always some light available in the mornings, but in the afternoons, with the sun behind the house, darkness came quickly, plunging me into the gloom of night well before sundown. I desperately yearned for the sunlight that was only inches away but out of reach.

The house in which I was being held, I surmised, was much more substantial than most Lao dwellings. No doubt it had been built for one of the former French governors of this remote province. The room was small, twelve feet east to west and fifteen feet north to south. The ceiling was about ten feet high. In the southeast corner, to my right and just behind me, was a small fireplace. On the wall to my left were several nails that apparently had been used to hang pictures. Just beyond my feet was the only door to the room, old and wooden, the green paint long since faded. The floor was made of red tiles, each about eight inches square. Over the next few months I carefully counted the tiles each day, seventeen east to west, twenty-three north to south.

The window to my right was the most fascinating and seemed to hold the most promise for exploration. It was a large double window that ran almost floor to ceiling. The glass had been knocked out of the frames and tin nailed over them. A thin strip of wood about a foot long had been nailed to the frames to keep them from opening.

Any exploration would have to wait, though. I was as much a prisoner of my injuries as I was a prisoner of the Pathet Lao. My forays around the room would be limited for some time to visual inspections because of my lack of mobility. I could do little beyond lying on my back and staring at the ceiling, as I tried to look beyond it, into my past and into myself.

When the guards came in to check on me, I began pointing to the stretcher and then to the floor under me. They stood and looked at me for a while, unable to understand what I was trying to say.

"Bed," I said, hoping they knew some English since I knew little Lao.

They smiled and shook their heads. They didn't understand. The guards were young and appeared not to be hardened soldiers. They likely were conscripts from the surrounding mountains who were pressed into service, given a uniform and an old weapon, and told to guard an American prisoner. I was a curiosity to them and an object of some concern. Most probably had never seen an American, much less one so trussed up and helpless.

I continued gesturing toward the stretcher, making crude motions with my one good arm that I wanted to sleep on it. After some time, it finally dawned on them what I was trying to say. They smiled and nodded their heads, took the stretcher out of the corner and lifted me onto it. I was still flat on my back, but at least now I was several inches off the cold tile floor.

However small the victory, it was still a victory. Not only had I managed to communicate with the guards but also I had gotten what I wanted. Whatever control I could exercise over the guards gave me a decided advantage. It was necessary to maintain that advantage and exercise it whenever possible. I might be their prisoner, but I refused to be their captive. I would resist their attempts to make me submit in whatever fashion I could.

By the end of my first full day in Sam Neua, it was apparent that food was going to be a problem. I had been without solid food for a week, subsisting on warm water and watered-down condensed milk. The prospect of death by starvation crossed my mind, but it seemed unlikely that I had been brought to Sam Neua to be starved to death. They could have done that elsewhere.

It was well after dark on the night of 31 March 1961 when I heard guards shuffling around in the hallway and saw streaks of light under the door. They wrestled with the lock for a few minutes before the door opened and two of them came into the room. One carried a lantern. The other held two small objects. The light was so piercingly bright compared with my day in the darkened room that I had to shut my eyes. One guard leaned over next to the stretcher and put the two objects on the floor. One was a small ball of rice wrapped in tin foil and the other a cup of canned fish. The guard motioned me to eat, then turned and left. When the door shut behind him, I was again shrouded in blackness.

I reached out in the darkness and pinched off a small portion of the rice ball. It was cold and sticky but tasted wonderful. I chewed slowly, savoring each piece. I didn't know how long it would be before there would be more. The fish was salty, some type of salmon or sardines, I thought. I couldn't tell for sure in the darkness. The smell nearly made me wretch, but I choked it down.

When I had finished, my stomach seemed bloated, as if I had eaten a huge meal. I lay back on my stretcher, content for the moment, waiting for the blissful solace of sleep to overtake me and free me from the cell, if just for a few hours.

However minuscule that meal seemed, it was a feast compared to what I would receive in the days to come. The fish was a luxury. The small ball of sticky rice was to become the staple of my diet, the lone meal of the day for many of the long days ahead.

8

The Field Marshal and Number One

The interrogations that began at the clinic in Phonsavan resumed 3 April 1961, three days after my arrival in Sam Neua and the day after Easter Sunday. I had passed Easter Sunday as I would pass many more days, flat on my back, trussed up in the cast, staring at the dirty plaster on the ceiling, and waiting impatiently for the small ball of sticky rice and a canteen cup of warm water. It was, to the Pathet Lao, merely another day, as forgettable and uneventful as the day before.

Already the passage of time was beginning to weigh heavily on me, and I could do nothing to speed it along. Time quickly had become a test of my will, my endurance, and my spirit as the seconds passed with agonizing slowness, carrying me deeper into a captivity that stretched out before me like a blank, black slate.

Sunday slowly drifted into Monday. The soft gray light of day had come into my shuttered cell for a few hours and then slowly dissolved into blackness. My meager ration of rice had been delivered, and I was preparing for another long, dark night when I heard shuffling in the hall outside the door and the guards struggling with the lock.

When the door opened, several guards came into the cell. One carried a lantern. Its brightness made me squint as I watched with growing concern this sudden and unexpected flurry of activity. Several more carried a dinette table, a blanket to cover it, and some chairs. They put the table and the chairs close to the east wall. Then they brought in cookies, candy, and hot tea and set them on the table.

The guards left and Number One came into the room, trailed by a Pathet Lao officer in uniform. I assumed he was an officer because he wore a .45-caliber American pistol in a holster with a webbed belt, which was about as close as the Pathet Lao came to displaying rank.

"Are you hungry?" Number One asked. I nodded my head. Of course I was hungry. I had had nothing more than a few meager helpings of rice the past ten days, and I was beyond hungry. However, I was also skeptical. The tea, cookies, and candy appeared to be a crude effort at bribing me into cooperating and telling what I knew—or telling what I had not told the interrogators in the hospital at Phonsavan.

"Please, eat what you like," Number One said, putting the food and tea within my reach. Tentatively, I began eating the cookies and candy.

Number One sat in one of the chairs. The Pathet Lao officer remained standing. He had not spoken while Number One dispensed with the formalities. When Number One was finished, the Pathet Lao officer took over. His English was better than Number One's, although his attitude left something to be desired.

"I am field marshal," he said proudly, his left hand on his webbed belt, his right hand on the butt end of the .45.

The Field Marshal wanted me to be impressed with him, but I immediately sensed that he was far more show than substance. Here was a man whose self-imposed rank far surpassed his abilities. He had an exaggerated sense of self-worth and was trying to make me believe he was something he was not.

"Why are you here?" he asked.

"You brought me here," I said.

"How many Americans are there in Laos?" he asked.

"I don't know. We have people in the embassy, the attaché people, the United States Information Service, places like that."

"Do they report information?"

"It depends on what you call information. If there's a battle somewhere, or an explosion, certainly they tell their boss about it. It gets to the ambassador."

"Are they training Lao policemen?"

"I understand they're being taught to direct traffic and things like that."

"What kind of intelligence do they report?"

"They just train in what the aid program calls for."

"How many American soldiers are in Laos?

"I don't know."

"How many are in the PEO?"

I caught my breath and felt a sinking feeling in my stomach, which I had been slowly stuffing with candy and cookies. If they suspected I was a member of the PEO, I could be in for a long, difficult stay. I was not surprised that my Pathet Lao captors showed a special interest in the PEO because they knew it was involved in Laos and they knew some of the people in it. They weren't exactly sure what its goal was, however. I was no expert on the PEO, but I knew just enough to get myself in a lot of trouble.

"Who is the head of PEO?" the Field Marshal asked.

"Mr. Boyle is head of PEO," I replied. Shortly after my arrival in Laos, General Heintges had been replaced as head of PEO by Brig. Gen. Andrew Jackson Boyle—at least he was a brigadier general until he got to Laos. Once he set foot in the country, he was "Mister Boyle."

"What is his rank?"

"He has no rank. He is a civilian."

"Why does America send civilian people out to do a military job?"

"That's because we are not training military tactics," I said. "Someone has to teach the Lao army to maintain the equipment and how to operate it. The people who do this are technicians in their field and they are hired by the Department of the Army as civilians."

As the questioning about the PEO dragged on, I tried to deflect the direction of the interrogation. To my surprise, I managed to do so with little trouble. I realized that if I was able to manipulate the Field Marshal this easily on the first interrogation I should be able to do so in later sessions. Besides, if I didn't cooperate, what were they going to do to me? Tie me up and throw me in a dark, dirty cell? I was already suffering through that. They couldn't make me suffer any more than I already was.

"What is the American policy in Laos?" the Field Marshal demanded.

"It's a policy of neutrality," I replied.

"What will the American Ambassador say at the SEATO meeting?"

"I don't know."

"Will SEATO enter the war?"

"I don't know."

"If SEATO enters the war, will they remain in Laos?"

"I don't know."

"Where is the Seventh Fleet?"

I hesitated for a moment. The same question had been asked repeatedly while I was in the hospital, and I had no better knowledge now than I had had then. "I don't know," I finally replied.

"How many ships are in the Seventh Fleet?"

"I don't know."

The questioning droned on for several hours. The Field Marshal kept going back to questions about American policy in Laos, about the location of the Seventh Fleet, and about the PEO. He must have gotten as tired of hearing me say "I don't know" as I was tired of saying it. By the time the Field Marshal quit for the night, I was exhausted.

The guards gathered up the table, chairs, tea, and what little remained of the cookies and candy and took them out of the cell. When they had gone and the door closed behind them, the suffocating blanket of blackness closed in on me again.

Although it was late and I was tired, I was strangely stimulated by the encounter. I had actually enjoyed the experience, despite feeling uncomfortable with some of the questions. It was a pleasure to talk to someone in English again, and I felt revived by the mental exertions I had put myself through to avoid revealing any of what little classified information I possessed.

The line of questioning had not helped me answer the one question that had nagged at me since the transfer to Sam Neua: Why was I being held? If, as the questioning seemed to indicate, they thought I was a good source of intelligence, they were going to be sorely disappointed. My knowledge as an assistant attaché was quite limited on the matters that would be of concern to them. Besides, they likely had intelligence sources of their own scattered throughout the American embassy and our compounds in the guise of cooks, clerks, and maintenance people who were supplying them with far more information than I ever could.

The only possible reason for them to hold me was as a bargaining chip. I was an officer, an embassy official, and an assistant attaché. Perhaps they thought they could use my presence on the C-47 as evidence that American military personnel were actively engaged in the war against them and thus gain some advantage in the truce talks that were sure to come. Yet aside from the photos taken shortly after the shootdown, there seemed to be no efforts to exploit me for that purpose, nor would there be in the days to come.

The reasons the Pathet Lao kept me captive were never clear to me or to the U.S. government officials who worked for my release. As I learned from my captivity, however, the Lao often have their own reasons for doing things that are terribly difficult for Westerners, with our linear logic, to understand.

The Field Marshal and Number One returned early the next morning, both in a foul mood. The previous night's session apparently had not gone as well as either they or their superiors thought it should have. They wanted more information and were intent on getting it. They brought their chairs and my day's ration of rice with them, but there were no cookies, no candy, and no hot tea as inducements to talk.

They were frustrated. I was not being a cooperative or compliant prisoner, despite being relatively helpless and at their mercy, and they were still not sure whether I was truly a simple military attaché, as my identification indicated, or a spy. No doubt they would have preferred the latter.

The Field Marshal began the session with a harangue against the U.S. government and living conditions in America. He had all the stereotypes down pat. He described the country as a decaying superpower, bereft of morals and conscience, brimming with social strife and racial polarization, and intent on subjugating the oppressed peoples of the Third World to increase its economic and political control. The Field Marshal paced around the room as he talked, his speech sounding as if it had been rehearsed. Number One took notes, as he had the night before. Finally, the Field Marshal stopped the discourse and looked directly at me.

"How many Thai soldiers in Laos?" he demanded.

"I don't know," I said defensively.

"How many Filipino soldiers in Laos?"

"I don't know."

"How many South Vietnamese soldiers in Laos?"

"I know of only three."

"What do they do?"

"They are attaché people."

"What are their names?"

"I know the name of only one, Colonel Kong."

"How many American soldiers in Laos?"

"I don't know."

"You know well these things!" he shouted. "You are attaché! It is your job to know these things!"

The Field Marshal started pacing again, visibly upset.

"I am a poor man and I am your God, your master," he said angrily, his heavily accented English deteriorating as he became more frustrated. "Mr. Kennedy is not poor like you. Mr. Kennedy is ha-pee. He lives in a big house. His house is bigger than yours. Or is your house bigger than Mr. Kennedy's?"

I chuckled in spite of the circumstances. His pronunciation of *happy* was unusual. I had never heard another Lao pronounce it that way, and the Field Marshal's pronunciation struck me as being rather bizarre.

"Well, Mr. Kennedy's house is a bit bigger than mine," I said.

My amusement only enraged him more.

"You're a poor man!" the Field Marshal said, snapping out the words. "You are sick! You are crippled! I am your God! I am your master! You not tell truth! When I come back, you tell truth or I kill you!" The Field Marshal stormed out of the room theatrically, as dramatic an exit as I'd ever seen. My captors had threatened to kill me several times previously, but I never considered the threats to be very serious. If they wanted to kill me, they would have done so long ago.

I looked over at Number One, who was sitting in one of the chairs he had brought into the cell. He had something in his hands, but I couldn't tell what it was.

"No one cares about you," he said. "Not even your family knows you are here."

He leaned forward and showed me what he had in his hands— my wallet. He opened it and took out photographs of my family. He held the photos in one hand and put the other hand over them. Then he pulled away the top hand and began flashing the photos at me. The faces of Betty and my three children, Barbara, Larry, and Elaine, the youngest, flickered in front of me and then were gone.

It was a terribly crude effort to make me homesick and induce me to cooperate. Instead of sapping my strength, however, seeing the photographs of my family used in that fashion only incensed me and strengthened my resolve to resist. Torture me if you like, I thought, but leave my family out of this. It was the last time I would see those photographs, but I was able to retain the faces of my family, capturing them in my mind as a camera captures the images on film.

Number One ran through the photos several times before the Field Marshal returned. His anger had dissipated somewhat, and he seemed more confused than angry.

"You must be more cooperative," he said.

I remained silent.

"Where is the Seventh Fleet?" he said.

"I don't know."

"What is your guess?"

I saw an opening. He was asking me for a guess, not an answer.

"The last I heard, off the coast of France," I replied.

The Field Marshal nodded, and Number One dutifully recorded the information. So what if I had no idea that at that particular moment the Seventh Fleet was in the South China Sea preparing to provide support to ground troops being shipped to the region in the event the United States decided to commit to a ground war in Laos!

"How many ships in the Seventh Fleet?" the Field Marshal asked.

"I don't know."

"What is your guess?"

"Oh, maybe five thousand," I said.

The Field Marshal seemed pleased. Number One again carefully recorded my response. The location and size of the fleet got to be a game with me as the interrogations continued over the next few days. The Field Marshal would ask me the fleet's location, I'd tell him I didn't know, and he'd ask to me to guess. One day I'd guess it was in the Mediterranean and had a dozen ships. Another day I'd guess it was in the South China Sea and had five thousand ships. Another day its five hundred ships would be anchored off the East Coast of the United States. Each response was carefully noted and recorded. If either the Field Marshal or Number One caught on to my little game, they never let me know. But if they used my figures, the Pathet Lao must have had some interesting planning sessions.

The interrogations had no discernible pattern. Most times the Field Marshal came alone; some days he was accompanied by Number One. On occasion I had consecutive days of interrogations; sometimes there were days between the sessions. Sometimes they were held early in the morning; sometimes they were in the late afternoon.

On several occasions they brought a tape recorder, but we argued long and hard over what I would or would not say on tape. I was intent on not saying anything detrimental to the United States that could be rebroadcast and used against me or my country.

The Field Marshal and Number One were unable to break through my resistance on the issue of the tape recorder. To complicate their problems, the tape recorder often did not work. After hours of wrangling they turned on the recorder and found it was even less cooperative than I. Like the balky lock in the door, it never worked properly, and they fought with it as much as they fought with me. Even with the tape recorder in working order, the questions never varied much. My answers were equally as repetitive. I said, "I don't know" so many times it became like a mantra, a source of power.

I was still trapped in the cast and confined to the stretcher on the floor, but the interrogation sessions somehow strengthened me. I enjoyed talking to someone in English and was buoyed by the repartee. Rather than dreading the interrogations, I actually looked forward to them. The Field Marshal occasionally stomped out of the cell, threatening to kill me, but I came to see this as part of his theatrics.

They made no effort at political indoctrination during any of these sessions. Occasionally the Field Marshal was accompanied by some minor Pathet Lao official, who ranted and raved about how terrible life was in the United States and how we were corrupting the Lao people, but my interrogators never lingered on questions of politics. They were more concerned with questions of intelligence and the apparatus that had been set up in Laos by the United States to collect it. How many agents does Souvanna Phouma have on the border? How many Americans are in Laos? How many Lao do the Americans pay for intelligence? Who is the head of PEO? When I would not cooperate as fully as the Field Marshal thought I should, he would either stomp out of the cell, threatening to kill me, or he would nervously pace back and forth, reminding me that he was my master and that I was a poor man in his control. After all, he reminded me frequently, he was a Field Marshal.

"Kennedy, he is ha-pee in his home," the Field Marshal told me. "You are not ha-pee here. You are far from home. You need to tell us what we need to know so we can send you home and you can be ha-pee."

"I don't know any more," I would say. "I am an attaché, assigned to your country at the invitation of your king."

I often invoked the name of the king because despite the political differences among the Pathet Lao, the Neutralists, and the Royalists, some still revered the king. Although I realized many of the hill tribes who lived around Sam Neua knew nothing of the king, I was hoping to get lucky and find someone among my guards who might be impressed by my mention of the king's name. I was trying anything I could think of to make them believe I was less than a spy but something more than the average embassy staffer.

The more the Field Marshal interrogated me, the more frustrated he became, but he never got to the point of physical violence, despite his threats. I came to believe that he had orders to do no more harm to me physically than had already been done in the airplane crash. His mission, it seemed, was to do no more than find out what little I knew, but in the process he irritated me more than he frightened me.

So, I irritated in return. I began goading him, and each session I pushed him a bit further. The give-and-take with the Field Marshal became essential to my psychological well-being in those early days of captivity, and I did what I could to take advantage of the opportunities.

On one occasion the Field Marshal launched into a lengthy diatribe against the United States and its lack of morals.

"Too many girls have babies without husbands," he said.

I looked at him and smiled. "I know you wouldn't go out and get some pretty little Lao girl pregnant and then run off and leave her, would you? You're too nice a fellow for that, aren't you?"

"Oh, no," he said quickly, embarrassed that I broached the subject of his sex life.

The Lao, I was beginning to learn, do not like direct confrontation or losing face. I knew the Field Marshal was not really a field marshal and that his rank was self-imposed in a vain effort to impress me. I began including "Field Marshal" in virtually every answer to his questions just to annoy him. Physically, I was constrained and no threat to him. Mentally, if I could best him in these interrogations, I would have at least some small measure of control in our relationship.

"How many Americans are in Laos?" he would ask.

"I don't know, Field Marshal," I would say.

"How many PEO people in Laos?"

"I don't know, Field Marshal."

It was "Field Marshal this" and "Field Marshal that" throughout the interrogation. One day he looked at me sheepishly and lowered his eyes. "I am really not Field Marshal," he said quietly.

"Oh," I said feigning surprise, "you're really not a Field Marshal?"

"No," he said. "I am not Field Marshal."

I smiled to myself. I had just won a major victory. I had bested the Field Marshal. I had forced him to submit. Psychologically, I now controlled him and the interrogations. Whenever he came into the room, he and I knew who was in charge. He may have physical control over me, but mentally I was now the aggressor.

Within two weeks, the Field Marshal was gone. Once I had gained control of the interrogations, his effectiveness had diminished to the point where he was useless. I never saw him again.

The interrogations continued for several more weeks, well into May 1961, with several different questioners. I was still in the cast, still confined to the stretcher on the floor. My legs still were not working and I was able to move only slightly. My terrible, frustrating existence was made only worse by my lack of knowledge about what was going on outside that twelve-by-fifteen cell.

Throughout the interrogations, I wrestled with my conscience every waking moment. Was I doing the right thing? How would I be treated when I returned, if I returned? I had signed a statement in the hospital attesting to my medical care. Had that gone beyond the bounds of the Code of Conduct? Did the Code of Conduct even govern me under these circumstances?

The Code of Conduct was still considered inviolate by military authorities. I was to do everything possible to resist, to escape, and to fight back. I was to give only name, rank, and serial number. Nevertheless, this was a different war—war on the fringes and in the shadows, without ethics, without codes of conduct. The rules were made up on the fly, as the situation demanded.

I had no one to talk to about my concerns. There was no POW camp chain of command to consult. There was no one to lean on, no one to hear my pleas and complaints. I was isolated from the military structure to which I had grown accustomed. I realized that the circumstances required me to set my own standards, establish my own code of conduct, and make up the rules as I went along as long as I maintained my honor, my dignity, and my loyalty to my country.

I was exploring new territory here for American military men and was uncertain how to proceed. I was operating under old rules of conduct in a war that seemed to have no rules. This was not World War II or even Korea. I had no idea what this was. Nothing I had learned to that point in my army career had prepared me for this because I was of another era, another generation. The army had not taught or even talked about how soldiers should handle themselves in the face of the enemy in these shadow wars.

What little I learned about life outside my cell during the first few weeks of my captivity came from the questions of my interrogators. Their fascination with the location of the Seventh Fleet indicated to me that it was on the move somewhere in the region, and their focus on the PEO and American military advisers told me there was great concern about additional U.S. assistance being brought into the country. Beyond that, I was in a vacuum, without any news of the world beyond the four walls that enclosed me.

Nevertheless, I was confident that the Pathet Lao hierarchy knew of my whereabouts and treatment and could easily pass this information on to their diplomatic counterparts in the United States. I was reassured in this regard by an event that occurred within a few weeks of my arrival in Sam Neua.

One morning I heard the guards rattling the balky lock on the door. I composed myself as best I could, figuring it was an early delivery of rice or another interrogation. When the door opened, a man I had never seen before came in. He was an older man, obviously well fed, with a thick mane of salt-and-pepper hair. He looked very much like the pictures I had seen of Prince Boun Oum, although I know it was not he. Later investigations failed to uncover this man's identity, although it was evident he had considerable power and stature and most likely was among the upper levels of the Pathet Lao leadership.

The man came into the room, glanced down at me, and then walked around the stretcher as if inspecting my accommodations. The guards remained outside but hovered around the door; they watched the man with a deference that bordered on fear. I tried to read the expression on the man's face, but there was nothing there. It was blank, impassive, and he never looked directly at me. I started to speak, but something told me to keep my mouth shut. I said nothing and just looked at him as he continued his matter-of-fact inspection of the captured American and his surroundings.

He was in the room no more than a minute. After satisfying himself, he left and the door closed behind him, the darkness engulfing me once again. I listened to the sounds of the guards ushering him out the front of the building, trying to figure out what the visit meant. Then it was silent again.

I never saw the man again and never learned who he was. Although the purpose of his visit was unclear at the time, it appears now it may have coincided with the call for a cease-fire in the civil war on 3 May 1961 or the start of the negotiations in Geneva two weeks later. The United States had been pushing hard for a negotiated settlement in the war and wanted prisoners on both sides released. My guess is that this particular visit was to ensure the Pathet Lao power structure I was alive, if not well, and could be used as a negotiating pawn if needed.

About that time the interrogations ended. I did not realize that neither the Field Marshal nor Number One would be returning to the cell until several days had passed without either of them appearing. It was not like them to go so long without questioning me about something.

When the realization finally sank in, the darkness and loneliness of my tiny cell weighed even more heavily on me. The Field Marshal and Number One had been a link to the outside world. Through them I had been able to glean tiny bits of information, and I had someone with whom I could converse in English. Now, there was nothing but blackness at night and twilight during the day behind the shuttered windows of my cell. The only thing I had to look forward to was my daily ration of rice.

The rice, usually in a lump about the size of a grapefruit, was carried in by an unsmiling guard and unceremoniously dumped into one of the dishes beside my stretcher. Occasionally, there was some condensed milk or canned fish, the latter either tuna or salmon, but my isolation was so complete that the guards would not even allow me to see the cans of milk and tuna. They would come into the room with their hands around the can, grab one of my food bowls, turn their backs, and dump the contents into the bowl. The remainder of the milk or fish was left in the cans outside the door. The guards apparently had instructions to give me only half a can a day and not allow me to see the labels of the cans.

Not being allowed to see the cans and their labels seems now a minor concern, but it was made a major concern by the circumstances of the forced isolation and deprivation of all outside stimuli. In the absence of virtually everything, anything becomes significant, no matter how trivial. So it was with those cans. I needed to know whether that food was Vietnamese, Russian, or American.

As the weeks wore on, the pain in my feet and legs gradually decreased, although there was a constant ache in my left shoulder and arm from the cast and the slowly healing break in the bone. I was continually testing the strength in my feet and legs. The stretcher was four or five inches above the floor and as the pain lessened I would ease my feet over the edge and start putting weight on them. If the pain was too great, I would lie back and wait for another day. As the pain became bearable, I put more weight on my feet.

At that point in my captivity, being able to walk again was the most important thing in my life. Even though I was confined inside the cell, being confined to the stretcher was far worse—a double confinement. I was a prisoner of the Pathet Lao, of the cell, and of my own injuries. Walking again represented freedom, even if that freedom was limited to the darkness of my small cell.

Despite the starvation diet, each day I could feel my legs getting stronger. Near the end of my first thirty days in captivity, I was able to roll into a sitting position on the stretcher and then push myself to my feet. At first, I could stand for only a few seconds before the pain knocked me back onto the stretcher. Then, gradually, I could shuffle a few steps in my bare feet on the cold tile floor.

The process of learning to walk again was made no easier by the bulky cast that kept my left arm thrust into the air. It threw off my center of gravity and made me compensate by leaning to the right while attempting to keep my weight evenly distributed on my aching legs.

The shuffle slowly progressed to a limp and the limp to a halting walk. The simple act of getting up off the stretcher and moving around the room was at that time a momentous event. It made life that much more bearable. I had expanded my horizons from the stretcher to the room and now could explore the room and seek to expand my horizons even more. It was a minor victory, to be sure, but in my eyes it was a significant step forward.

While lying on the stretcher, it seemed as if time stopped. Time was a dead weight around my neck, dragging me deeper into depression, loneliness, and the darkness of self-pity. When I began moving around the room, time moved with me. The more I moved, the faster time moved. After a while it became imperative that I move, or else the passage of time ceased.

Escaping the confinement of the stretcher was a personal victory, but it also provided a sense of triumph over my guards. I did not want them to know I could stand on my own, much less walk. The longer they were ignorant of my mobility, the longer I was in control of that part of my life. I had knowledge they did not have, which gave me an important advantage. For the next few weeks, whenever I heard the guards rattling the lock on the door, I would shuffle back to the stretcher, lie down, and pretend I still could not walk.

With my newly discovered freedom, it was time to begin expanding my limited horizons. It was time to look beyond my cell, to see if the world was still out there, to see if I could rejoin it, even in some small way. I needed to know there was life outside the walls of my cell.

9

Window to the World

The stream of light was little more than a sliver, as fine and transparent as a single strand of a spider's web. It came through a pinhole just above eye level in the tin covering the window. I had not seen it while I was confined to the stretcher, but once I regained use of my legs and began shuffling around the cell, it quickly caught my attention. The cell was so devoid of other distractions that I quickly spotted any cracks in what was otherwise a seamless vacuum.

If I stood on my tiptoes the pinhole was at eye level. It was not large enough to see through, but it was large enough to give me hope that life existed outside the dark, cramped confines of my cell. More important, it provided something to think about, something to occupy my mind, and something to make time pass. That tiny beam of light was my lifeline to the outside world.

Once I discovered the pinhole, finding a tool to enlarge it was my next concern. The nail I had seen earlier embedded in the west wall would do the job just fine. It took several days to work the nail loose. I did not want to work too quickly for fear I would be discovered by the guards. If I heard footsteps in the hallway or someone rattling at the lock, I would lie down on the stretcher until they were gone.

I also wanted to make sure that I did not simply rip the nail out of the wall. I wanted to be able to put it back when I was not using it so the guards would not know I had a tool. The more I kept from them, the more advantageous for me. As much as I was at their mercy, I felt it important to maintain some edge.

The nail was a common carpenter's nail about two inches long, but to someone bereft of virtually all other possessions it was a thing of beauty. It was a tool, a writing instrument, possibly a weapon, and one of the few things I could call my own.

The first thing I did with the nail was start a calendar. I had no paper or pencil, so I used the nail to scratch a calendar on the west wall of the cell. I had tried to keep time in my head until then but probably was off a few days when I began. Still, the mere presence of the calendar on the wall provided some structure in my life, which had been stripped of all sense of time and order.

I worked on the calendar from late morning to early afternoon. There was enough light in the cell during that time to see what I was doing. By one o'clock in the afternoon, the sun had started to slide behind the house, and darkness slowly filled the cell again until the next morning.

Working on that calendar and marking off time became a major part of my daily activity. It was like having a cup of coffee at the same time every day, an event I looked forward to with great anticipation. It provided continuity and became one of the foundations on which I built my days in captivity.

I would look at the calendar and wonder how soon I should go over and scratch off the date. Once I did it, I could not do it again that day. As long as I did not do it, I had something else to do, something else to look forward to. The more time I took with the calendar and the more attention to detail I paid, the more time passed, and the object of each day was to make time pass.

The nail also gave me a tool to enlarge the hole in the tin so I could see outside. The decision to enlarge the hole gave me a new set of questions to ponder. As insignificant as they may seem now, at the time they were questions of vital importance: What time of day should I work on the peephole? Would anyone outside be able to see what I was doing? How much noise could I make without being discovered? How large could I make it without being discovered?

I wanted to make the hole large enough so I could see out, but I didn't want it so large as to be evident as soon as someone came into the cell. I stood and studied the window to see if there was some other way to provide a view of the outside world.

The double window was large, stretching almost from ceiling to floor. Each of the windows had a piece of tin nailed over it to keep out the light and block my view of the street. The windows at one time opened out to the street. Now, a foot-long piece of board was nailed horizontally across the frame to keep them shut. A transom above the window also had a piece of tin nailed over it to block the light.

The pinhole was in the piece of tin that covered the right window. Enlarging that hole seemed to be the only way of gaining visual access to what was beyond my cell. I decided to do most of the work on the hole around midday. The guards generally disappeared after lunch, and street traffic was greatly reduced. It was quiet during this time, but there was still enough noise to cover the sound of the steel nail grating against the tin.

If I worked early in the morning, I ran the risk of making too much noise and being discovered. If I worked late at night, there was not enough light to see what I was doing, and I might make the hole so large that it would be easily seen by the guards when they entered the cell to feed me.

I worked slowly and quietly, gently testing the pliancy of the tin. Each squeak of metal on metal caused me to stop and listen for the sound of the guards approaching. Satisfied that no one else had heard, I pressed on, stopping frequently to inspect my handiwork and worrying that I was making the hole too large. I knew this would be my only opportunity. If this hole was discovered, there probably would be more frequent inspections. Putting a second hole in the tin as a backup would double the risk.

I was still working on the peephole when the guards learned I was up and moving around the cell. Their discovery prompted no special precautions—no extra security at mealtimes and no added guards at night to watch for escape. In fact, the guards rarely carried weapons when they came into my cell, and those who did usually had them slung over their shoulders with casual indifference.

On one occasion a guard came into the cell with an aging carbine. He set it in the corner while he delivered my rice and then left without the weapon. I sat on the bed looking at the carbine. I considered hiding it under the mattress to see how long it took him to remember where he left it, but, just as I got to the point of getting up and grabbing the carbine, the guard returned and sheepishly retrieved it.

Their indifference to my mobility puzzled me briefly. Yet, it was in keeping with their attitude through most of my captivity. These were not battle-hardened Pathet Lao soldiers. They seemed more like conscripts from mountain villages, assigned to a thankless, burdensome duty.

The threats of death ended when the interrogations ended. When the Pathet Lao cadre went away, so did the concern about who I was and what I knew. The guards I had now were workers, and I was little more than an animal that had to be fed once a day and kept under control. Someone, somewhere within the Pathet Lao hierarchy had to know I was being held and for what reasons, but those reasons continued to baffle me. It seemed to make no sense to keep me if they were not going to use me in some fashion to better their position in negotiations to end the war or to release me.

The only times the guards got upset was when an enemy airplane flew over. Occasionally the Soviet An-2 Colts landed at the Sam Neua airport, but three times during my captivity I heard other airplanes that clearly were not Colts. One was a propeller-driven plane and the other two jets. They probably were on reconnaissance flights because I never got any indication they were trying to attack the village. No sooner would I hear a plane droning overhead, however, than antiaircraft guns all around the city began firing. For several days following the sightings of those airplanes, the hostility of the guards increased noticeably, as if I was responsible for them. The guards would sneer, occasionally shake their fists, and on some occasions point their weapons at me and dry fire.

For the most part, though, hostility from the guards was not part of the daily routine. Their attitude was either indifference or a shy curiosity about the balding American in their midst. Several guards in particular regularly found excuses to linger in the cell longer than they should. Sometimes they would just watch me eat or smoke a cigarette; other times they would try to converse in sign language or their limited English.

One of the more curious guards was named Thong Seng, the other I came to know as Sweetavong. Sweetavong was in his late teens or early twenties. He apparently took a liking to me because he was from Vientiane and knew I had served there. He was taller than the other guards and projected a sense of self-confidence that the others did not. He was always smiling and friendly when he was alone with me.

One reason Sweetavong apparently felt drawn to me was that I was one of the few people with whom he could converse in English.

Some weeks after my arrival in Sam Neua, Sweetavong came into the cell smiling broadly and pulled himself up to his full height.

"I speak in grease," he said proudly. I was puzzled because I had no idea what he was saying. His accent was thick, and my ear was not yet tuned to Lao English.

"I speak in grease," he said again, still smiling. Finally, it dawned on me. The man could speak some English.

"You speak English?"

His eyes lit up and he nodded his head vigorously. "Yes, I speak in grease."

"Well," I thought to myself, "you don't speak much English, but it's a start."

What little English Sweetavong knew had been learned from the U.S. Information Service in Vientiane, where he apparently had been a schoolteacher before siding with the Pathet Lao and being sent into the mountains. How he came to be guarding an American prisoner in Sam Neua was never quite clear, but it obviously was not because of his command of the English language.

Over the next few months I tried to get Sweetavong into the cell whenever possible. It allowed him to work on his English and enabled me to pump him for information. Still, the conversations were stilted, and I learned very little from him. It also was impossible to tell how much of what he told me was propaganda and how much was the truth.

The guards frequently underwent political indoctrination from one of the Communist cadre. On occasion, I would hear them gathered in a room above my cell, being harangued, reciting their lessons, and then singing "Pathet Lao! Pathet Lao!" with a forced enthusiasm no doubt prompted by those lessons.

On one occasion Sweetavong started talking about the U.S. and Soviet space programs, although I'm sure his knowledge of them was quite limited. He indicated whatever the Russians were doing at that point was far superior to anything the United States had attempted.

"What about the Americans?" I asked.

"Monkeys," he said, motioning with his hands that they had been sent into space and returned. "Come back. All dead," he said with a smile, pleased that the socialist system in which he had been indoctrinated had once again demonstrated its superiority over the capitalists.

That was one of the few occasions after the Field Marshal disappeared and the interrogations ended that any note of political indoctrination was injected into my limited conversations with the guards. Most of the time I was just trying to understand them or make myself understood and trying to pick up even the slightest bit of information about the war that might give me some frame of reference and a reason to believe there would be an end to this someday.

My efforts to obtain information were greatly hindered by my lack of knowledge of the Lao language. I do not have a good ear for languages, and guards were not in my cell often enough or long enough to allow me to pick up much of their language. My vocabulary in Lao was restricted to a few useful phrases:

Sabaidii—hello.
Khawp jai—thank you.
Khao nio—sticky rice.

> *Jhawp lai*—good.
> *Baw jhawp*—bad.

The word I used most frequently during the seventeen months of my captivity was not even a word, but an English corruption of *fire*. I pronounced it "fie," which apparently was close enough to the Lao word for fire or light, *fay*, that the guards understood what I wanted. The guards allowed me no matches in my cell, and whenever I needed to light my cigarette I had to call them. I'd pound on the door and yell "Fie! Fie!" until one of them reluctantly came with a light. Usually it was nothing more than a small branch from their cook fire with enough of an ember to light the cigarette. They apparently had no matches either.

They were not happy to have to light my cigarettes. I had a ration of ten cigarettes a day, although I seldom received that many, and without matches the guards had no choice but to bring me a light to shut me up. I knew enough not to disturb them during their early afternoon siestas or late at night. At all other times, getting a light was a matter of persistence.

Thong Seng, the only other guard with whom I developed a relationship, was short and wiry. Unlike Sweetavong, Thong Seng had no pretense at sophistication. He was a farm boy recruited to fight the Royal Lao Army, but instead he had been sent to unload rice in Sam Neua. Now he was guarding the Pathet Lao's American prisoner.

Thong Seng was truly curious about me and often would come into the cell just to stand and watch. He looked at me as if he had never seen another American before, and I don't doubt he had not. I was an object to be studied and inspected. After several months of this, Thong Seng apparently decided all the propaganda he had heard about Americans was not necessarily true. As my captivity dragged on into the winter, he became a source of extra food and kept alive a fading belief that if escape was not possible, perhaps release was.

Several times early in my captivity the guards would come into the cell as a group and start showing off. It was as if they wanted to impress me with their positions of responsibility or were trying to prove themselves to me.

The leader seemed to be a guard I called Shandee. He was quite impressed with himself. Although I did not see him often, whenever he came into the cell, he made a point of strutting around, pulling a huge wad of *kip*, the Lao currency, out of his pocket, and waving it in my face. He wanted to show me he was the treasurer, the keeper of the kip, and the man who had been entrusted to control the finances of this unit.

Through sign language, he told me I had an allowance of ten kip a day for food and cigarettes. I doubt they ever spent that much, considering what little food I received. On occasion, they would bring me a few small water buffalo sausages or some green bananas. Most of the time, though, my lone meal of the day was a lump of glutinous rice plopped unceremoniously into my bowl.

The daily routine had a spirit-numbing sameness to it—silent twilight during daylight hours interrupted only briefly by a guard bringing a ball of rice and some water and then suffocating blackness. The guards seemed relatively secure that I was nailed into that cell without hope of escape. No doubt they, more than I at that point, realized the futility of escape. It was too far to walk out, and a lone American in this part of Laos would be quickly spotted and recaptured.

Soon after the guards learned I could walk, they took out the stretcher and replaced it with a bed and a chair. The chair was made of wood with a straight, high back and wooden slats on the seat. The bed was of a similar simple design, wooden with narrow slats on which there was a thin mattress that served not only as my sleeping pad but also as my hiding place.

Everything I owned went under the mattress for safekeeping: the blue-striped civilian shirt I was wearing when captured, the nail, whatever extra cigarettes I had scrounged from the guards. Hiding my belongings there made no sense because it was the first place anyone would look during an inspection, although there never was one.

The bed also had posts at each corner with a mosquito net draped over them. The net was important not so much for keeping out the mosquitoes, which were not that bothersome here in the mountains, but for keeping the rats off me. Several times during the first few days in the cell, rats had scurried across my face and chest in the middle of the night, waking me with a start and putting me in a cold sweat because I could do little to avoid them or defend myself.

The chair became my table and nightstand. I kept my food bowls and drinking cup on the chair, sitting on the bed to eat my rice and whatever other small bits of food they might throw into the bowl. The bed and chair were pushed close to the west wall, providing some space to walk and think.

During construction of the peephole, I began to pace. Pacing helped me think and helped time pass. When I sat in the chair or the bed, time seemed to stop, and thinking became more difficult. I had to be in motion, doing something, moving, thinking, and worrying about my peephole. As the hole in the tin grew larger by infinitesimal fractions, I would inspect it from all angles while pacing the cell. The pacing was in a racetrack pattern, counterclockwise. From the bed on the west wall to the south wall, then past the fireplace to the east wall and the window, north past the door and back to the west.

When I wasn't inspecting the hole during the pacing, I'd put my head down to count the red tiles on the floor. The counting became hypnotic, almost like a comforting mantra in which I could lose myself and ease the burden of time. Seventeen tiles east to west, twenty-three north to south; seventeen east to west, twenty-three north to south.

When the hole in the tin was about the size of a dime, I decided to stop enlarging it. Any larger and it surely would be discovered. Even at that size it seemed as large as a picture window. With the door closed, the beam of light came through the hole like a spotlight after the sun crested the hills on the east side of the valley. The light would start as a spot on the west wall, moving slowly down the wall before sliding onto the tile floor.

I would sit in bed and watch that beam of sunlight—my personal beam of sunlight—walk across the floor. When the light was on the fifth tile, it was time for food. When it was on the seventh tile, I would begin thinking about the first cigarette of the day. The light marched across the floor with relentless regularity and I would know time was passing. But by noon the light was gone, and the cell began to fill with the gradually thickening darkness.

That peephole became my window to the world. It was like being born again. After more than a month of darkness and deprivation, I could once again participate in the world outside my cell, if only as a voyeur. I had a whole new perspective on my captivity.

With the peephole completed, I began inspecting that world beyond my cell. To the east, about fifty feet in front of the house, was a dirt road running north and south. Directly across the road was a long, low wooden building. To its right was an opening, and beyond that was what appeared to be a small lake. I later discovered it was a rice paddy.

To my left and across the road was another wooden building that appeared to be a town hall. Two flags flew in front of the building: the Lao flag and a blue flag with a white dove on it. Beyond the buildings to the east were the brush-covered hills that rose steeply from the valley in which the village of Sam Neua lay.

That was all I could see, but the new vistas provided a whole new meaning to life and a sense of excitement for things to be discovered and learned about Sam Neua. Although it was a provincial capital, Sam Neua was no more than a crossroads river town in the jungle highlands. Highway 6 came in from Vietnam to the east, turning south at Sam Neua on its way through thick jungle and steep mountain ridges toward the village of Ban Ban and the Plain of Jars. The road in front of my house was just an access road through town. It faded off into a jungle path north of town. The Sam River, little more than a stream at that point, ran roughly north and south through the town behind the buildings across the street from the cell, just out of my view.

At that time the village had no more than about three thousand people. They were mostly Black T'ai, White T'ai, and T'ai Neua. They lived in a collection of ramshackle bamboo huts along the river and crossroads and scratched out a living with rice and opium. There were virtually no ethnic Lao in the village.

The house in which I was imprisoned undoubtedly had belonged to one of the former French administrators, if not the governor of the province. As best I could tell, it was one of the more substantial structures in the village. At the time of my captivity, it was being used not only to hold me but also as a distribution point for rice. On numerous occasions I heard trucks backing up to the house and sacks of rice being loaded or unloaded by the guards.

Sam Neua was so far removed from Vientiane that it was more like Vietnam than Laos. The people here had far more in common with the Vietnamese and exhibited the centuries-old fears and suspicions of the lowland Lao, who rarely ventured far from the Mekong Valley.

Because of its location, Sam Neua was a key choke point on the invasion route from North Vietnam. Its isolation made it the perfect place for the Pathet Lao to plot their strategies against the government in Vientiane. Although Sam Neua had previously been the scene of much fighting between French and Viet Minh troops over the years and later would see fighting between factions of the Lao insurgencies, it was relatively peaceful now, immune from surprise attacks from the ground because of its remoteness.

Sam Neua was clearly established at the time as the Pathet Lao headquarters, but I did not realize that the guards were unaware that I knew where I was. When I mentioned one day to Sweetavong that I was in Sam Neua, he turned and said sharply, "How do you know you are in Sam Neua?"

I smiled and said nothing. The less he knew of me and what I knew, the more I could confuse him and retain some sense of power, some sense of self-worth. That is why the peephole was so important to me. It was mine, and it belonged to me. I had labored over it, worried about each fraction of its enlargement. More important, I, not my captors, controlled when and how long I would look through it.

Building the peephole and keeping it secret from the guards became a major victory that helped lift me out of the dark depression in which I wallowed for the first thirty days I was confined to the stretcher. The peephole gave me light. It gave me a window to the world. And it gave me hope and a reason to look forward to the next day, despite the crushing boredom that was sure to accompany it.

One of the first things I discovered through the peephole was a morning market down the street to my right. Early in the morning, long before dawn, I would hear someone walking down the street. I rushed to the peephole and saw a man walking south toward the market and carrying a Coleman lantern. Rightly or wrongly, I told myself that he was the town butcher, going early to get the meat prepared.

At first light other townspeople began moving toward the market. There were Lao, North Vietnamese, even three Indians with large white turbans and black beards who appeared regularly. I thought at times of yelling to them but decided it would do me no good. I was being isolated from other prisoners and from the general population for a reason. To draw attention to myself at that point would be counterproductive and could lead to the discovery of my peephole, my only source of freedom in this wretched confinement.

Unknown to me, the peace talks aimed at negotiating a cease-fire in this latest fighting and terms for an extended settlement had opened in Geneva, Switzerland, on 16 May 1961. Had I known, my spirits would have been buoyed immensely. Of course, knowing that the Chinese Communists had taken out six-month leases on their villas and limousines in Geneva, apparently expecting lengthy negotiations, would just as effectively have negated any enthusiasm.

Still, the mere knowledge that peace talks were being held would have given me some hope. As it was, I had nothing but great uncertainty about the length of my captivity. The only thing certain in my life at that point was that the sun would come up every day. Beyond that, nothing was certain. I tried not to think about how long I might be there. It was too depressing to have to live without a goal, without an end in sight.

The peephole became my salvation. The people I saw through it were my link to a world from which I had been excluded. I tried to live vicariously through them, eagerly watching them go to morning market and trying to anticipate what food they would return with. Some would bring back live chickens. Some would bring back vegetables. Others would be carrying large chunks of meat when they came back up the road. I looked forward to seeing the same people each morning. If they didn't show up, I'd worry about them, wondering where they had gone or what they were doing.

The peephole was my escape. I would stand there for hours on my tiptoes, listening and watching for anyone or anything to pass by. When I wasn't at the peephole and I heard something in the street, I'd rush to the window and press my eye to the hole.

That dime-size hole enabled me through my imagination to leave the cell and participate in the lives of those people I saw in the street. By escaping into their lives, I escaped my own life. Instead of lying on my bed, staring at the ceiling, and sinking deeper into depression and self-pity, I was able to escape into the fantasies I constructed: What did they do? Where did they go? How many children did they have? What would they have for dinner that night?

I gave them families. I gave them jobs. I gave them lives. It was like watching people on TV; they didn't know I was there, but I could watch them and monitor them. After a while, I came to believe I knew them as well as I know the TV newscasters I now watch nightly. They don't know I'm there or that I'm watching, but I am there, beyond what they can see and beyond what they know.

I realized that in the absence of hope, I would have to create hope for myself; in the absence of life, I would have to reconfigure mine so that, if this ordeal ended before I died, I would be able to emerge physically and emotionally intact.

Now that I could see what was outside my cell, I began to entertain thoughts of escape. To consider it seriously, I would first have to get rid of the bulky cast. Then, I would have to be able to open the window without the guards knowing it. Without any tools, that could be a difficult task, but it was worth a try. It would give me something to do, something to think about, and something to help time pass.

10

Learning to Live Without Life

By early summer I was moving easily around the cell. The pain and stiffness in my feet and legs were gone, although I retained a few scars as permanent reminders of the shootdown. The only other remnant was the bulky cast that encased my left arm and upper torso.

I felt my arm had healed sufficiently to remove the cast. The muscles were atrophied to the point I could move the arm around inside the cast without pain, but I had difficulty convincing the guards it was time to be rid of the cast.

Every morning for several weeks I would point to the cast and make sawing motions when the guard came into the cell with my daily ration of rice. He would merely grunt, plop the ball of rice into my dish, and leave the room, as if he understood but didn't care.

In late June the guards finally ushered a small, dirty man into the cell. He carried a handsaw, and at first I thought he was a carpenter. He was missing several front teeth and had a haircut that looked as if it had been done with a dull knife. His hands were incredibly filthy, with grime embedded under his nails. He looked like someone's addled child who had just spent the day rolling in the dirt. Even I—who did not have access to a toothbrush, comb, or enough water to bathe; whose hair and beard were long and matted; and who was terribly filthy in my own right—was appalled by this man's appearance.

Whatever his shortcomings in sanitation the man had some expertise with the saw. It took him some time to remove the cast, and the guards came in and joked and laughed about it as he worked. Nevertheless, the cast came off without any additional wounds.

When the guards and the man with the saw had gone, I examined my left arm closely. It was sore and stiff and shriveled from its confinement in the cast. I thought perhaps that is how I would look when freed from my prison. The doctors who had set the arm had not done a particularly good job. My left arm now was at least a half-inch shorter than my right.

Still, it was a great relief to be free of that cast. I could breathe freely again, and I could move around the cell unencumbered. Most important, I had use of my arm again.

I saw the dirty little man two other times during my captivity. On those occasions I was unable to get out of my bed for several days. It was probably little more than the flu that made me ill, but the lack of basic medicines, even aspirin, made me feel much worse. In my weakened condition, with so little protein and no vitamin C in my diet, any minor illness could quickly become a major problem.

On those occasions I would shout to the guards that I was ill, and after a long wait they would bring in the dirty little man with the bad teeth and bad haircut. He'd study me for a few minutes as if he could divine the nature of my illness by sight and then give me two pills and leave. That would be the extent of my treatment. I don't know what the pills were, but I took them. I recovered no more quickly, but I also got no worse.

Dysentery and the terrible aches and cramps that accompany it were constant companions during my captivity. The guards had neither medicine nor food to help ease the gut-twisting pain that accompanied the attacks, which left me too weak to do anything more than squat over the bedpans to relieve myself.

The dysentery attacks would quickly fill the bedpans with runny, mucus-laden stool. The stench was like a thick cloud inside the cell, lingering long after attacks. Waving their hands and holding their noses, the guards winced at the smell when they came into the cell, but they refused to wash the bedpans, and I had neither paper nor water to clean myself, making the problem even worse.

I knew that prolonged dysentery attacks would weaken me to the point of being susceptible to a host of other diseases and infections. The only thing I could do to keep the situation from getting any worse was to insist that what little water the guards allowed me must be sterilized.

Initially, the guards brought my water in a GI canteen cup.

That's all I had for the day. It was barely enough to drink, let alone wash, and brushing my teeth was out of the question. Toothbrushes seemed to be an unknown commodity in Sam Neua.

When the canteen cup developed a leak, it was replaced by a small black kettle. It held more water but still not enough to clean myself. Only after some particularly virulent dysentery attacks, when I had fouled myself to the point that I could no longer stand my own smell, did I permit myself the luxury of using some of my drinking water to wash.

Getting sterilized water soon became an obsession. If the guards brought the water into the cell and it was not warm, I'd hand it back to them, point at it, and shout, "Fie! Fie!" in my pidgin Lao to indicate I wanted it boiled before it was brought to me.

If the guards got out of the cell before I had a chance to check the water, I'd sniff it and sip it. If it smelled or tasted as if it had come straight from the river, I'd go to the door and begin pounding on it and shouting, "*Baw jhawp* water! *Baw jhawp* water!"

The water usually came in the mornings with my single meal of the day. I had to ration it to make it last. Every day during the guards' siesta period after lunch, as the darkness in the cell began to thicken, I would take inventory of my supply of water to see if I had enough to last me through the night and on into the next morning.

If I felt I would run out of water during the night I would wait until after the siesta and then begin banging on the door, trying to get the attention of the guards. Even if I did, there was no guarantee they would bring me more water or that they would boil it first. Sometimes I was successful in getting water more than once a day, and often I was not.

Curiously, the guards could be intimidated fairly easily. The more angry and obstreperous I became, the more cowed they were. It was apparent that they had been ordered to keep me alive but without any frills or luxuries. I was to be given the minimum of food and water necessary to sustain my life, but no more than they received, and what they got was very little.

Mealtime generally was a highlight of the day, even though the meal consisted of nothing more than a ball of glutinous rice, what the Lao call *khao nio*. I knew when the guards gave me my food it would be the last time that day the door would be opened and that I was on my own until sometime the next day.

I made each meal into a singularly significant event. The anticipation of what might accompany the rice heightened the excitement of its arrival. Something more than the usual—a bit of sausage or a handful of greens—provided what amounted to the makings of a feast.

During the entire seventeen months of captivity I received bits of sausage no more than three times. On other occasions, only slightly more frequently, I received a leafy green vegetable that resembled mustard greens or turnip greens. Three times the guards brought in a handful of small, green bananas, the only fruit I received during my captivity. I savored the bananas, chewing them slowly and feeling the sweet pulp fill my mouth and slide sensuously into my stomach.

Beyond that, there was nothing but rice to fill my rapidly shrinking stomach. Ice cream and a cold drink with ice cubes rattling around in a frosty glass became recurring daydreams that haunted me throughout the captivity.

It took some time to sense any weight loss. I knew I was losing weight rapidly, but I didn't have any means of judging it. The hospital clothes I still wore were loose and baggy before I began losing weight, and the weight loss was hidden in the clothes. Without a mirror I had no sense of how much weight I had lost.

The weight loss bothered me less than the lack of sanitary facilities. My toilet continued to be the two permanently fouled bedpans. I had no toothbrush and nothing to wash myself with. Still worse, my hair and beard had become long and matted after only a few months. No doubt, if I had had access to a mirror, I would have been stunned at the specter that looked back at me.

The only amenity was cigarettes. Although my allotment was supposed to be ten cigarettes a day, I seldom received that many. On those days when the cigarette ration was fewer than ten, I usually managed to make at least one additional cigarette by conserving enough tobacco and paper from the butts of those I smoked. If the cigarettes were the last few in the pack, the guards would often leave the pack, providing enough paper for two or three additional cigarettes when I could save sufficient tobacco.

Working my way through the daily cigarette ration became a major part of each day. Smoking each cigarette became an event unto itself. I would think about how deeply to inhale on each puff, knowing if it was too deep I would not be able to enjoy this one cigarette as long.

Inconsequential questions became significant in that vacuum that was my cell: How soon do I smoke the first cigarette? How much time should I allow between cigarettes? How long will it take the guards to come and light it? When I get my daily ration, will the guard give me the pack so I can make extra cigarettes from the paper?

Sounds also become major events under those circumstances: a rifle shot, a guard shouting in the street. What did they mean? How would they affect me?

Three propaganda broadcasts each day could be heard over loudspeakers throughout town. The first usually was early in the morning, the second from shortly before noon until well into the siesta period, and the last just before dark. Usually these broadcasts consisted of little more than martial music or someone talking in Lao. But one morning quite early in my captivity I was awakened to the strains of "Sunrise Serenade." "Are they doing that for me?" I wondered. "Do they know what they're playing?"

I waited for weeks to hear "Sunrise Serenade" again but never did. After a few months, the broadcasts ended altogether. That in itself was a source of considerable speculation: Why had the broadcasts ended? Was the system broken? Did they not want me to hear what was being said? The possibilities were endless.

Another event early in my captivity that evoked a great deal of speculation was the installation of poles and lines for electric lights. Through the peephole, I watched as crews installed poles along the road and ran lines into the building where I was being held and into the long, low wooden building across the street. That building, I had determined, was a supply point. Through the peephole I often saw Pathet Lao soldiers go into the building and emerge with a canteen, a rifle, or some other piece of military gear. Number One also was a frequent visitor there, although he never came out with anything; perhaps he was checking on supplies being stored there.

After a few weeks of work, a generator cranked up nearby. It sputtered for a while and then stopped. It sputtered again and stopped. The third time they cranked it, the generator came to life and began feeding juice to the lights. The guards began clapping and cheering for the single low-wattage bulb that had just been installed outside my door. The Pathet Lao were creeping slowly into the twentieth century. Silently, I cheered with them.

I would see these things and hear sounds in the night and think about them for hours, examining the possible consequences or benefits to me. When I wasn't doing that, I created elaborate scenarios involving the people I saw through the peephole.

One old Lao man with a pack mule was a regular visitor to Sam Neua. When I did not see him for a few days, I would invent trips for him, following him step by step as he wandered up into the mountains, stopped to eat a handful of cold rice for lunch, searched for wild game in the mountain highlands, and warmed himself by a fire at night.

These excursions into elaborate fantasy worlds somehow kept me rooted in reality. If I could have no life of my own, I would live in the lives of all the people I saw through the peephole. As long as I could escape the cell through the lives of other people, I could deal with the wretched conditions in which I found myself.

I pondered many times how insignificant my life was, how little it mattered whether I lived or died to anyone other than my family, my friends, and me. Rather than depress me, that realization brought with it a sense of peace. I became comfortable with myself and my thoughts. I was secure in my belief in myself and my God, able to deal with death if it came, and willing to bear whatever burdens life dealt me.

The Lord's Prayer I said each day gave me great solace. I would walk to the northwest corner of the cell, stand facing the wall, and begin the prayer: "Our father, who art in heaven. . . ." I would say it aloud, knowing the guards either would not hear me or would not understand what I was saying. No one was going to interrupt me; no one was going to stop me.

I said the Lord's Prayer and then prayed for the safety of my family, for the souls of the men on the C-47, and finally for strength for myself. Despite the circumstances in which I found myself, I thanked God he had spared me for whatever reasons.

I had, through some miracle of divine intervention, escaped the C-47. I had been given another life, such as it was in this vacuum. But each day, each hour, each minute, I slowly began to fill the contents of that vacuum with what I knew and what I felt.

The guards saw nothing when they came into the cell: the chair, the bed with the mosquito net and mattress pad, and an aging, dirty, smelly man in ragged hospital garments. When they closed the door and darkness descended, however, that cell became my world, filled with thoughts and people and fantasies that the guards could never have. Deprived of everything, I built my own world—part fantasy, part reality—that only I could see and only I could feel.

I built the world as I paced, seventeen tiles east to west, twenty-three north to south, seventeen east to west, and twenty-three north to south. My attempts to enlarge that world never ceased. Once I regained use of my legs, I took the chair over to the window and pushed away the loose tin that covered the valance. That gave me an unobstructed view of the street. On occasion I would be standing on the chair and looking out into the street when passersby would notice me. They'd see me, look away, and then do a double take. When they looked back, I was gone, ducking down out of sight. I was like an apparition. I was there, but I was not there.

The guards took a while to discover what I was doing. Whenever I heard them rattling the lock in the door, I would get down from the chair, move the chair over by the bed, and sit in the bed waiting for them to come in. I looked for all the world like an innocent child.

When the guards learned I was pulling the tin away and looking through it they came in and nailed it back into place. There was never any physical retribution, but they let me know that they were not happy that I had showed myself to some of the residents of Sam Neua. For whatever reason, they were trying to keep my presence in town a secret.

With the tin securely nailed back into place, I began reexamining the window as a means of gaining additional light or as an escape route. The possibility of being trapped in the building if there was a fire frightened me, and I wanted to know that I could get out if I had to. Escape was more an idea without any substance at that point. I was too unsure of myself and my situation to have any clear idea of what to do or where to go. The idea of escape remained an elusive apparition until after midsummer 1961, when I seriously began to consider it.

Late on the morning of 15 July, long after my rice and water had been delivered, four guards came into the room. Accompanying them was a short, older Lao man who obviously had not missed many meals. He eyed me curiously and then motioned for me to stand in the middle of the cell. Pulling out a tape measure, he began measuring me. Although he spoke no English he pointed to me and said, "Hanoi. America."

Was he telling me he was measuring me for a suit of clothes for a trip home via Hanoi? I had nervous flutters in my empty stomach, my heart was racing, and my mouth went dry as I considered the possibilities. Dare I think of home? Of my wife and children? Of ice cream and steak and cold iced tea? The guards enjoyed themselves immensely, giggling and laughing, as the fat old tailor measured me.

"Hanoi!" one guard said, pointing and laughing uproariously.

"Mossacow! Mossacow!" another said.

"America! America!" said a third.

The tailor held up five fingers, indicating I would be leaving in five days. I tried to control myself and my emotions but could not. I was almost trembling by the time the tailor finished his work and left. I let myself believe I was going to be released, and it didn't matter to me where I would be going. I just wanted a change. I wanted out of that dark cell.

Two days later I was standing at the peephole when I saw a man come to the front door and hand some clothes to one of the guards. Were these my clothes? Was this the day I was to be moved?

I waited impatiently on the cot. Finally, I heard someone fumbling with the lock on the door. A guard came in, put the clothes on the chair, and quickly left. It was a traditional guerrilla uniform: jet black cotton trousers with a drawstring waist and a pajama-like black cotton top with two chest pockets and two side pockets.

There was no ceremony and no explanation. As I examined the new clothes, I felt that these were not suitable for any transfer or release. I realized I was not going to be shipped out of Sam Neua after all. I was not going anywhere. This was simply my new prison uniform to replace the ragged hospital clothes I had worn for the last several months. New clothes of this type could mean only one thing: They were going to keep my butt locked up for a long, long time.

The realization hit me hard. I had allowed myself to get too excited about the prospects of release without any real evidence that it was going to happen. Anticipating too much and then having it yanked away could be psychologically destructive. I realized then that I could not afford to look too far into the future. I would have to attend to the tasks at hand, the simple things, and let all else happen as it might.

I went back to pacing—seventeen tiles east to west, twenty-three north to south, seventeen west to east, twenty-three south to north—looking for something to take my mind off the depression that was settling over me. As I paced, the idea of escape that had been lingering in my mind began to take shape.

Escape had been impossible for the first thirty days. The leg injuries that kept me confined to the stretcher and the cast on my arm made me helpless. Now, escape seemed a reasonable possibility well worth exploring. The windows opened from the inside out. Only a foot-long piece of half-inch board nailed horizontally across the frame kept the windows shut. If I could work the window loose from that board without disturbing the nails, I might be able to push the windows open.

After testing both windows, I decided to concentrate my work on the right side, which seemed more pliant than the left side. I had enough space to get my fingers around the edge of the frame so I could push it out a fraction of an inch, then pull it back. I worked on the window for days, pushing and pulling by fractions of an inch, until the window came free of the nails in the board.

Late one night in September, I finally got the window open— a great victory. I was elated. I opened the window slowly and looked out. It had been five months since I had seen the sky, except for what I could see out the peephole. I poked my head out the window and breathed deeply, freely. Above me, the stars glittered in the night sky.

Now, I had an escape route. I had a way out. I had an option to pursue if I thought it worth pursuing. Still, I had to weigh the costs of captivity and slow deterioration against escape and possible quick demise.

The next step was to break off the nails flush with the back of the board so that the window, when closed, would appear to be still nailed to the board. This took more long days of work, bending the nails up and down, up and down, hours on end, until metal fatigue won out and the nails broke off. The nailheads were still in the board, but I could open and close the window at any time. There was enough tension to keep the window closed when I pulled it shut so that when the guards came into the room they wouldn't be able to detect anything.

Once I was able to open the window, I began planning my escape. The guards had no set routine. They were terribly disorganized, and initially I saw no problems slipping out of the building past them and into the village of Sam Neua.

But then what? The military supply point across the street presented a significant problem in that soldiers were coming and going from it at all hours. Up the street to my left was the town municipal building, which also had constant activity.

I didn't know what was beyond there, but I knew a round-eyed white face in this landscape would not go unnoticed long. If I did escape, the only sensible route was through the jungle, which presented another set of complex problems.

If I was able to get out of the building undetected, would I be able to get out of the town and into the jungle undetected? If I got into the jungle, where would I go? The Plain of Jars was being fought over. The Pathet Lao controlled the roads. More important, how would I navigate? I did not know this area of the country at all. I had only a general sense of direction: Vietnam was east, the Plain of Jars was southwest, and Vientiane was some distance southwest beyond that.

I was looking at weeks of walking, possibly months. The only thing I could be sure of was that a lot of people would be trying to kill me. I would be on my own the whole way until I penetrated friendly lines, which in itself held out the possibility of being shot by one side or the other.

I would have to stick to the jungle, although I knew the terrain between Sam Neua and Vientiane was dangerous and deadly, offering no assurances of food, water, or safe haven. From Sam Neua to the Plain of Jars was inhospitable jungle and steep mountains filled with Pathet Lao, villagers who most likely would be unfriendly to an American, snakes of every description, and tigers.

Several times I asked Sweetavong how far it was to the Plain of Jars and Xieng Khoung province. Each time he gave a different answer. One time he would say fifteen days. Another time the response would be sixty days. He apparently knew as little as I did about the distance from Sam Neua to freedom.

Still, I began hoarding rice and cigarettes in anticipation of an escape. Water would be a major problem. I had nothing to carry water in and did not know the terrain well enough to chart a route that would ensure I would be close to water during a journey south.

The prospect of escape, while exhilarating, was also worrisome. I was not the picture of health. My endurance was sapped by the lack of protein and fresh fruit. Yet I was honor-bound by the Code of Conduct to attempt an escape if it was within my power to try.

I struggled with that requirement. Was I, an American military man, bound by the Code of Conduct under these circumstances? This was not war, but what was it? I had done nothing to aid the enemy, if in fact the Pathet Lao were our enemy. I had done nothing to shame my country, my family, or myself. I had resisted efforts to get information out of me during the interrogations until we got to the point that I felt I had psychologically bested my captors.

The idea of escape nagged at me. Was it better to try to escape and risk what seemed like sure death at the hands of the Pathet Lao or be swallowed up by the jungle? Given the fact we were not at war, should I ride out the captivity with honor, maintain my dignity, and struggle to survive so I could tell the world about what had happened here? I was the only witness. Without me, who would tell my story, and who would know the fate of Ed Weitkamp and the crew of the C-47?

Early one morning in September, I awoke about daylight and opened the window. Usually none of the guards was up at that hour, but this morning one of the guards who liked me the least, the dour-faced Kong Phong, was standing in the doorway just to the left of the window, looking out into the street, and watching the sunrise.

We looked at one another in surprise. Then he yelped something in Lao, rushed inside, and began shouting to the other guards. I quickly shut the window. All hell was breaking loose in the house. Guards stumbled down the stairs, shouting to one another, as someone began frantically working the lock to get in the cell.

As usual, getting the door open took several minutes. I sat down on the cot with a sick feeling in my stomach. The guards had not resorted to beatings or physical torture to this point. All the torture had been psychological, even if unintended. Now that I was out of the cast and, in their eyes, relatively healthy, would this be the excuse they were seeking to beat or torture me?

When the guards finally opened the door, four of them rushed into the cell with their weapons drawn. While three watched me, Kong Phong took a hammer and nails and redid the window while shouting at me in Lao, his face red with anger. Within minutes, the window was repaired. Kong Phong glared at me, then said something to the other guards, and they all left the cell.

It was a relief to escape the beating I fully expected, and having the window repaired was actually a blessing. Working it open again gave me something to do. No sooner was the door locked than I went back to work, and within a few days, I had it open again. Nevertheless, the incident with the window gave me pause about any escape. If catching me looking out the window was that easy, finding me scurrying through the countryside undoubtedly would be just as easy, even if I did get out of the house.

In the end, I decided escape would be the worst-case scenario in the event a major war broke out. I did not think I would survive heavy fighting trapped in the house. I would try to get to the jungle in the confusion and take my chances there, even though those chances were quite slim.

Still, having the ability to open the window and get out gave me an option. I wasn't trapped. I wasn't confined. I wasn't a prisoner. I was a free man who could choose to stay inside, where it was safe, or risk whatever being outside brought with it. The mere fact that I had the choice excited me. No matter how bad things got, I knew if they got any worse I could get out of the house and try to get away. It was one of those intangible things that kept me going, even in the worst of times, no matter how unrealistic escape was at that point.

I thought of escape constantly, but I knew it was something I would attempt only as a last resort. There were many reasons to believe it would end in disaster. If I get out of the house, do I get shot? If I make it to the forest, how long before I die of starvation?

Every move, every gesture, and every action had consequences, and I had to figure out those consequences before I took the action that would bring them on. I figured an ill-advised or poorly timed escape attempt would produce consequences too great to risk. Escape would be the final solution, the last act of a desperate man who preferred quick death in the jungle to slow death in that cell.

The decision not to attempt a hasty escape was a decision based on the practical reality of the situation, not on the inflexible idealism of the Code of Conduct. I would wait them out, no matter how terrible the waiting.

11

States of Mind

The day begins. It is yesterday. It is tomorrow. It is every day I have known and every day I ever will know. It begins as I drift slowly out of sleep's warm, comforting blanket into the suffocating blackness of my cell. I lie in the darkness, my eyes open to the void that surrounds me, seeing nothing, wondering if what I hear is real or a dream from which I only think I am waking.

I am somewhere between sleeping and waking, never quite sure which is which because of the blackness in my cell. I stay there as long as I can. To be fully awake is to begin to think, to think is to ponder the passage of time, and to ponder the passage of time is to have time stop in place and refuse to move. The longer I am able to avoid waking, the shorter the day and the less of a burden time is.

If I hear the butcher coming down the street on his way to market in the predawn darkness or see the light from his lantern, I rush to the peephole just to catch a glimpse of another human being. Once I am awake, it is impossible to lie in bed and think of what might be or what might have been. Time stops when I am in bed. Only when I am up and moving does time pass.

Even in the dark, I begin pacing to make the clock move: seventeen tiles east to west, twenty-three north to south, seventeen west to east, twenty-three south to north. I hope the guards begin to stir soon so I can get a light for my first cigarette of the day.

At first light I stand by the peephole and watch the people on their way to the morning market: the Vietnamese, the Hmong, the Indians in their turbans, the old man with the pack mule. Then I watch them return with a handful of greens or a slab of meat or a fresh chicken or duck, and I wish I could walk from my cell and join them for breakfast. I envy them in their richness, knowing all I will receive this day—all I receive every day—is a ball of cold, sticky rice.

When morning market has ended, I wait for the sun. When it is out, I have a beam of light by which to measure time. The closer to the west wall, the earlier in the morning. As the beam approaches the fifth tile I listen for the guards in the hallway and the rattle of the lock that signals the arrival of my day's ration of rice and cigarettes and a kettle of tepid water. When the rice arrives, I eat slowly, dragging out the simple act of chewing the sticky grains simply to have something to do.

As the sun approaches the seventh tile, I begin to think of my first cigarette of the day. I lift the bed pad and check my supply. I select which one I will smoke and hide the others. Then I go to the door and begin pounding and shouting for a light for my cigarette. "Fie! Fie!" I yell to the guards. They pretend they do not hear.

"Fie! Fie!" I yell again. Still they are reluctant to produce a light for my cigarette.

"I need a light, goddammit!" I scream through the door as I pound on it with my fist. Finally, I hear someone rattling at the lock, untwisting the wire that holds the door shut. The guard opens the door and reluctantly, if not sullenly, offers a stick from the cook fire with a burning ember at the end to light the cigarette. I motion that I want to go outside. The guard shakes his head no for the hundredth time.

"Khawp jai," I say when the cigarette is lit, "thank you," but only if I am being particularly magnanimous.

Then I pace: seventeen tiles east to west, twenty-three north to south, seventeen east to west, and twenty-three north to south, an endless cycle to make the stubborn clock move. I wait for something to happen: a shout in the street or scattered rifle shots in the distance.

The afternoons are the worst part of the day. They are twice as long as the mornings, three times longer than the nights because nothing happens in the afternoons. The guards sleep, and the town disappears. I count my cigarettes, measure my water, and pace: seventeen tiles east to west, twenty-three north to south, seventeen west to east, and twenty-three south to north.

I have somehow obtained two old towels and have turned them into mules for my feet. Two pieces of braided cloth serve as straps to keep the mules in place. Each morning before I begin pacing, I make a ritual of carefully tying on the mules. I fold and refold the towels, positioning them perfectly, then tie them on. The tiles are not so cold on my feet with the mules, but, more important, working with the mules provides another means of making time pass.

I itch continuously. My hair, stringy and matted from lack of a combing or washing, is well below my shoulders; my beard is full and bushy and eventually will reach the middle of my chest. I am filthy and unkempt, a miserable human being by my appearance, but a man not yet broken by the loneliness, isolation, or darkness.

By the time the cell begins to sink into complete and absolute darkness early in the afternoon, I begin to think of sleep. In sleep there is no loneliness, no despair, and no imprisonment; in sleep there is release. Time passes and I do not worry for its passage. When it is dark, I lie on my bed and wait for sleep to capture me and take me away from this cell. So it has been every day I have been here, and so it will be every day for the rest of my life.

By late September I had been imprisoned for six months. I had not seen the sky over my head or felt the warmth of the sun on my face or breathed anything but the fetid air of my cell. I frequently asked to be allowed outside to work. I was willing to work and would have gladly planted and grown my own food. It would have enhanced my diet, given me some exercise, and enabled me to get out in the sun once in a while.

When the guards opened the door, I would point outside and make motions to demonstrate that I would chop wood or hoe in a garden—anything to be allowed outside this cell. The guards never thought much of the idea. "I will ask," Sweetavong said each time I asked him, but nothing ever came of those hundreds of requests. I remained locked away from the sky, the sun, and any sense of life.

One afternoon in early October I went to the door and began pounding on it to get the attention of the guards. I wanted a light for a cigarette. "Fie! Fie!" I shouted.

When the guard opened the door, I motioned again that I wanted to go outside. This time the guard nodded and with his rifle motioned me out of the cell.

Surprised, I cautiously walked into the darkened hallway. The guard motioned me toward the back of the house. Two guards playing cards picked up their weapons and joined us. They led me out the back door and into a small courtyard. At last, after six months, I was outside.

I looked around in bewilderment. The sun had slipped behind the mountains to the west, casting shadows on the water covering a rice paddy just behind the house. The air was warm but tinged with a hint of the brittle chill that was to come. I looked up at the sky—a cloudless blue dissolving into purple and black. It looked wonderful. Then, I breathed deeply and freely for the first time in six months. Guards lounged around the courtyard, but they appeared unconcerned that I might try to escape.

One young guard thought he should tell me what would happen if I did. He began to raise his weapon and point it in my direction. The weapon was older than he was, a rusty relic of the French occupation. As he lifted the weapon to his shoulder, the stock fell away from the barrel and clattered to the ground. The guard stood there in shock, unsure of whether to cry or run away. I stifled the urge to laugh and continued to look around, enjoying every precious second in the warmth of the late afternoon sun.

I had been outside no more than three minutes when the guards motioned me back inside the house. As I trudged down the hallway, I could see myself inside the cell even before I was in it, surrounded by darkness, pressed in by loneliness, and unable to breathe. There was a sinking, hollow feeling in my stomach as the guards shut the door and the curtain of darkness descended. Then the guards twisted the wire around the doorknob to lock it and it was quiet. I was alone again.

The days passed with slow, numbing regularity. Any small aberration in the day—any change in the routine, in the food, in the parade of people to the morning market—was enough to make it a special day, but there were few special days. The ordinary days began to run together, one into the other, each as terribly long as the one before but not quite as long as the one that will come tomorrow.

I began to wonder what was going on in the world beyond what I could see and hear. Were there peace talks? Was there still a United States? Did anyone know I was here? Did anyone care? I was losing touch with home and what I knew of life before my capture.

One day, in a fit of patriotic fervor, I decided to list all fifty of the United States on the west wall of the cell to remind myself of home. With my trusty nail, I began slowly scratching the name of each state in the soft white plaster next to my calendar.

"A-L-A-B-A-M-A," I wrote in large block letters. "A-L-A-S-K-A." Then I told myself, "Slow down. Take some time. Make time pass." I wrote, "A-R-K-A-N-S-A-S."

On I went, slowly, meticulously scratching each name into the wall. The game of states became a major project. I took the better part of two days to put the names on the wall. When I was finished, I stood back and admired my work, counting to make sure I had all fifty.

The count was forty-nine. I was puzzled; I was sure I had fifty. I recounted: still forty-nine. I closed my eyes and visualized a map of the United States. I was missing one state, but which one?

I began pacing and reviewing the states. Which state was missing? I'd pace and look at my list, pace and look at my list, but the fiftieth state eluded me. Finally, I went to bed, still reviewing the states, trying to find the missing one.

The morning brought no help. I went back to pacing and thinking. The better part of another day passed before it finally dawned on me—Iowa was the missing state.

No sooner did I scratch those four letters on the wall than a sense of depression began to settle over me, replacing the momentary excitement I had felt when I discovered that Iowa was the missing state. The game was over and could not be played again. It had taken nearly three days but now was finished. I would have to find something else to occupy my mind to make time pass.

By October the weather had turned cold in the highlands. Mornings were always cold and damp in Sam Neua, but the coming of winter brought a constant wet chill that permeated the cell much as the blackness did. My feet had hardened from the months of pacing on the tile floor and could barely feel the cold through the threadbare cloth of the mules, but my lack of clothes and lack of body fat made the cell feel much colder. I was given nothing more to wear than the black cotton pajamas and nothing more to keep me warm at night than a light cotton blanket.

One night in mid-October I was lying in bed, trying not to think about how cold I was, trying not to think about how hungry I was, and searching for sleep when I saw a light approaching the front of the house. I rushed to the peephole and saw four men approaching the front of the building carrying a lantern.[1] The guards immediately began undoing the makeshift lock, and I turned away from the window and sat on the cot.

The guards came into the room and began making elaborate preparations, much as they had during the initial interrogations with the Field Marshal. A table was brought in and covered with a blanket. A Coleman lantern, an empty pitcher, cups, ashtrays, and an empty flower vase were put on the table. Four chairs were arranged around the table. As they worked, the guards smiled and talked among themselves. Then they pointed to me and indicated with sign language and a few words of English that I would be signing some papers regarding my release. "You lucky boy. You going home," one guard said.

Could it be true? After the depressing disappointment of the summer, when I had allowed myself to get too excited about a possible release while being measured for new clothes, I was reluctant to get my hopes too high again. Something did not seem quite right about this, but I would play along with the game. If I was to be released, I would get excited when it happened. If it did not happen, I would not suffer the same disappointment as I had several months earlier. I suppressed my excitement and decided to try to exploit the situation. I made smoking motions. "Cigarette?" I said to the guards.

Still smiling, one guard pulled out an entire pack of Vietnamese cigarettes and handed it to me. It was a great windfall. If I rationed these as carefully as I rationed all my other cigarettes, I would have enough for a week; with my regular ration thrown in, I could indulge in an extra cigarette each day.

The guard lit my cigarette, and I puffed away while the preparations continued. When the guards were satisfied with the arrangement of the table and chairs, they ushered in my four visitors.

One was Number One. He had not been in the cell since May, but I had seen him frequently through the peephole going into the supply center across the street or the municipal building up the street.

Another Lao man in the group was older. I had also seen him through the peephole and had ascribed to him some position of authority within the Pathet Lao hierarchy in Sam Neua. Number One treated him with a certain deference that made me believe the older man outranked him.

The third member of the party was Vietnamese. He was taller than the two Lao. He had piercing black eyes and carried himself with a great deal of authority. He spoke Vietnamese, Lao, French, and reasonably good English, and he served as interpreter.

The fourth man, a European, was never introduced. He simply came into the cell with the other three and began speaking French. He appeared to be in his late thirties and wore a wrinkled business suit that was too small for his stocky frame. At first I thought he was a Russian. Only later did I learn he was a Hungarian journalist named Gyoergy Mate who had come to Sam Neua to interview me for the Budapest Communist party newspaper *Nepszabadsag*.

Mate and the two Lao spoke French while the Vietnamese translated into English. It seemed more like a conversation than an interview or an interrogation. Mate took no notes the entire time. He asked me the perfunctory questions about my name, rank, serial number, and assignment, which I gave him. "How are you treated?" Mate asked.

"I have one meal a day, cigarettes almost every day, a bed to sleep in, and a mosquito net for the bed," I replied. "But the cell is very dirty. Plaster falls from the ceiling all the time."

I pointed to spots on the ceiling where the plaster had cracked and fallen. I had not seen the cell this well lit in some time and was unaware of how dirty it was. Cobwebs and piles of dirt were stacked in the corners. "It's very dark in here and I'm never allowed outside," I went on.

"You are better off than many Lao people," the Vietnamese retorted.

"You are a long way from home," the Hungarian said soothingly. "Do you regret what you have done?"

"Regret what?" I thought. I had not done anything to regret. "No," I said, staring at him.

"Do you regret being on the plane?" the Hungarian went on.

"Of course."

"What would you think if an ambassador was shot down over the United States?"

The question didn't make any sense, but I didn't want to risk irritating him too much. "I'd have to know more about the situation," I said as diplomatically as possible.

"You are a diplomat," the Hungarian said. "You do not have to fly combat missions."

I said nothing. There was an uncomfortable silence in the room. All I could hear was the breathing of the four men and the hiss of the Coleman lantern.

"Do you know of the misery you cause the Lao people?"

"Any time there is a war, it creates misery for people on all sides," I said.

Again there was silence in the room, save for the sound of the Coleman lantern. I looked across the table at the Hungarian, who looked at me and then shrugged his shoulders. The interview was over.

The four men got up and left the cell as quickly as they had come. The guards removed the table, chairs, and other objects. I bummed one last light for my cigarette just before the guard closed the door and blackness descended on me. I lay in my bed and watched the orange glow from the cigarette as I tried to figure out what had just happened.

It didn't make any sense. There had been no papers to sign, there was nothing about any release, and if this was an interrogation, it was done even worse than the previous ones. Not until more than a year later, long after my release, did I learn that Mate was a Hungarian journalist. When he returned from his journey into the heart of Pathet Lao country, he filed one dispatch about me that was picked up by American wire services and carried in my hometown newspaper. In his eyes, I was the prisoner from hell: I refused to cooperate with my captors, I refused to be cowed by their threats, and I refused to be intimidated or coerced by their propaganda.

Mate wrote that when he asked one guard about me, the guard replied: "Don't talk to me about him. I try to explain everything, but it goes in one ear and out the other. He thinks we are savages who hardly deserve the name of men."[2] Of their efforts at political indoctrination, Mate wrote that the camp commandant had been "trying to teach him, but no result seems to be showing."[3]

After the embarrassment caused by some Korean War POWs who defected to the Chinese, Mate's story about my efforts to resist my captors played well back home. Of course, his article had a number of inaccuracies, not the least of which was his observation that the room was furnished with a "petroleum lamp and a supply of books in English."[4] I would have killed for a lamp and some books.

Mate also quotes me as saying I was being given enough food, cigarettes, and medicine and that I was receiving regular letters through the Red Cross.[5] Mate portrayed my treatment and my captors as far more humane than they actually were. The truth, in this instance, was something Mate could manipulate to suit his own purposes.

A few days after Mate's visit, I was standing by the peephole in the middle of the afternoon when a Lao man dressed in civilian clothes came to the front door of the house. I had never seen the man before, but he apparently was an official of some rank. He said something to one of the guards and immediately was ushered into the cell.

Without saying a word, he handed me two envelopes, turned, and walked out. I stared dumbly at the envelopes. In the dim light of the cell, I could barely see them in my hand, much less read them. What were they? I walked over to the peephole where some light was available and held the envelopes close to my face. They were Red Cross telegrams! Someone knew I was alive! My hands shook as I opened the first one and held it to my face to read. It was from Betty. "Wife, children are well, entire family thinking of you and hoping to hear good news soon," it read in the stilted, formal style of telegrams. I closed my eyes and held the telegram to my face, trembling with excitement and relief. They knew I was alive! They knew I had not died in the crash! They were not suffering the terrible uncertainty of not knowing whether I was alive or dead. I saw Betty's face, and the faces of my children, and breathed a silent prayer of gratitude.

I hurriedly ripped open the second envelope and held it close to read in the dim light. It was from my mother and said much the same as Betty's telegram. A great sense of peace settled over me, not for me, but for my family. I knew from these telegrams that they knew I was alive and they would be able to deal with my captivity in their own way. Knowing there was some certainty in their lives provided me with the first moment of true happiness since I had been taken prisoner.

As I held the telegrams in my hands, I began to think about all those things I had not allowed myself to think about before then. I shuffled over to the cot and sat down, my mind a blur of images of home and family and food and the soft, comfortable warmth of my own bed.

I walked back to the peephole and held the telegrams up to the light, read them again, and reveled in the warmth of love and caring that emanated from them. Someone cared; I was not alone.

I returned to the cot. I was elated at having some word from my family, but at the same time a shadow slowly began to intrude on my elation. The telegrams said something more. They said I was destined to be here for some time to come. They said: "Hey buddy, here's some mail. You're going to be with us for a while."

Despite the dark reality the telegrams brought concerning my future, they became treasured possessions, my only link with the outside world. They went under the bed pad for safekeeping, along with my nail and my blue-striped civilian shirt. Some days I would pull out the telegrams just to look at them and run my hands over them. They were my contact with home, my bond with my family, and proof that life still existed outside my dark, rank prison cell. They were justification for surviving.

I received mail only once more that year, on 5 November. The same Lao man delivered it in the same unfriendly, unsmiling manner. As he handed two envelopes to me and turned to go, I said, "Does this mean the war is over?"

"No," he said curtly, moving for the door.

"I'd like to work. I'd like to get outside each day," I said hopefully.

"I'll check with the authorities," he said, closing the door. I never saw him again.

Instead of telegrams, the early November mail consisted of a birthday card from my children for my thirty-eighth birthday the previous 24 May and a letter from my cousin Margaret White. Margaret's letter was bright and cheery. It told about her family and the goings-on back in Waycross, Georgia. She talked about her husband, referring to him as "my sweet Willie," although everyone else in the family called him Snowball. I permitted myself a smile and a chuckle as I read Margaret's letter. It was good to know people still had normal lives and that life as I once knew it still existed.

The days dragged on into late November with a mind-numbing sameness. I could tell nothing about the war or the peace talks or anything else from the guards. I continued to press them for occasional trips outside the cell, but to no avail. The days were a constant struggle against time, worrying about the water, counting my cigarettes, trying to get a light for my cigarette, and pacing, pacing, pacing.

I began to wonder how much longer I could endure this dark

isolation. Except for the telegrams and letters, I was shut off from all outside contact. The attacks of dysentery were infrequent but violent. My weight had dropped dangerously low on this subsistence diet. I was slowly starving to death.

Thanksgiving 1961 proved a turning point in my will to survive. I had been held eight months in conditions that were subhuman; the Lao treated their mongrel dogs better than they treated me. "Surely for Thanksgiving," I thought, "I'll get something more than a lump of cold rice." I violated my own rules and began thinking of what wonderful food I might receive on Thanksgiving, even though there was no logical reason for me to believe the Pathet Lao had the slightest idea of what the holiday meant or that this day was even a holiday. It was simply my mind spinning beyond the bounds of common sense and rational thought.

Perhaps I'd receive some real meat, I fantasized. Turkey would be wonderful, chicken would do quite nicely, maybe some vegetables or fruit, something other than bananas. I began the day with great hopes of a sumptuous feast. The beam of light moving across the floor was painfully slow. It reached the fifth tile and I strained to hear the guards in the hallway fumbling with the lock. There was nothing. The light hit the sixth tile and moved on, and still nothing. I went to the door and pounded on it. "Food!" I demanded.

Still no reply. I pounded again. "Give me some food!" I shouted. I put my ear to the door and listened. No one was moving in the hallway. "Food! Food!"

I pounded my hand against the door and continued to shout. "Food, goddammit! I want some food!"

"*Bhaw mi,*" came the faint reply from somewhere down the hall.

No food? I was enraged. "This is my Thanksgiving, you dirty sons of bitches! In America we wouldn't treat a dog like you people are treating me!"

There was no response from the other side. The faint voice was gone. There would be no Thanksgiving; in fact, there would not be any food. Angry and bitter, I retreated to my cot, my stomach churning and my head spinning. Was this another form of torture? Were they doing this deliberately? I was nothing to these guards, less than human, an irritant in their lives that had to be tended and kept locked up. I was an insignificant speck.

Angry at the guards, I brooded all day. My wish for Thanksgiving was my way of keeping alive my ties to who I had been and to what I remembered of my former life. I was now deprived of all else, and my thoughts of Thanksgiving were my way of retaining some sense of who I was and where I came from. I had no reason to think that they would understand anything about Thanksgiving, except that I wanted them to because that would have meant they acknowledged me as a human being.

Recognizing my beliefs and my rituals would have forced them to acknowledge me as a human being. Instead, I was a prisoner from a culture they neither knew nor understood. I was to be handled with no small amount of disrespect, as they handled their own prisoners. They had no real concerns about me as a human being, and that, in retrospect, is what bothered me most of all about that day. It was not so much that they denied me food on the day that I thought, perhaps mistakenly, was my Thanksgiving; it was that they denied my existence as a human being.

As the day wore on, I paced to work off my anger at the guards, and as I paced I thought of Thanksgivings past in Hebardville as a child and with Betty and my own children at the various places we had lived over the years. I made up my own menu of turkey with dressing—soft, with plenty of onions—and fresh greens from the garden and one of my grandmother's fruitcakes. I saw myself carving the turkey, as I did in so many of those years, inhaling the rich smell from the steaming bird, and then sitting down and giving thanks for all the blessings in our lives.

Instead of trying to suppress thoughts of home and family, which usually depressed me greatly, that day I dredged up every memory I could. The more I thought about those Thanksgivings, the more thankful I became and the more forgiving of the guards. Instead of wanting to kill them for depriving me of my food, I began to fantasize about taking them to America, away from this environment of economic deprivation and political indoctrination. I would clean them up, give them new shoes and clothes, and take them to nice restaurants to show them how we lived. I was angry at the guards but felt no malice toward them. They were doing what they were told by people who saw me as a product of a political and economic system they despised.

Yet no one, I told myself, should be treated like this, not even a dog. I had to survive to tell others what had happened to me, to warn them should a similar fate befall them. If I could survive the cold and lack of food during the coming winter, I would reassess my situation in the spring. I set my goal for 22 March 1962. That would mark my first anniversary in captivity. If I was released before then, so much the better; if not, I would take stock of my situation and move on.

That day seemed a million years away, but the date gave me a goal. That goal gave me hope to sustain me during a winter that promised to be terribly long and bleak, darker than any I have ever known. I went to the corner of my cell and began reciting the Lord's Prayer. I prayed for my family, I prayed for forgiveness, and I prayed for strength to make it through the winter.

12

Deeper into Black, Deeper into Night

Not long after the Thanksgiving incident, the dangerous lure of escape began to entice me once again. The humiliation and degradation of that day had unleashed anger and bitterness that lingered for weeks.

I knew the longer I waited to attempt an escape, the less likely it was to succeed. I was becoming steadily weaker from the skimpy rations of rice. I was healed of my injuries, but was not sure how much my strength and ability to survive had been eroded, and once out in the jungle, how much more quickly would my strength be stripped away?

I also had come to the realization that I would not be able to escape alone. There were too many guards in and around the house, too many soldiers in Sam Neua, and too many obstacles in the countryside that worked against the survival of a lone American wandering through the wilderness. I needed a guide, an interpreter, someone who knew the country, and someone who could tell me which villages to avoid and which would help me.

I began to cultivate a relationship with Thong Seng expressly for that purpose. He spoke little English, but Thong Seng had demonstrated a friendliness toward me that the other guards had not. Although Sweetavong knew more English, he also seemed a more devoted party member who was less likely to risk helping me.

As my captivity dragged on into winter, the number of guards in the house was drastically reduced for reasons unclear to me. For several weeks Thong Seng was virtually the only person I saw. He brought my food and cigarettes every morning and on several occasions made other unexpected visits to the cell.

During those unannounced visits, Thong Seng gave me extra rations of food and cigarettes. He demonstrated a generosity and a sense of humanity I had not seen in the other guards. He also washed my clothes and gave me a pair of old socks, which were a godsend. My mules were in tatters, and my feet, although toughened from months of pacing the tile floor of the cell, welcomed the addition of the socks for the cold, damp nights that came with winter in Sam Neua.

Thong Seng's attitude was markedly different when other guards were with me in the cell. He would hang back on the fringes of the crowd and let others take the lead, but when he was alone with me he demonstrated what I perceived to be a genuine curiosity. He never got angry with me, even when the other guards did.

On those occasions when Thong Seng and I were alone in the cell, I broached the idea of escape through a combination of sign language and my limited Lao vocabulary. Earlier, I had tried to talk to him about Vientiane and an infamous night club there, the Vien La Tri, also known as the Green Latrine. During Kong Le's occupation of Vientiane, troops from the Neutralist and Royal Lao Army factions had partied there at night when they were done fighting one another for the day.

When I first mentioned the Vien La Tri to Thong Seng, he smiled and immediately began doing a native dance known as the *lamvong*, which involves slow steps and graceful and intricate intertwining of the hands and fingers.

As I became more confident in my relationship with Thong Seng, I began to pantomime my escape plan. He watched with great seriousness as I mimicked sleeping, then waking, and slipping out the window. I made walking motions with my fingers and said: "Vientiane. Vien La Tri." Then I pretended to drink a beer, smoke a cigarette, and break into my version of the *lamvong*. Every time I got to the *lamvong*, Thong Seng would smile and imitate me.

This word game and pantomime went on for several months without any apparent results, but it also brought no retribution from Thong Seng, and he obviously did not tell any of the other guards of my plan or of my overtures to him.

One day well into winter, Thong Seng came into the cell in an unusually serious mood. He took his rifle and began using it to point out various guard positions within the building and walking patrols outside. Then he pointed south, indicating the road forked not far from the house. One branch went east to Vietnam, the other south to freedom. "Vietnamese," he said, pointing east and south.

He held up his hands and started an exaggerated trembling as if to say he was deathly afraid of the Vietnamese.

"Many Vietnamese?" I asked.

"Beaucoup Vietnamese. Beaucoup Vietnamese," Thong Seng said, using his sparse French and pointing in all directions to indicate we were surrounded by Vietnamese. He was trying to tell me that any escape attempt would deliver me into the hands of the Vietnamese.

I had absolutely no knowledge of the tactical situation at the time. There seemed to be little fighting in our area and no nighttime blackouts to indicate the town was under threat of attack from the air or the ground.

However, there were occasional indications that what Thong Seng told me about the number of Vietnamese soldiers in the area was not entirely an exaggeration to keep me from making an escape attempt. Several times I saw armored vehicles and other heavy weapons moving through town that clearly were of Russian design and appeared to have Vietnamese crews.

Another time in that winter of 1961–62, I had slipped into bed and pulled the blackness over me like a shroud, but I was unable to sleep. There was a strange stillness in the town: There was no pedestrian traffic in the street. No dogs barked. Even the chickens had ceased their incessant cackling and scratching. It was as if the word had been passed that everyone and everything should stay off the street.

Then came a strange shuffling sound from the street. It was a rhythmic, hypnotic sound. I lay in bed for some time listening, wondering what it was, before I decided to get up and investigate. I went to the peephole and looked out. I had just enough moonlight to see columns of troops marching north past the house. The only sound they made was the shuffling of their sandals or tennis shoes on the dirt road. There was no jingling of equipment and no cursing or muttering in the ranks. The march discipline was incredible.

From what I could see, the troops carried rifles and had fully loaded packs. I don't know how many passed the house before I got out of bed, but I counted 136 during the short time I watched. It was at least a company, perhaps more. My initial reaction then, and my belief today, is that these were North Vietnamese troops. I had never seen any Lao troops, not even Pathet Lao, exhibit this type of rigorous march discipline.

Equally as fascinating as the silent shuffling of the marching soldiers was the silence in town. There were no sounds or movements that night except for the soldiers. It was terribly eerie to stand there and watch them march past the house and through the deserted town in complete silence. Some time after they had passed, the town slowly began to return to normal. A few lights appeared here and there in houses, people emerged into the street, and the dogs began to bark again. This unsettling experience led me to believe that the Vietnamese were even more numerous than Thong Seng had indicated.

There were other indications of fighting around Sam Neua, although that fighting was, at most, sporadic. Several times I saw small groups of Pathet Lao soldiers hurriedly assemble into a patrol and head out of town. Sweetavong also told me he sometimes led patrols to fight against anti–Pathet Lao groups in the area.

"I like to fight," he told me.

I smiled and nodded, wondering all the while if this was nothing more than boasting to impress me, but on one occasion Sweetavong disappeared for several days. When he came back, he was wearing a red beret much like those worn by Kong Le's paratroopers. He also had some cigarettes he said he had taken from rebel soldiers and a piece of rope he said he would have used to bring them back if they had surrendered. They had not surrendered. "General Phoumi's soldiers," he said proudly.

General Phoumi's soldiers this far north? They obviously were not part of an offensive, or there would have been much more military activity in town. I doubted it was any sort of rescue attempt because even in my wildest dreams I did not believe any military force would be sent to try to rescue me. I was not worth the lives it would cost. So I doubted Sweetavong's story but pressed him for details.

He told me he had been sent out on patrol with ten other Pathet Lao soldiers to capture three of General Phoumi's soldiers who had been seen in the area. The patrol marched for approximately eight hours, arriving at its destination about midnight. They surrounded a building and ordered the soldiers inside to surrender.

The soldiers refused and began shooting at the patrol. Sweetavong said he then opened fire with his Browning Automatic Rifle. In the ensuing battle, Sweetavong claims he killed two of the soldiers and wounded the third in the leg. The wounded man escaped, even though the house was surrounded, which led me to wonder about the veracity of the story and the effectiveness of his patrol. Still, I could not dispute the red beret and the extra cigarettes. Something had happened; exactly what, I'm not sure.

The signals from these events were mixed and confusing, but they were enough to tell me that I had little chance of survival outside Sam Neua. If the jungle did not finish me off, surely hostile mountain villagers would, and even if I managed to escape both of those, I would still have to deal with Vietnamese and Pathet Lao troops.

The decision of whether to attempt an escape was an incredible burden that weighed heavily on me. Should I attempt an escape, as was my duty as a soldier, even though I knew the chances of survival were virtually nil? Was it better to try to survive the captivity so I could tell others what had happened to me? There certainly was no guarantee that I would be able to survive this confinement, given the rate at which I was physically deteriorating.

The question gnawed at me as the winter dragged on into 1962, with no end in sight to the war or my captivity. These were terribly bleak days. They were cold and dark and lonely, broken only by an infrequent incident that had little bearing on my captivity or, it seems, the war.

One day I heard the rumbling engine of a tractor in the street and went to the peephole to see a low trailer loaded with Chinese laborers being hauled into town by a Massey-Ferguson tractor. The laborers were dressed alike, in black pajamas and conical straw hats, but the tractor drew my attention. It was just like the Massey-Fergusons I had seen plowing the fields of south Georgia when I was a boy.

The sight of that tractor brought back a flood of boyhood memories of friends, family meals, and the warmth of summer nights that kept me happily reminiscing for days.

On another day I watched in fascination as a large group of ragtag, barefoot soldiers was issued new tennis shoes. The soldiers were in a loose formation in the street in front of my cell. One man who appeared to be Vietnamese watched as another man tossed pairs of tennis shoes into the ranks from the supply building across the street. The soldier catching the shoes would quickly try them on. If they fit, he kept them; if they didn't fit, it was his responsibility to swap them with another soldier. When they were finished, all the soldiers had new tennis shoes. They were happy, the Vietnamese supervisor was happy, and the supply man was happy.

During my entire captivity, I was able to speak with only one woman. One female soldier occasionally worked with my guards but never came into my room. One day the guards left the door to my cell open for a few minutes. The door to the room across the hall also was open, and I saw the woman in there cleaning the floor. "Sabaidii," I said, offering the traditional Lao greeting.

She looked up, momentarily startled at the dirty, bearded American speaking to her, then went back to her work.

"Sabaidii," I said again. She did not bother to look up this time.

I was determined to make her speak to me, though. I was determined to hear a female voice.

Finally, after a few minutes of my repetitions of *"Sabaidii,"* she turned and said slowly and sweetly, *"Sabaidii."*

That was all, but it was enough to remind me that there were still things worth living for, still things soft and sweet and warm, and still things waiting for me back home.

On yet another cold night during that long, black winter, I had fallen asleep when four guards burst into the cell carrying their weapons, a lantern, and some firewood. I sat up in bed, wondering what was going on. They ignored me and went directly to the fireplace. After much chattering and laughing, they started a fire.

Once the fire was lit, they sat on the floor, put their weapons aside, and pulled out a deck of cards. The guards played for cigarettes. Each time a hand was won, the winner would pass three or four cigarettes to me, apparently my share of the pot for allowing them to use the fireplace. I sat on the bed and watched them play, smoking my sudden windfall of cigarettes and stashing the rest under the bed pad.

The guards were interested only in the fire and their card game. They said nothing to me and didn't disturb anything else in the room. I could not follow the game they were playing, not being much of a card player. They would each put a card on a pile, and then one would slam the card down on top of the pile and they'd all cheer and hand me more cigarettes. By the time they quit several hours later, I had several days' worth of cigarettes tucked under my bed pad.

After that, I began asking the guards for their cards. On occasion, they would let me have them. The first time they did, I went through the cards and counted them. One was missing. I scrounged up some paper and made a fifty-second card so I could play solitaire. Very seldom did the guards allow me to keep their precious cards, however. They had almost as little as I did, and the cards were one of their treasures. "Cards?" I would say.

"Bhaw mi," they'd say, telling me they didn't have the cards. Only if I was persistent enough would they allow me to use the cards for a few hours.

The memories of that winter are scattered and ill-defined, like those in a bad dream. I remember only fragments of those months, for it became a tremendous psychological struggle to endure the cold, the deprivation, and the lonely blackness of the cell. My personal deadline for survival to 22 March seemed a distant point on the horizon that got no closer, no matter how many days passed.

I remember at one point Sweetavong telling me that peace talks were in progress. He said Prince Souvanna Phouma and Prince

Souphanouvong had gone to Vientiane to negotiate but had not been able to agree on anything. I was not sure whether to believe him. I was never sure whether to believe anything Sweetavong told me. I just filed it away for possible future reference.

On another occasion during that winter, a civilian friend of Sweetavong's was allowed into the cell. He told me peace talks were going on in Geneva, Switzerland. It was the first I had heard of them. Again, I was not sure what to believe. Why had this man been allowed into my cell? Why was he telling these things?

I refused to get my hopes up because those expectations could easily be dashed. I retreated into my shell of pacing and pondering, walking and thinking, making time pass.

I do not even remember Christmas 1961. Thanksgiving remains with me as a searing memory of all that was psychologically brutal about my captivity. The experience that day was so traumatic that I believe I convinced myself that Christmas would be just another day. I would expect neither extra food nor additional privileges that day. There was no reason to expect them from my Communist captors. I believe I passed Christmas Day without any special ceremony, except for my daily prayer for my wife and children and thanks that I was still alive, though barely.

I was constantly trying to avoid dwelling on thoughts of family and home. When I allowed myself to think of those things, I would begin sinking into a state of depression from which I was not sure there was an escape, like being sucked down into a whirlpool. I didn't know how long I might be held there or if I'd ever be able to pull myself free. Being confined to the cell was bad enough, but allowing myself to become a captive of depression and self-pity would only worsen the situation and lessen the chances for survival.

I continued my daily prayers. I prayed for my family and their well-being, I prayed for my friends and their happiness, I prayed for the souls of the men who had gone down with the C-47, and, selfishly, I continued to pray for the strength to survive this ordeal.

In the lonely blackness of that cell, I began to understand for the first time how insignificant a speck of humanity I was. In the course of life and time, I was nothing more than a whisper in the wind. Neither my life nor my death would mean much to anyone except my family and friends.

Gradually, reluctantly at first, I began to confront and accept the fact that I was neither important nor significant in the swirl of international events in which I had been caught up. I also began to come to terms with my own mortality. If I could accept death on its terms, I could accept life in whatever fashion it presented itself, even in this cell.

The winter dragged on. The cold, damp days became a blur. It seemed as if everything I had ever known was in that cell. The cell was my entire life, my whole existence, and the sum of everything I had been and was to be.

I was becoming weaker and more gaunt by the day. I was beginning to question my own ability to survive much longer. By late February I was even beginning to question my own sanity. The days spent staring at the walls of the cell and the nights spent peering into the blackness that engulfed me left me balancing precariously on the edge of sanity.

Then came the dream within a dream. It was a dream so real, so vivid, and so unnerving that it haunts me to this day. I went to sleep one night shortly after it got too dark to see anything in the cell. My sleep was restless and uncomfortable, and I began to dream. In the dream I was a free man, going where I wanted, doing what I wanted, and eating what I wanted. I was happy and content in my dream.

Then within the dream I went to sleep, and within that dream of sleeping as a free man, I began to dream again. In that dream within a dream, I was a prisoner. I was trapped in blackness, ill-nourished, frightened, and trying desperately to maintain my grip on reality. It was a startling portrait of myself and what I had become.

When I awoke in the center dream as a free man, I had a great sense of elation and joy. I was not a prisoner. I was free. "Hey, I just had a bad dream," I told myself. "I dreamed I was a prisoner. This was all behind me."

A great weight was lifted from me. My heart was racing. I was a free man. There was no black cell. There were no guards. There was no Sam Neua. Then, slowly, I began to drift out of the dream of freedom and back into reality. I opened my eyes to the blackness of the cell. The walls pressed in on me. Chickens were cackling and dogs barking outside. I smelled the soiled bedpans in the corner. I was still a prisoner. The great elation of a moment before was gone. In its place was a despair so crushing I was not sure I could bear its weight.

The dream within a dream left me wondering more than ever about how much longer I could survive this ordeal. I had been hanging on to hope by only the slimmest of threads that now seemed to have been broken. I was drifting within the blackness, more lost and alone than ever.

13

False Dawn

On into March the days of captivity crawled with agonizing slowness. The first anniversary of my capture, the arbitrary survival deadline I had set Thanksgiving Day, was now just a few weeks away, but it seemed an eternity. The mere thought of trying to look into the future provoked a nervous anxiety within me that made it difficult to attend to the daily tasks that until then had helped me occupy time.

I began to doubt that I could survive to the anniversary date. My morale and will to survive were at new lows. I needed something to rescue me, lest I be lost in the whirlpool of hopelessness and despair that was dragging me down.

That rescue came in a rather unusual fashion. I was sitting on my cot late one afternoon, pondering my fate, when the door burst open and Sweetavong walked in. He put his hands on his hips and looked around the room as if he were inspecting it. "This building in bad shape. They fix," Sweetavong said.

"Will they work on this room?" I asked hopefully.

"No, you stay here," he said, turning and leaving the room.

As with many of the decisions of the Pathet Lao during my captivity, this made no sense. Why repair the building and leave this one dirty, dingy, smelly cell intact? Why not repair the whole building?

In the year I had been confined in that cell, it had changed little. Plaster still occasionally rained down from the aging ceiling. The dirt piles in the corners were a bit larger and the cobwebs somewhat thicker. The rancid smell from the bedpans had permeated the cell with an odor that no amount of remodeling or fumigating could eliminate.

If they repaired the rest of the house and left this room as is, that might mean there were plans for my release in the foreseeable future; if they repaired my room, I was sure they were planning to hold me even longer. For days I wrestled with the inconsistencies and the uncertainty of this news about repair of the house. What did it mean for me? The answers finally came early one evening a few days after Sweetavong's visit.

Ten armed Pathet Lao soldiers came to my cell and motioned me to gather my belongings. While one of the soldiers rolled up my sleeping pad and blanket, I grabbed the blue-striped civilian shirt, my water kettle, my rice bowl, and my precious supply of cigarettes.

The guards surrounded me and motioned me outside. We went down the steps of the house where I had been a captive for nearly a year and out into the street. The guards surrounded me in a tight cordon. It was dark, and few people were in the street, but the guards kept motioning me to hurry along. They did not want anyone to see the captive American. I had no idea where they were taking me or what was going on. Was I about to be released? I would not allow myself to consider that possibility too long. I knew expectations not fulfilled could be extremely damaging to my already fragile psyche.

I tried to drag my feet and enjoy the sensation of being able to breathe fresh air and look at the sky for only the second time in a year. I wanted to slow down and look around, but the guards kept motioning with their rifles that they wanted me to hurry. We turned left on the street and kept walking. I needed only a few steps to realize our destination was the long, low wooden building I could see from my peephole and assumed was a municipal building.

The guards ushered me into the building and then directed me to turn left down a short hallway, to an open door. They motioned me inside. The guard carrying my bedroll walked in ahead of me and threw it on a low, wooden platform. I walked into my new cell, stunned and confused for a moment. The door closed behind me.

I stood in the middle of the cell clutching my meager belongings to my chest like a lost child. I was trying to make some sense of what had happened, but my mind was not working properly. Was this a temporary residence before release? Was I being moved here while my other cell was renovated? There was no one to answer my questions and I certainly had no answers of my own.

I was uncomfortable and nervous in my new surroundings. The

old cell had been my home, and I had adjusted to it and its minuscule proportions. The west wall had my calendar, the window in the east wall had my peephole, my window to the world, and the floor with its seventeen tiles east to west and twenty-three north to south was my universe. I knew the sounds of the house surrounding my old cell and the sounds in the street outside. Now, it was all gone. I would have to adapt to this new cell.

I groped through the darkness to the platform and my bedroll. I slowly unrolled the bed pad, slipped underneath the blanket, and tried to sleep, but my sleep that night was fitful. The excitement of the move, the uncertainty of what it meant, and the alien surroundings of my new cell made for a restless night. It was near dawn when I finally fell into a brief, troubled sleep.

In my sleep I heard someone singing in a sweet, rich tenor, "Qué será, será; whatever will be, will be." At first I thought I was dreaming, but then I realized I was awake. This was no dream. I listened for a few moments, enjoying the voice and the song, which seemed to be coming from somewhere down the hall to my right. I went to the cell door and pushed aside the canvas flap covering the bars.

"Who is singing in English?" I demanded loudly. The singing stopped.

"I am Jan," a voice replied.

"Who are you?"

"I am a soldier from South Vietnam."

"How many are with you?"

"There are four others. We parachuted into Laos and were captured. My leg is broken."

The acoustics in the hall were terrible, and we had to shout to make ourselves heard, often repeating the questions and answers. Still, after Sweetavong's fractured English, the sound of a friendly voice buoyed my spirits like nothing I had experienced the past year, and to know that after all this time I was not the only prisoner in Sam Neua was a wonderful blessing. I was not alone.

"Who are you?" Jan asked.

Before I had a chance to reply, the guards came rushing down the hall. One of them yanked the canvas back into place and began berating me in Lao. I understood none of what he was saying, but clearly he was angry that I had been talking to the other prisoners. Another guard went down the hall to scream at Jan and the prisoners with him.

Now I knew there were other prisoners here, at least one of whom could speak English. At last I could share my burdens with someone rather than shoulder them alone. After nearly a year in dark solitude, I at last had some company.

The mere sound of Jan's voice gave me hope that things were about to change for the better. Had not Sweetavong said some months earlier that peace talks were in progress? Perhaps an agreement had been reached, prisoners were being consolidated for release, and the end of this nightmare was in sight. The move to a new cell and the fact that I was being kept with other prisoners gave me reason to hope that might be true.

My new cell was a far cry from the crumbling room in the house down the street where I had spent the past year. Its most significant feature was a small barred window high on one wall above the wooden planking. The window was about three feet wide and eighteen inches high. I stood on the planking and looked out.

The window faced east, toward a network of rice paddies and mountains. My view of the street and the people I had grown accustomed to watching through the peephole were gone, but there was nothing covering this window to block the light. I would have sunlight and fresh air every day.

Near the back of the building and just to the right of my cell window was an outhouse. As I stood looking out the window that morning, I saw a soldier under guard hobbling toward the outhouse on crutches. As one of the soldier's legs appeared to be broken, I assumed the soldier was Jan. I considered calling out to him but thought better of it. We could talk later. I went back to inspecting my cell.

The floor was concrete. The wooden planking against the east wall was about six feet by twelve feet. It would have to serve as my bed, chair, and table because no other furniture was in the room.

The cell door was a wooden frame with vertical steel bars six to eight inches apart. A large piece of canvas was nailed to the outside of the frame but was loose enough to allow me to look up and down the hallway when the guards were not around.

To my right on the same side of the hall were other cells. To the left, toward the front of the building, there appeared to be an entryway with a manned guard station and a desk. I could barely see a corner of the desk from my vantage point.

As I was inspecting my new surroundings, the door to the cell opened and a guard motioned me outside. I dutifully followed him down the hall and out a side door. We walked around behind the building and he pointed to the outhouse. I was ecstatic. After a year of using the bedpans to relieve myself, I now had a real toilet, however ramshackle.

I thought if this was going to be part of the routine my new surroundings would be far superior to the house. I had more light and a window, and I was allowed to go outside to the toilet. Although my calendar, states, and peephole were gone, I had new territory

Lt. Sabab Bounyavong (left) of the Royal Lao Army and assistant U.S. Army attaché Maj. Bob Freeland chat during a reception at the U.S. embassy in Vientiane in 1960. Soon afterward, Sabab sided with the anti-foreigner Neutralists in the complicated, three-sided Laotian civil war and interpreted for Lawrence Bailey's Communist Pathet Lao captors after Bailey's capture in March 1961. State Department

In December 1960, fighting intensified in Vientiane between the Royal Lao Army and Neutralist forces that had seized power in August. Although he had only been in the country a few days, Bailey was made responsible for organizing the American evacuation convoy. R. Freeland

Identifiable by white strips of cloth, Royal Lao Army troops loyal to Col. Kouprasith Abhay, commander of the Vientiane military region, pause during the fighting against Capt. Kong Le's Neutralists. The Neutralists wore red strips. R. Freeland

After the battle for Vientiane, the author stands in front of the famed Black Stupa (That Dam), which legend says houses a seven-headed dragon that protects the city. The gouges in the wall were caused by mortar or artillery rounds that also heavily damaged the U.S. embassy, just down the street. Bailey is wearing the blue-striped shirt he had on the day he was captured. It survived his captivity and hangs today in his closet, a reminder of grim days. R. Freeland

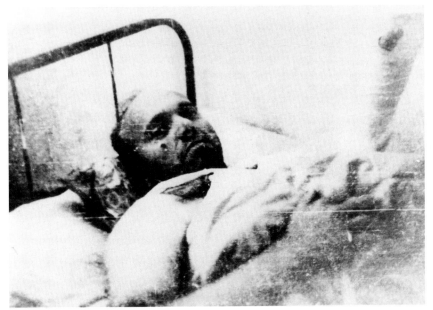

Unidentified for twelve years, the Defense Intelligence Agency's photo No. 109 shows Bailey shortly after his capture on 23 March 1961. His upper body and broken left arm are in a cast. Defense Intelligence Agency

The Pathet Lao finally released Bailey in August 1962, along with five other prisoners held separately from him. Here Grant Wolfkill (with sweater around his neck) and Bailey (the second person to his right, looking down) are escorted to the terminal of Vientiane's Wattay Airport. L. Bailey

En route to the Philippines following his release from captivity, the author enjoys his first cup of coffee in more than seventeen months. Department of Defense

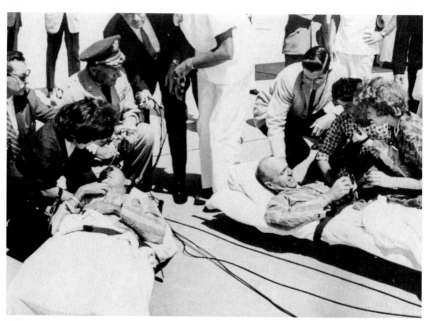

Sgt. Roger Ballenger (left) and Bailey surrounded by their families on the tarmac at Andrews Air Force Base, Maryland. AP/Wide World Photo

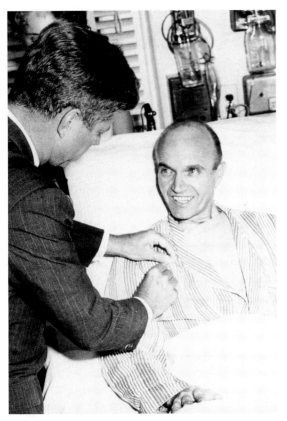

President John F. Kennedy pins the Bronze Star on Bailey at Walter Reed Army Hospital in Washington in August 1962. It was the first one awarded since the Korean War. Department of Defense

Wolfkill, Bailey, and Ballenger (left to right) at a press conference in October 1962. Association of the U.S. Army

In March 1992, Bailey returned to the village of Sam Neua, Laos, thirty-one years after his imprisonment there. R. Martz

One of the many caves in the limestone karst near Vieng Xai, Laos. It is said to have sheltered American POWs during the Vietnam War. R. Martz

The author in Vieng Xai before a memorial to Pathet Lao fighters. R. Martz

An aerial view of the crash site of Bailey's C-47, outside the village of Ban Li near the Plain of Jars. It had been excavated shortly before his visit by members of the Defense Department's Joint Task Force Full Accounting.
Department of Defense

Members of the MIA search team at the graves of Bailey's comrades.
Department of Defense

to explore. The only major drawback to my new cell was that I could not get out of it as I could the previous one, but finding a means of escape would help occupy my time.

Despite the initial excitement over the transfer, it soon became clear that it was not a temporary home, that release was not just down the road, and that life would go on with all the uncertainty of the past year. The food remained the same, a single ball of cold, sticky rice dumped into my bowl once a day.

The guards were all new. Sweetavong was gone, and so was Thong Seng. I never saw them again and never learned any of the names of the new guards. None spoke any English, and they rarely spoke to me in Lao. They were even more businesslike than the guards in the house, harder, and tougher. They were either combat veterans or had had some experience with prisoners.

Then, the outdoor toilet privileges stopped after about ten days. Someone had screwed up. I was not supposed to be outside in daylight where people could see me. The bedpans and their rancid, choking smell were returned to the cell.

Within a week of the move into the new cell, time once again began to inflict its onerous weight on me. If I lay on the wooden platform to take a siesta at midday as everyone else did, time stopped. If I did not move around the cell, time did not pass. While they rested, I paced the cell to keep time moving. I was nature's pendulum; without my pacing, time ground to a halt.

By late March it became clear that this cell would be my home for some time. In an effort to ward off the deep depression that I knew would accompany that realization, I had to find something to occupy my mind and give myself some hope. I found that glimmer of hope in a wooden pole inexplicably left in the cell. The pole was about four feet long and an inch and a half in diameter. I do not know for what purpose it was used, except perhaps as a means of propping open the door when the guards washed out the cells.

Whatever the reasons it had been left behind, it provided a useful tool to attempt to fashion some means of escape. I needed to know that I could escape if that was my final option. I had devised an escape route from the first cell, and I wanted one here in case getting out became necessary.

The bars on the window were too short and too stout to try to work free from the plaster walls. There was no room for leverage. Besides, any work on the window could easily be seen by any of the guards pulling back the tarp or anyone walking behind the building.

The bars in the doors offered more of a possibility. They were long and were somewhat pliant. Although they were rigidly rooted in the door frame top and bottom, I began experimenting with the pole to see if I could get some leverage between two of the bars to bend one of them.

There was just enough space to slip the pole between two bars and still get a good grip. If I worked the bars back and forth long enough, using the pole as a lever, I might be able to produce metal fatigue and break one of the bars.

It was a long shot, but it would provide me with many hours of useful entertainment and recreation. I was terribly weak from lack of food, and my weight was continuing to slide dangerously low. I needed food and exercise.

I worked slowly and deliberately, usually during the siesta period when the guards were the least attentive. I sat on the floor and worked the bars near the bottom of the door frame. Trying to break them in the middle, where they were most pliant, would be too noticeable. I would have to take the more difficult but less easily discovered route.

It was some weeks before I was able to break one of the bars. It snapped near the door frame. As I looked at it, I realized that even if I bent it back I would not have enough space, even in my emaciated condition, to crawl through. I would have to bend another bar. And so, without hesitation, I began to work on the second bar.

Late in March, not long after I discovered the pole and went to work on fashioning an escape route, one of the Lao guards came to my cell. He carried an American .45-caliber pistol in a holster on his hip, an indication to me that he had some authority. The guard had some paper and a pencil, which he handed to me and made writing motions. *"Mia! Mia!"* he said. He was telling me to write my wife.

I was momentarily taken aback. Why now, after more than a year in captivity, was I being told to write my family? Was there hope? Was the end in sight? Using the wooden planking as my desk, I sat on the concrete floor and began writing a letter to my wife, Betty. I wanted to sound calm and in control in the letters. I wanted my family to believe the situation was not as bad as it actually was because there was no sense dragging them into my despair.

I still had some paper left after writing the letter to Betty and decided to write another to my mother. I told her many of the same things I told Betty. When I finished, the guard brought me two envelopes. I addressed them, put the letters inside, and handed them to the guard without sealing them. He took them and left the cell.

The next day the guard returned with the letters, which he handed to me and then left the cell. They had been rejected and would not be sent. I was confused more than angry in that once again the actions of the Pathet Lao made no sense.

Why would they tell me I could write letters and then reject them? They couldn't read the letters anyway. What were they rejecting? All I wrote about was my broken arm and my concern that it would have to be broken again and reset when I got home. Discouraged, I returned to the regimen of working on the bars in the door and seeking an escape route.

About that same time, a guard came to the cell and handed me a stack of mail, which I counted carefully. There were forty-five pieces. Christmas cards, birthday cards from the previous year, thinking-of-you cards, letters from friends and relatives, and notes of encouragement from people I did not even know. I felt an overwhelming sense of frustration at having to deal so suddenly with so much mail. What should I read first? After months of being denied anything to read, I now had too much. I began going through the stack, sorting it for priority, and racing the sunlight in the cell. When the sun went down, I was even more frustrated because I had not gotten through the stack. I lay awake that night, thinking of who else might have written and of what they had to say.

Although I was angry at the length of time it had taken the mail to reach me, I was pleased to know that my family and friends had gotten word that I was still alive and being held prisoner.

At some point in April 1962, a pair of green Pathet Lao tennis shoes were tossed into my cell. Except for the cloth mules and the socks Thong Seng had given me during the winter, I had been barefoot all of the past year. My feet were tough and hard, and I found the tennis shoes uncomfortable to wear. I did find another use for the tennis shoes, however; the rubber soles made a wonderful eraser.

I had obtained a stub of a pencil and some leftover scraps of paper over the previous few weeks, and the acquisition of the tennis shoes enabled me to go into the design business. I began designing my dream house. After all these years, the details of that house have long been forgotten, but I clearly remember sitting in the cell and carefully working on the floor plan.

I would pace for a while, thinking about some special feature of the house, then sit down, and draw it, or I'd think of some alteration, use the sole of the tennis shoe to erase what I had done, and start all over. I spent hours working on that house. It was not necessarily something I actually intended to build when I got home. Instead, like almost everything else I did, it was something to pass the time, occupy my mind, and keep me mentally alert.

The guards continued to be terribly unnerved by the infrequent appearances of aircraft over Sam Neua. Not long after the transfer to the new cell, I was looking out the window when I heard a jet. I began to scan the skies for it. A Lao man squatting by a paddy dike picked up a rifle and began motioning for me to get my face away from the window and back down in the cell. He did not appear to be angry or threatening, but he was insistent on getting me out of sight. He motioned several times with the rifle before I dropped out of sight. There was no way the pilot of that jet could have seen me, but the Pathet Lao still were taking no chances that my presence in Sam Neua would be discovered by anyone.

A curious incident occurred in May 1962 that made no sense to me then and still makes no sense. I don't know if it was for real or a ploy by the Pathet Lao to trap me into committing some offense that would either add to my sentence or result in increased punishment.

I was looking out the cell window one day when I saw a man approaching the rear of the building. He saw me and waved. I waved back, and the man smiled and walked on. Several days later, the man came back. He walked up to the outhouse and stood behind it so that only I could see him. We began trying to converse in sign language. From what I could understand, he was telling me that there was fighting all around Sam Neua and that paratroopers were being dropped in the vicinity. I could believe the story about the paratroopers because of Jan and his fellow prisoners, but I had not heard weapons being fired in some time and there was no indication of any urgent defensive measures in and around the town.

The man returned frequently to that position behind the outhouse, where he signaled me with his hands. I signaled him in return. I don't know if he was a prisoner or simply a local citizen with a dislike for the Pathet Lao. Whatever the case, I decided to push him to see what I could learn.

One day he walked by the cell window and whispered in French: "Tomorrow."

"Tomorrow? What's tomorrow?" I thought. I took a scrap of my paper and wrote him a note asking if peace talks were in progress. I dropped the note out the window the next day as he approached. He picked it up, read it, and nodded his head in affirmation. Maybe there was hope.

I then wrote out a long list of questions for the man and dropped them out the window. He picked up the note and took it into the outhouse to read. When he was finished, he motioned that he was going to write a note to me. I waited all day, eagerly anticipating what he might be able to tell me of the progress of the peace talks or my chances of release.

I did not see the man again for two days. When he finally came walking past the back of the cell, he appeared nervous. I made a motion of writing a note, but he shook his head and walked on.

I saw the man a few times after that, but he never came close to the cell window again and never gave me any answers to my note. I don't know if he was caught with the note or was afraid he would be caught, but that was the end of our communications. I was just as much in the dark as ever about the progress of any peace talks.

I went back to working on the bars in the cell door and sneaking an occasional conversation with Jan. Talking with Jan helped keep up my morale, even though our conversations were hampered by his stilted English and the watchful guards. We tried to talk during the siesta period, but usually we were able to get in only a few questions and answers before a guard came storming down the hall to shut us up.

During this time Jan and his cell mates became the objects of concerted political indoctrination by a man who appeared to be a North Vietnamese military officer or political cadre. He wore civilian clothes but had a military bearing about him, and the jailers treated him with the appropriate respect. The man claimed he was Lao, but Jan insisted he was North Vietnamese. Jan and his cell mates frequently were taken from their cell to another building, where Jan said they endured hours of political lectures about the quality of life in North Vietnam.

I tried to get Jan to press him for information about the peace talks but he was never successful. Jan knew as little as I did about what was happening beyond our cells.

By early June my morale had reached a low ebb. I began to believe my captivity would end only with my death. Physically, I was a shambles. I could feel my skin stretching over my bones, and I was more than emaciated. I was absolutely skeletal.

Time became more of a burden than ever. When I sat and tried to think, my mind would not function because I was obsessed with the passage of time. Sitting made time stop, only pacing made it move, and only when I paced could I think.

Once again, I began to question my own sanity. I had reached my lowest ebb. I knew I could not last much longer on this subsistence diet and without any hope. Then came a series of events that, despite the overwhelming sense of despair and isolation that surrounded me, helped pulled me through. The first came in mid-June and was as unexpected as anything the Pathet Lao had yet done to me.

I was in my cell one night, about to go to sleep, when I saw the light from a Coleman lantern coming down the hall. The cell door opened, and a young guard motioned me outside. I obeyed, and he pointed down the hall to the right of my cell. It was rare to be taken out of the cell at night, and I began to question what was going to happen, although I knew I had no control over whatever it was.

At the end of the hall was a small room with a table, a chair, and a No. 2 corrugated metal washtub filled with water. The guard motioned me to sit in the chair, then put the lamp on the table, and pulled a pair of scissors from his pocket. To my astonishment, the guard began cutting my hair and beard. My beard was down to the middle of my chest, and my hair was way past my shoulders. Both were terribly matted and tangled, and they smelled bad because I had neither washed nor combed them in more than a year.

As the guard snipped away, large clumps of hair dropped into my lap and onto the floor. This guard was by no means a professional barber, but his efforts had a miraculous effect on me: I began to feel human again. I was no longer just an animal in a cage to be guarded and fed once a day. I was being accorded some sense of respect as a man.

When the guard was finished with my hair and beard, he handed me a bar of soap and motioned me to undress and take a bath. This was almost too much to handle at one time: first a haircut, now a bath.

I quickly stripped off the worn black pajamas that had been my only clothes since the previous July. I was shocked at what I saw in the stark light of the lantern. I knew I had lost a tremendous amount of weight during captivity, but I was not prepared for the sight of my own once well-fed body. My skin, although dirty, was a luminescent white from the months spent in darkness. My arms and legs were little more than sticks covered with skin. Was this really me?

I eased myself into the warm water of the tub and felt a sense of relief flow over me. After having been denied the simple, decent courtesy of a bath for so long, I was allowed to rejoin the ranks of humanity. The guard watched in great amusement as I splashed water on myself and worked up as much lather as I could with the coarse soap. He made obscene gestures with his fingers, apparently trying to tell me I would soon be released. I tried to ignore him and concentrate on my bath. I washed every part of my body, happily splashing water on myself and the floor. I was going to enjoy this bath as long as I could because there was no telling when I would have another.

The guard allowed me to take my time, with no sense of rushing and no sense of urgency. I washed until I ran out of soap and the water was ice-cold. Then I stepped out of the tub and back into the dirty black pajamas.

That night I slept a contented sleep. After being denied simple pleasures for so long, the haircut and bath had made me feel human again.

I was reluctant to try to make too much of this event. My eager anticipation of events that had not come to pass on other occasions had tended to make me despondent. Still, I could not help but wonder about the meaning of these events. Why a bath and a haircut now? Then came another of those events that helped keep me from sliding into hopeless despair.

Several days after the bath, I was sitting in my cell when the door opened and a guard dropped a blanket filled with something on the floor. The door shut, the guard was gone, and I eyed the blanket suspiciously. "Now what?" I wondered.

I carefully unfolded the edges of the blanket and looked inside. I couldn't believe what I saw: food—more food in one place at one time than I had eaten the previous year—a can of condensed milk, a large can of fruit cocktail, a can of sliced pineapple, a tin of chocolate, a two-pound box of sugar, a jar of Tang, a jar of bouillon cubes, and a military can opener. There were also a pair of gray socks, a pair of black socks, and some underwear. And matches— more matches than I knew what to do with—twenty-four boxes of book matches. Now I would not have to run around yelling "Fie! Fie!" whenever I wanted a light for my cigarettes. Now I had the unprecedented luxury of lighting up whenever I felt like it.

I sat down hard on the floor and stared at the sudden windfall. It was like Christmas. After months of hoarding every bit of string and every scrap of paper, I now had a treasure that threatened to overwhelm me. I had difficulty comprehending the riches and the wealth suddenly in my possession. Where should I start?

There was a card in the middle of the pile with a name on it. I lifted it out: "Grant Wolfkill, NBC," it read. "What a wonderful man," I thought. "If I get out of this I'll have to look him up and thank him for sending this." What I did not realize at the time was that Wolfkill, a cameraman for NBC television, was also a prisoner of the Pathet Lao, and the package had been intended for him. The Pathet Lao, either not caring or unable to read, had sent the package to me. No matter who it had been intended for, I planned to make good use of it.

The beef bouillon cubes were a godsend. I dissolved them in my warm drinking water and sipped them slowly, feeling the nourishment race through my bony frame.

The following day I received another package, this one containing a cheap suit, some underwear, a pair of socks, a belt, and a cap. It was clear now that something was in the works. They were not giving me extra food and new clothes to keep me in prison, at least not here. Some move was in the offing, and where, I did not care. I just wanted to leave Sam Neua. Even if it was Hanoi, Peking, or Moscow, I wanted out of Sam Neua.

I cautioned myself not to get too happy about things and too caught up in gorging myself on the goodies. I continued to ration the food in the first package and warned myself not to go overboard. I ate slowly and carefully.

Even the attitude of the guards changed. There was a sense of relief among them, as if something had happened to ease their concerns about the war. They became less concerned that I might see something out the window.

Yet they never took down the canvas covering the cell door and never let me talk openly with Jan. I'm not sure which of the two of us they feared most, but I assume they did not want me spoiling their hours of Communist propaganda with a few ill-timed remarks about America.

Only later, after my release, did I learn that the improvement in my treatment coincided with the formation of the Tripartite Coalition in late June 1962 of the three warring factions and the announcement of a cease-fire presaging the end of the war. Only the details, including prisoner release, needed to be worked out.

Perhaps even more disconcerting than the uncertainty of my captivity was the frustration of waiting for something to happen those last few weeks. It was apparent that something was about to happen, but what, I did not know, and the Lao were not saying.

Trying to make time pass on those days became even more of a burden. I tried to do innumerable things to make time move. I read and reread all the cards and letters I had received in March. The books of matches I received in the Wolfkill package had pictures of birds and flowers on them. I sat and stared at the matchbook covers for hours, imagining I could hear the birds singing and smell the flowers. If time had been a burden before, it now was an onerous weight. The seconds ticked off with maddening slowness as I waited, waited, waited for something to happen.

In July I had another bath and haircut. I was given a new pair of shoes that were too small for my feet. The food continued to improve, another sign they were trying to put a few pounds on my skeletal frame. The guards kept teasing me. "You go home tomorrow," they would say, but tomorrow always stretched into another tomorrow and a tomorrow after that.

On 26 July 1962, I was taken from my cell by a guard who led me to a table and chair set up in the hall. Waiting for me was Number One. I had not seen him for many months and wondered why he would now reappear. Number One motioned me to sit down at the table and handed me paper and pen. "Write your family," he ordered in French.

He stood there as I wrote a lengthy letter, again trying not to reveal too many of the details of my captivity and attempting to cheer up the family. When I was finished, Number One took the letter, but it was never mailed, or if it was, my family never received it.

The following day, 27 July, I was taken from the cell and again led to the table and chair set up in the hall. A guard handed me a news item indicating that an agreement had been reached in Geneva to end the war. I was not sure whether to believe it.

Then the guard handed me paper and pen and indicated I should again write to my family. Once again, I complied. "Dearest Betty," I wrote, "I am being permitted to write to you again today to tell you some good news. They showed me a copy of some news which states the government of Laos has been settled and that I will soon be released and can come home."

The three-page letter was similar to the one I wrote the previous day, talking about my injuries, my eagerness to see the children when I returned home, and my hope that no one had worried too much about me. I handed the letter to the guard, who looked at it and then motioned me back into my cell. Of the four letters I was permitted to write during my captivity, this last one was the only one that ever found its way to my family. Once more I waited, and waited, and waited. Time moved so slowly as to defy description.

On 11 August 1962 a guard came to my door and made flying motions with his arms. "Tomorrow, you go," he said. I looked out the window. There was a thick ground fog, and the clouds hung low on the tops of the mountains. I knew there would be no plane that day. Each of the next two days the guard came to the door and did the same thing: He made flying motions with his arms, smiled, and said, "Tomorrow you go."

The fog and clouds persisted, but hoping against hope, I sat in the cell, my ear cocked for the sound of an airplane engine that never came.

On 14 August the guard did not come, and, nervous and excited, I began pacing. Was the plane coming? Would I really be released? Then, in the distance, I heard the unmistakable growl of an airplane engine. From the sound it was an An-2 Colt, the same sort of Russian biplane that had brought me to Sam Neua.

"This is it!" I told myself. "This has got to be the day!" I listened carefully as the plane circled and landed. Then the engine was shut off. I was convinced from what the guards had been telling me that this was my plane, my ride out of Sam Neua, wherever it might be taking me.

A North Vietnamese officer came to my cell and motioned me to gather my belongings. He smiled and began talking to me in French. "I hope you have a good trip home," he said. I did not know how to respond and hurriedly wrapped my possessions in the blanket. I had replaced my black pajamas with the new clothes several days earlier to be ready for the trip and needed now only to grab a quilted Chinese coat that also had been given to me. I swung the bundle over my shoulder and walked out of the cell for the last time.

As we were leaving, one of the guards pulled down the canvas covering from the door. The bar I had broken could now be seen quite easily. The guard stopped short and said something in Lao. I don't know the exact translation, but the tone of it said something like "What the hell is this?"

I looked back down the hall, expecting to see Jan and the other imprisoned paratroopers following, but there was no sign of them. The officer led me out the front door to the street, where an American jeep was waiting. He got in the back with a guard and motioned me to sit in front. I climbed in and put the bundle on my lap.

The driver started the jeep, put it into gear, and took off. We had gone only a few yards when he stopped across the street from the house where I had first been held. The house was shrouded in bamboo scaffolding, still under repair. The driver and guard stayed with me while the North Vietnamese officer in back went into one of the buildings across from the house. I glanced nervously over my shoulder. "Surely they aren't taking me back to that house, back to the dark little room with the tin over the windows and the fireplace in the corner," I thought to myself. The longer we sat there, the more concerned I became that I was being taken back to the house.

Finally, the officer returned and we took off again. This time we did not stop until we got to the airstrip. Sitting there was a gray An-2 Colt biplane. Except for the color, it looked just like the plane that had brought me to Sam Neua. Several people were milling around the plane, including three European-looking men I assumed were the Russian crew. They were talking to one another and pointing to a thunderhead at one end of the runway. I knew the plane would not take off until that cloud moved on.

The driver, guard, and North Vietnamese officer left the jeep, and, with no one to guard me, I felt free to get out and approach the pilots. I heard one of the Russians say, "That American" in English. As I came near, the Russians looked up, startled. I must have been quite a sight with my bundle of belongings and emaciated body.

I pointed to the watch on the wrist of one of the Russians and said, for no apparent reason: "Do you have the time?" As if time mattered.

"Nyet!" the Russian shouted, turning his back. "Nyet!" The other two also turned their backs and returned to their discussion of the weather. They made it quite clear they wanted nothing to do with me. There would be no fraternizing with the passenger or the prisoner, whichever I was at that point.

As we waited for the weather to clear, I wandered around the fringes of the crowd unhindered, unguarded, and unwatched. After so many months in captivity, it was a strange sensation not to have someone with a rifle watching my every move.

A Lao official was in the crowd, as well as a Russian in a civilian suit, the North Vietnamese officer, women with babies, and several Pathet Lao soldiers. No one seemed the least bit concerned about me stumbling around lost and alone but at last rid of my captors.

After about three hours, the weather began to clear, and the Russians climbed into the plane and motioned for us to follow. I looked around again, expecting to see Jan and the other South Vietnamese prisoners on their way to the plane, but they were nowhere to be seen. As I followed the crowd to the plane, the North Vietnamese officer approached and handed me three letters, all from my wife. I accepted them without saying anything and climbed aboard.

The engines barked to life with a cloud of exhaust smoke, and the plane began bouncing along the grass runway. Slowly the Colt rose into the air and began circling in the valley to gain altitude. On one of the passes around town, I looked out the window and saw the house where I had been held, the bamboo scaffolding obscuring its exterior.

Then I turned to look ahead. I had no idea where we were going, but at that point I did not care. I was free of that house, of the jail cell, and of Sam Neua, even if I was not yet free.

14

Free at Last

Sam Neua slipped beneath the clouds and was gone. The Russian biplane continued to climb well above the mountaintops that thrust into the low-hanging cloud cover before turning southwest. I permitted myself a small sigh of relief. I had no idea where we were going, but I knew this was not the way to Hanoi, Moscow, or Peking.

At that particular moment I did not much care about our destination. I was moving. I was going somewhere. I was out of Sam Neua. I was out of that cell where blackness and the slow march of time had burdened me so. I knew if I had to start over again, if I had to face another uncertain sentence in a cell somewhere, I could do it and survive. I had beaten my worst enemy—time—and I could beat it again.

I looked around the plane, pleased with myself despite the uncertainty of the situation. The seats in an An-2 Colt are little more than benches along each side of the fuselage facing inward. Across from me was the Russian in a civilian suit, who seemed totally uninterested in me. A Pathet Lao officer in uniform stood in the doorway to the cockpit and provided a running commentary for the crew. He would tap the pilot on the shoulder, point out one side of the plane or the other, and say, "Pathet Lao" or "Phoumi," describing which side was holding a particular piece of real estate we passed over. The pilot ignored him.

Also on the plane were two women with babies and, near the

back, several young Pathet Lao soldiers. Occasionally the soldiers would stand and walk around, throwing the plane off trim and drawing angry shouts from the Russian crew, but there was no sense that these young soldiers or anyone else on the plane was serving as my guard or escort. No one seemed to be paying much attention to me. No one seemed in charge of me except me, a novel feeling after so many months of captivity. The soldiers were far more interested in a half-case of Tuborg beer they had found than they were in me.

We had been in the air only a few minutes when the soldiers popped the tops on several of the beers and began drinking. I must have been staring at them because one of the soldiers opened a beer and handed it to me. I smiled and took a swallow. It was warm and flat, but the most wonderful thing I had ever tasted. After all these years, I can still taste it. It tasted of freedom, of civilization, of life, and of all the things I had been denied over the last seventeen months.

I grasped the beer tightly in both hands and leaned back against the bulkhead. That simple act of kindness—one human being reaching out to another—touched me like nothing else in my seventeen months of captivity. It was the first time in those dark, lonely months I had been treated like an equal, like a human being, and not as a prisoner or an animal to be caged and guarded.

The plane flew southwest for about an hour before setting down at an airport I did not recognize. Only later did I learn it was Xieng Khoung airport, not far from where I had been shot down.

The Russians and the Lao got off the plane and left me sitting there alone. I was unsure what to do or where to go. I was so used to being herded around and guarded and held on a leash that it was difficult to accept the fact that I could now make decisions on my own. Eventually someone stuck his head in the door and motioned me to get out of the plane. I grabbed my bundle of belongings and complied.

Outside, the Russian crew members were shaking hands with other Russians who had come to greet them. They ignored me, and there were no Pathet Lao guards around to take charge of me. I was alone in the middle of the airstrip. No one came to claim me, and no one seemed to be in charge. Was I free? If so, where was I free? I began wandering around the airstrip, my bundle of belongings slung over my shoulder and no doubt looking like a beggar out foraging. After a few minutes, a jeep with two Pathet Lao soldiers slid to a halt near me in a spray of dust, and the soldiers motioned me to get in. My new escorts had arrived, albeit somewhat late.

The jeep left the airport and drove for about fifteen or twenty minutes before pulling up outside a small complex of concrete buildings surrounded by empty foxholes and strands of barbed wire—another prison camp.

As I stepped from the jeep, the face of a man appeared in the window of one of the buildings. He had long white hair and a flowing beard. He reminded me of Moses. "Major Bailey, I presume?" the man shouted in English.

I looked up, startled. It was the first American voice I had heard since the day I was shot down. "Yes, Bob Bailey," I shouted back.

The man's face disappeared and the guards motioned me to follow them. They led me to the largest of the buildings in the compound and pointed to an open door. I could see several people moving around inside. I slowly approached the door and looked inside.

Five relatively healthy, bronzed faces looked back at me. One was Filipino, the other four Americans. I was surprised to see other Americans because I had heard nothing about other American prisoners. I didn't know who they were or what they were doing there, but the sound of their American voices delighted me.

The five appeared in fairly good shape. They were thin because of the meager rations, but all had some muscle and meat attached to their bony frames. Compared to them, I was a ghost of a man, a walking stick figure with a death's-head.

The bearded man whose face I had seen in the window approached and offered his hand. "Grant Wolfkill," he said simply. It was the man whose name was on the package of food and clothing I had received several months earlier. He told me he was a cameraman for NBC television and had been captured 15 May 1961, when an Air America H-34 helicopter in which he had been riding was forced down by mechanical problems in Pathet Lao territory about seventy miles north of Vientiane. Two crew members of that helicopter, both Air America employees, Edward Shore Jr. and John McMorrow, were among the captives in the room. The other two prisoners were army Special Forces Sgt. Roger Ballenger and Air America employee Lorenzo Frigilano.

Ballenger was a demolitions specialist who had been working with the Royal Lao Army as part of a unit known as L-TAG, the Laotian Training Advisory Group, helping them clear mines from the roads. He was captured during fighting near Vang Vieng in April 1961.

Frigilano was a Filipino mechanic captured during the battle of Vientiane in December 1960. He had been reading comic books in a bomb shelter at the airport when Kong Le's troops, trying to escape the Royal Lao Army artillery barrage, swept through the area and took everyone with them. Friggi, as he was known, had been held longer than any of them. I shook hands all around. "You don't know how glad I am to see you guys," I said.

It was an incredibly emotional experience to see other Americans after seventeen months of isolation. It was marvelous to hear them speaking unaccented, understandable English. I was so deliriously happy that it was all I could do to keep from crying. I felt a tremendous sense of relief because I knew then that freedom was within reach.

I began talking that afternoon and did not shut up until well after midnight. Wolfkill said later he thought my mind had been affected by the months of isolation because of my incessant chatter, constant blinking, and furtive gestures. No doubt the others also thought I was a bit daft the way I carried on. Having been deprived of friendly companions for so long, I was unable to stop talking. I wanted to tell them everything I knew, everything I had gone through, and all I had endured.

They knew all about me and the circumstances surrounding my capture, but they appeared shocked at my descriptions of the loneliness and darkness to which I was subjected for so long. During their fifteen-month imprisonment, they had been able to communicate with one another in some fashion, lean on one another for comfort and support, and assist one another.

Although they had been confined to stocks for long periods and occasionally tortured by the Pathet Lao, for the most part they had endured their tortures together. When I told them of my experiences, they said, almost to a man, "No matter what we went through, I wouldn't trade places with you." But I don't know if I could have handled the stocks as well as they did.

Over the past year the members of this group had become relatively close, almost like a family that bickers frequently but pulls together when threatened from the outside. Wolfkill was the de facto leader, primarily because he spoke French fluently and therefore could converse with some of the guards and the Pathet Lao officials who occasionally questioned them. Wolfkill also was a veteran of the U.S. Marine Corps, and leadership seemed to come naturally to him.

Shore and McMorrow did not hide their employment with Air America, the CIA's proprietary airline. I could sense some tension between them and Wolfkill that I later learned stemmed from a long-standing disagreement over an escape that was planned but never carried out. At the time I joined them, however, Shore and McMorrow had put aside their feelings in order to ensure the survival of the group.

Roger Ballenger was the lone eagle, the quintessential Special Forces sergeant. He was short and lean and tough, with dark, hard eyes that defied his captors to the end. He had survived every torture and humiliation the Pathet Lao had thrown at him, including long stretches of solitary confinement in a dark room, and had come through it with his honor, his dignity, and his sense of humor intact. He got along with the others in the group, but he could have survived on his own if he had to because he had done just that for many months. His tough training had paid off.

While Wolfkill provided some sense of leadership, Ballenger seemed to be the rock who gave the group its structure, its sense of humanity, and its spiritual life. Each night before the group went to sleep, Ballenger led the men in reciting the 23rd Psalm. No matter how acrimonious the bickering of the day, no matter what petty feuds may have erupted, the evening prayers seemed to have a soothing effect.

That first night at Lat Huang, as darkness descended on the camp, the men gathered around Ballenger. Softly, slowly, he began reciting the 23rd Psalm. "The Lord is my shepherd; I shall not want. . . ." I felt a shiver go through me and I began to tremble. I felt as if I had been saved from my ordeal, rescued by my faith in God and my reliance on his wisdom. I felt as close to those men I had met only hours earlier as I have ever felt to anyone. We had become an immediate family there in that cell. And I began to recite the prayer along with them. "He restoreth my soul: he leadeth me in the paths of righteousness for his name's sake. Yea, though I walk through the valley of the shadow of death, I will fear no evil: for thou art with me. . . ."

Frigilano was something of an outsider because he had been held for many months with the Lao prisoners, but by 14 August he had been assimilated into the group of Americans, sharing whatever rice, fruit, or canned fish they were able to get their hands on.

Friggi was wonderfully gifted with his hands and could make the most marvelous creations out of seemingly useless scraps of wood and paper. One of his best inventions was a little machine that made perfectly rolled cigarettes out of bits of paper and tobacco he acquired. He also had somehow gotten his hands on a needle and thread and was constantly sewing, usually repairing clothes.

Two Thai soldiers captured in fighting the previous year also were being held in the same camp but were separated from the Americans. There was little contact between the two groups.

Ballenger told me the American group had lost one of its members early in captivity. Army Special Forces Capt. Walter Moon was captured at the same time as Ballenger, 22 April 1961. The convoy in which they and two other Special Forces soldiers were riding was ambushed by Pathet Lao forces near Vang Vieng. The other two, Sgt. Gerald Biber of Benkelman, Nebraska, and SFC John Bischoff of Mountain Rest, South Carolina, have never been accounted for. Ballenger last saw them hanging onto an armored car as it tried to escape an ambush.[1]

Ballenger became separated from Moon shortly after he was captured and did not see him again until several weeks later at this prison camp, a former agricultural school called Lat Huang. Ballenger said Moon's mental and physical health had deteriorated rapidly in captivity. He lasted little more than three months. He had been wounded once in the head during an early escape attempt and suffered greatly as a result. On 22 July he apparently tried to escape again, and a machete-wielding guard knocked him to the ground. As Moon lay helpless, he was shot several times in the back before his face was crushed with the butt of an M-1 rifle. Then his body was dragged outside the building, his blood leaving an indelible stain on the concrete floor. One guard shot him again in the back of the head with a pistol. Ballenger said Moon was buried just down the hill from the cell, although I never saw the grave.[2]

My sudden intrusion on the group disrupted its routine and gave the members one more hungry mouth to feed. They were running short of food and were unsure whether the canned fish and fresh pineapple they'd recently acquired would last until they were released. They had been told repeatedly that release was imminent.

"Any day now," the guards would tell them. But "any day" had stretched into more than a week.

Despite the food shortage, I was given an equal share of whatever the group had. We champions of free enterprise had become socialists when it came to food distribution. Everyone shared equally, no matter how small the portions. My inclusion made the portions even smaller, but there was no grumbling, no backbiting, and no angry glances in my direction.

They not only shared their food but also pressed on me small gifts that meant a great deal to me at the time: a cigarette from Wolfkill, a *Reader's Digest* from McMorrow, a helping hand from Ballenger on my way to the toilet. The smallest gesture on their part seemed the greatest blessing because they were true human beings who cared about me and my welfare. Their selflessness in view of all they had been through together was heartwarming, giving me hope that human decency could survive in the midst of inhumanity.

The only thing about me that bothered them was my refusal to shut up. I felt a compulsion to speak to someone, anyone, after so many months of enforced silence. I talked late into the night and began talking again as soon as the first streaks of dawn appeared through the shuttered windows. They listened to me ramble on as they went through their daily routines, never once telling me to shut up, although I'm sure they felt like it many times.

The camp itself, while a repository of horrors for my cell mates, was to me a marvelous place because I now had a great deal of freedom. I could go to the toilet whenever I wanted. I could walk down the hill to a little stream that ran along the edge of the camp and take a bath or wash my clothes whenever I wanted. I could go out into the sunshine whenever I wanted. The guards watched us, but they did so with a great deal of indifference.

My second day at Lat Huang, we were discussing the most equitable means of dividing what little remained of the fresh pineapple when I heard the distinctive sound of a single-engine jet flying overhead. I looked up to see if I could spot any markings. It was too high, a mere silver glint in the sky, but I knew it had to be either Thai or American because neither the Pathet Lao nor the Vietnamese nor the Royal Lao Air Force possessed jet aircraft at that time.

My first thought was that the jet might somehow delay our release or result in a return to some lonely, unlit cell. I mentioned my concerns to the other prisoners, but Ballenger and Wolfkill assured me that the jet had become a daily visitor that did not seem to pose any threat to our guards.

Just about that time a nearby antiaircraft gun began furiously pumping shells at the jet, the little black puffs of exploding rounds chasing it across the sky. Suddenly, there seemed to be a larger puff of smoke from the jet, and it appeared to lose altitude.

"He's trailing fire," Wolfkill said excitedly. I could not see any fire, but we all watched the plane until it flew into a cloud and disappeared.

Later that afternoon one of the Pathet Lao officials came into the room smiling triumphantly and carrying what appeared to be a crash helmet. I wanted to look at the helmet to see if it had any markings that might indicate the plane's origin or the identity of the pilot, but the official kept his hands wrapped around the helmet and would not permit us to look too closely at it.

"We have shot down your plane! Shot it down!" the official said in French.

"What happened to the pilot?" Wolfkill asked, translating for us as he talked.

"I don't know. I just know that we have shot down your plane. This will teach you Americans a lesson," he said, as he turned and left the room.[3]

We discussed the incident among ourselves but reached no conclusion about whether the official had actually been holding a crash helmet or whether the plane had actually been shot down.

We waited for another prisoner to show up in the compound, but none did.

Later checks revealed no American aircraft had been lost in Laos that day, and my debriefers had no knowledge of any Thai jets shot down on that date. That information led me to believe the incident with the Pathet Lao official had been a charade designed to impress the prisoners.

That day, however, our thoughts were consumed by the incident with the jet. The importance of such events are magnified beyond all reasonable proportions for imprisoned men whose hopes of freedom can leap or plummet in an instant, based on nothing more than a look, a misspoken word, or some unexpected incident. In retrospect, the appearance of the jet had little meaning in the overall context of my imprisonment, but at that moment in my life the fate of the jet and its pilot seemed inextricably bound to me.

We talked that day about what might have happened to the pilot and what might happen to us. We talked about Charles Duffy of the State Department, who had disappeared the year before while hunting; about Biber and Bischoff, both last seen alive; and about any other Americans we did not know of who had been captured after us.

Moon, we knew, was dead, brutally murdered by Pathet Lao guards. Duffy was still missing, as were Biber and Bischoff. Frigilano said he had heard a Royal Lao Army major imprisoned with him talk about an American who had been hacked to death by Pathet Lao soldiers with machetes. Was it Duffy? We never found out. For the next few days we waited for the other missing men to join us, but the wait was in vain.

On the morning of 17 August the guards brought us a tin of fish. We left half the contents in the can and distributed the remaining half into eight portions: one each for the Americans, one for Friggi, and one for each of the two Thai soldiers. Then we waited and waited and waited.

Ballenger, Wolfkill, and Shore were at the latrine when a Russian jeep pulled up outside the door. One of the Pathet Lao officials motioned us to gather our belongings. It was time to leave. McMorrow rushed outside and shouted down the hill to our three companions, "Hey! Come on up and pack! We're going home! Hurry! We're going home!"⁴ The three came scrambling up the hill as the rest of us hastily gathered our meager possessions. I stuffed my precious letters and the blue-striped civilian shirt into my blanket and hurried outside to the waiting jeep. We were like schoolkids going on a field trip. Everyone was talking at once. The starvation, the torture, the loneliness, the darkness, and despair were forgotten for the moment because we were going home.

As the jeep pulled away from the door, I noticed the four Americans and Friggi looking back in silence. I knew they were looking at the dark stain on the concrete floor that was Moon's blood.

The jeep took us to Xieng Khoung airport, where we were loaded onto an Ilyushin transport plane, the Soviet version of the DC-3. In addition to the prisoners to be released, two Russians in civilian clothes were on the plane. One of them told us the plane was due to land in Vientiane at 10:00 A.M.

The plane took off and circled briefly to gain altitude before turning southwest toward Vientiane. There was a large clock on the bulkhead above the cabin door, and all of us watched nervously as the hands slowly crept around the dial. I had flown in this area many times and knew from the landscape that we were heading for the capital and freedom. My flying companions were not as confident. "Ed, I'm not sure this damn plane is flying toward Vientiane," Wolfkill said.

"Me neither," McMorrow said. "It doesn't seem right."

"I think it's headed right, now," Shore said.[5]

"It's right," I said, looking out the window, calm and relaxed, now that I knew we were headed for release. "It's right." My words seemed to have a calming effect on the others, and they went back to watching the clock and discussing what they should or should not say to the media that surely would be waiting at the airport to record our arrival. As a journalist, Wolfkill wanted all of us to tell everything.

"Don't keep anything secret from the newsmen at the airport," Wolfkill urged. "The only reason anyone would want you not to talk is for fear you've been bad prisoners, that you've signed confessions or told traitorous tales. Well, you haven't. So even if the military doesn't like it, start telling everyone what we've been through. Grab the nearest newsman at the airport and talk like a blue streak."[6]

As a military man, I knew I needed clearance before I talked to anyone about anything, no matter how badly any of us had been treated. Ballenger felt the same way. "I'm not talking to anyone until I get military clearance," Ballenger said defiantly, ever the Special Forces sergeant.

"Goddammit, Roger," Wolfkill said, "you'll be talking to American newsmen, not the Pathet Lao."

"Doesn't make any difference," Ballenger said.[7]

I stayed out of the discussion and closed my eyes. Images raced through my head: the sack lunch I had never gotten to eat, the shootdown, the capture, the Pathet Lao field hospital at Phonsavan, the transfer to Sam Neua, the dark and dreary loneliness of the cell there, and the hundreds of hours and miles of pacing, trying to make time move.

I opened my eyes with a start. For an instant I was not sure whether I was back in the cell dreaming of this release or I was living it. The drone of the airplane engines and the happy chattering of my companions reassured me this was no dream.

I knew then there was something inside me, something I would never shake for as long as I lived, something so dark and terrible that it would be a part of me forever. I had escaped the cell, but I would never escape what it had done to me. It would be there whenever I awoke in the darkness, wondering for just an instant whether I was a free man or back in the cell in Sam Neua.

For now, however, there was freedom and all its warm and wondrous delights to savor. The clock hands slowly slipped on toward the appointed hour. The longer we flew the farther we seemed to get from Vientiane. I knew it was a trick of my impatient imagination because I was eager for the trip to be over and thinking it would never end.

Finally, out the windows we could see the land drop down from the mountains to the Mekong River Valley and the brilliant green rice paddies shimmering in the tropical sun, the approach to Wattay Airport and Vientiane.

"There it is!" McMorrow shouted.

Exactly as the clock hit 10:00 A.M. the wheels of the aircraft touched down on the pierced steel planking of the runway at Wattay. In grudging admiration, I saluted the Russian pilot. The man knew how to keep an airplane running on time.

We all pressed our noses to the windows, as excited as McMorrow. We scanned the crowd, looking for friends, looking for any faces we recognized. There were dozens of Special Forces soldiers there, bronzed and muscular and wearing their green berets at a jaunty angle. "Look at all those guys in green berets," Ballenger said. "Those are my boys, Special Forces."[8]

I was stunned at how large the American soldiers looked after so many months of seeing nothing but diminutive Lao and Vietnamese. They looked like giants.

The plane rolled to a stop, the door opened, and a ladder was brought. United States Ambassador Leonard Unger and a representative of the new Lao government came on the plane and shook our hands. "We're going to have a very brief press conference and then we've got a plane waiting to take you to the Philippines," Unger said.

The Philippines? I didn't want to go to the Philippines. I wanted to stay in Laos. I wanted to go back to my quarters, say hello to Ho, the cook, and to Bob Freeland and Colonel Hollis. I wanted to pick up my life where it had been interrupted seventeen months earlier.

It was not to be, however, because neither the State Department nor the army wanted me to stay in Laos. They wanted me out of Vientiane, out of the country, immediately. In Laos, I would be too much of an embarrassment to the new coalition government that already was struggling for acceptance and survival.

There was no time to question the orders and no time to protest a decision that had been made for me. I was suddenly caught up in a whirl of events over which I had no control, almost like being a prisoner again, only this time in friendly hands.

As we stepped off the plane, faces pressed in on us in a confusing blur. Most were strong American faces, pink and healthy from a regular diet of meat and fish and proteins and vitamins, freshly shaved faces smelling of aftershave and cologne. Unger tapped me on the shoulder and leaned close to my ear. "There's your airplane!" he shouted above the din, pointing across the runway at the L-23. I looked at it wistfully, knowing I would never get to fly it again.

The crowd continued to press in on us as Unger led us to an area where there was to be an official ceremony marking our release. A Pathet Lao official, Gen. Phone Sipraseuth, smiled and shook hands all around, although he spoke no English. Wolfkill fixed the general with a cold glare, shook his hand, and said: "Thanks for nothing whatsoever, general."[9]

A Lao woman wearing a Red Cross uniform was introduced as "the Red Cross lady who sent you all the packages."

"What we needed was the SPCA, not the Red Cross," Wolfkill snarled.[10] We all laughed. The remark apparently wasn't translated because the Lao kept smiling.

There was still no indication from anyone as to why any of us had been held so long. Whether we had served the purposes of the Pathet Lao as bargaining chips during the peace negotiations was unclear at that moment and has remained unclear. Their reasons for doing what they did were known only to them.

It was clear from the crowd that greeted us that the new government intended this release to enhance its image in the eyes of the world, but we certainly were not about to allow ourselves to be used for additional propaganda purposes. No one was about to say anything nice about our captors just to get out of the country, especially not with the death of Moon still fresh in the minds of Ballenger, McMorrow, Shore, and Wolfkill and especially not with the image of that black cell in Sam Neua permanently imprinted on my mind.

After the short session with the Lao officials, we were led to a table where reporters with cameras and microphones jostled one another for position. Wolfkill, Ballenger, and I were the only ones to be interviewed. Shore, McMorrow, and Frigilano, the Air America employees, were separated from us and taken to the plane, away from the prying eyes of the media. The two Thais also had disappeared. I still wasn't sure what I could or could not say so I let Wolfkill and Ballenger do most of the talking.

They talked about the stocks and the black cell and the brutality of the Pathet Lao guards. Anger and bitterness oozed from Ballenger's voice as he talked of the dehumanizing conditions of his imprisonment. "They kept us in cages side by side," he said. "They tried to drive us crazy. They kept me in a dark room with no windows and at night they threw rocks at the door to keep me awake."[11]

"There were three of us in one small bathroom of an old house without windows or light," Wolfkill recounted. "We had ropes tied around our necks and our arms tied behind our backs. We were led outside twice a day.

"In September we were moved to Nong Het, where the three of us lived in a small, windowless cell. We were kept in wooden stocks like Salem witches for twelve hours a day."[12]

The reporters said little as the descriptions of our imprisonment went on. They dutifully scratched in their notebooks or took photos. Jim Robinson, a friend of Wolfkill's from NBC, asked where I had been held. I said something about the house in Sam Neua and its cell. "Tell me about this hotel you were held in," Robinson said innocently.

"Hotel?" I exploded. "It wasn't a hotel! It was a little room without any light! It was a cell! A prison!" The American officials sensed the press conference was becoming embarrassing for the Lao and quickly brought it to an end. Ballenger and I were hustled off in the direction of a C-118 waiting to take us to the Philippines. Wolfkill went in the other direction; NBC had chartered a plane to take him to Bangkok.

"How's Bailey doing?" someone shouted from the C-118.

Unger waved, put one hand on my shoulder, and with his other hand reached into his pants pocket and pulled out some American coins. "Put these in your pocket and jingle them around," he said. "It'll help you feel more at home."

I took the coins, shook Unger's hand, and climbed the ladder to the plane. Ballenger, Shore, McMorrow, and Frigilano were already inside. As soon as I stepped aboard, the door closed and the engines began cranking. A young air force officer approached and shook my hand. "We've been waiting a month for you guys," he said. "These bastards kept promising you were going to show up. If there's any-thing we can do for you, just let us know. We've got anything you need."

I thought for a moment and then smiled. "Coffee," I said. "I'd like some coffee, please." I had not had a cup of coffee the whole time I was a POW.

The officer turned to fetch my coffee, and I sat down in one of the cushioned seats. I shook my head, trying to find myself in the midst of the events that had suddenly thrust me out of a prison camp and onto a U.S. Air Force plane bound for freedom.

A great sense of warmth enveloped me like a comforting blan-ket. I yielded to its friendly embrace and closed my eyes. I was finally free.

15

Learning to Live with Life

The plane ride to the Philippines unleased a flood of emotions: pure, unrestrained joy that at long last I was truly free, sadness that I returned without the remains of the crew of Rose Bowl, and fear of the unknown. What had I missed and what awaited me? I was seventeen months behind the rest of the world. The time spent in prison in Sam Neua had been like living in a vacuum that nothing had penetrated: No news of the outside world, of progress, of anything that pertained to life in a civilized society prior to capture was allowed into the cell. My life stopped on 23 March 1961, and only now was it being resumed.

My first concern was what had happened to my family during my imprisonment. I had received only a few letters from my wife with sketchy information about home and the kids. "Do you know anything about my family? Are they OK?" I asked one of the young officers assigned to care for us during the trip. "As far as I know," he said. And my mother? She, too, was fine. What about orders? Where was I going?

I would be checked by doctors in the Philippines and then sent to Walter Reed Army Hospital in Washington for more tests. Eventually, I would return to duty at Fort Meade, Maryland, near my home in Laurel, I was told. I walked around the C-118 in a daze. Things were happening too fast. Information was coming at me in a blur, and I was having difficulty dealing with it. I had spent so long with so little that I found myself overwhelmed by the sudden glut of information and experiences.

The C-118 had bunks with fresh sheets and soft mattresses, and I retreated into one of them to try to impose some order to the chaos engulfing me. I tried to sleep, but every time I shut my eyes I was looking into the blackness inside my cell in Sam Neua. The cell sat there behind my eyes and waited for me to try to escape so it could pull me back in. I got out of the bunk and grabbed another cup of coffee. I was nervous and edgy. I hopped from seat to seat, talking first to Ballenger and then to Shore, McMorrow, and Frigilano. Only they knew what I had been through. Only they knew what I was feeling. Only they understood.

When we arrived at Clark Air Force Base in the Philippines, we were given individual rooms in an isolated part of the hospital. There was a common sitting room where the other four POWs and I would meet to talk and fill out forms, but otherwise we were held separate from everyone else, away from the prying eyes of the press and curious civilians. The government wanted only the hospital staffers to see us for the first few days after our return to civilization. My room was filled with the aroma of fresh soap and clean sheets, things I had not smelled once during the months in captivity, things I thought I would never smell again. "Is there anything I can get for you?" a young officer asked.

"I'd like to take a shower," I said. He smiled and shut the door behind me. As I stripped off my POW clothes I caught a glimpse of my reflection in the bathroom mirror. I looked up, startled. Was that really me? Not once during my captivity had I seen myself in a mirror or even seen my image in a pane of glass. I knew I had lost a great deal of weight, but I was appalled at what I saw. That stick figure of a man staring back at me was not the Bob Bailey I knew. My face was a death mask, the pale skin drawn tightly around my cheekbones. My chest was hollow, the ribs clearly visible through the thin layer of flesh. My arms and legs were thin poles without muscle. I weighed a robust 185 pounds when captured, and I now weighed a skeletal 117 pounds. One of the first air force physicians to examine me, J. P. Darby, had to avert his eyes when he saw my condition. "For the first time I've truly seen man's inhumanity to man," he said.

Except for the weight loss and occasional bouts with dysentery, however, I was relatively free of major illnesses. My refusal to drink any water unless it had been boiled first had limited my exposure to the organisms that cause dysentery. Had I not done that, I probably would not have survived captivity.

In addition to a battery of physical examinations, we were given a series of psychological tests, the only psychological examinations

I received following release. All were geared to the Korean War–Cold War perspective. Had I been brainwashed? Had I been politically indoctrinated? Had there been efforts to convince me to become a turncoat? After the unpleasant and politically embarrassing experiences with some American POWs in Korea, military officials wanted to know if the Pathet Lao were using similar interrogation techniques, but, based on what Ballenger and I told our doctors, the Pathet Lao were quickly dismissed as unsophisticated captors unschooled in the arts of interrogation or psychological intimidation.

The doctors who examined me and the military officers who questioned me later saw my POW experiences as an extension of what had occurred ten years earlier in Korea, not the beginning of a new era of prisoners of war. Although the army later made a training film about my captivity and the things I did to survive solitary confinement, I was never consulted on it, saw it only one time, and met virtually no one else who saw it. By the time American pilots were being shot down over North Vietnam and taken prisoner in 1964, what Ballenger and I had learned about captivity seemed to have been forgotten. Not once during the Vietnam War was I asked by military officials to talk about aspects of my experiences that might help them understand what POWs in North Vietnam were being forced to endure.

Some doctors in the Philippines had a concern that my time in solitary confinement had left me mentally unbalanced. I felt totally in control of my mental faculties and told the doctors that the captivity had had no adverse psychological effects on me. Then one of the doctors asked me to reconstruct my life from my earliest memories up through captivity. I quickly bogged down in the details of my own life: Some early events would not fit into their proper order. The more I tried to fit the pieces into place, the more I failed and the more frustrated I became. Was losing track of the important events in one's life a sign of mental instability? I began to cry. What had happened to the order in my life? What had happened to me?

Psychologically, the captivity had more of an effect on me than I realized or was willing to admit. My concern at that point was not so much with my own mental state, though. I felt that the long hours of loneliness and isolation were playing tricks on me and that eventually everything would fall into place. My primary concern was satisfying the doctors so I would be allowed to fly again. Being taken off flight status would mean the end of my career as a pilot.

The doctor sensed my frustrations during these sessions and reassured me that the lapses were normal, even for many people who had not undergone the same sort of grueling psychological stresses as I had. He said it would have no bearing on my flight status and predicted, correctly as it turned out, that I would be able to fly again soon after I was returned to full duty.

The hospital personnel tried to help us adjust to some semblance of normal life as quickly as possible, but there were certain events so jarring that they made me feel like an outsider, far off the pace of the rest of the world. At one point I overheard some of the doctors and nurses talking about a Dr. Ben Casey. I thought he was a doctor in that hospital. "Who's this Ben Casey I keep hearing about?" I asked one day.

They looked at me as if I had just returned from the far side of the moon. "Why, he's the lead character in a TV program," they laughed. I laughed with them, but I felt lost.

We were permitted to leave the hospital for brief periods, but I never did. I remained in the isolated ward. I had no desire to get out and mingle with other people. I was content to sit in the room and read or talk with the other POWs. I was still trying to catch up with a world that had passed me by for seventeen months.

My biggest problem in adjusting to freedom was learning to deal with the normal passage of time. In prison I tried desperately to make time move. I spent every waking minute goading time into moving more quickly. Every event in prison, no matter how minor, took on great significance. The slow passage of time allowed me to examine everything that happened, delve into its complexities, and figure out what the ramifications might be for me.

Now, I was trying to reverse that and make time slow down. I wanted to examine each new thing, each new event, and take from it what I thought important. I tried to grab onto things as they sped past and enjoy them, but things were moving too quickly. Events swirled around me with no order or opportunity to reflect on them. I was on a treadmill that moved at its own pace, and I could not keep up. I was frustrated and frightened by what was happening. I wanted to stay in that hospital until I was ready to confront the world on my own terms, at a pace I could handle, but it was not to be. After a few days of tests, we were told it was time to return home.

I sent word ahead to Washington that I didn't want anyone but my wife, Betty, to meet me at the airport. I wanted no children, no mother, no friends of the family, and no reception of any kind; I was uncertain how I would handle crowds pressing in on me. I had learned to deal with my aloneness, but it would take some time to deal with people again, even my own family. I did not want to embarrass them, myself, or the army. I did not know how I would react to anyone or anything, so I decided to try to avoid it.

I was emotionally giddy that I was free again but concerned about what I should or should not say about what had happened to me. I had no idea of how I was going to be viewed by members of the public or my fellow army officers. I wanted no publicity or attention. I simply wanted to slip back into a normal life, return to work, and resume flying. I envied Ed Shore and John McMorrow in their anonymity. As Air America employees, they could simply disappear behind the protective walls of the CIA and have nothing to do with any of the public commotion that I could feel beginning to close in on me. Ballenger seemed to handle the sudden, jarring transformation from POW to free man with far more equanimity than I did, perhaps because of his Special Forces training. He seemed able to take on events as they presented themselves and deal with them in an appropriate fashion, whereas I found myself overwhelmed by those events.

Then, too, there was a certain amount of guilt attached to coming home as a POW. I had not completed my assignment, and I was concerned that I might have told the Pathet Lao something during the interrogations that may have helped them politically and prolonged my captivity and that of the other Americans. I felt I had done the best I could as a POW under the circumstances in which I found myself, but I was uncertain whether others viewed me that way.

In later years, whenever the subject of my captivity was brought up, I treated it with some trepidation. It required a lengthy explanation for people to understand why I had returned, and that explanation often was greeted with no small amount of skepticism. The implication was that I had somehow failed my country because I had allowed myself to be taken prisoner and survived. Like many others captured during the war in Vietnam, however, I was a victim of circumstances over which I had no control. I had not run in the face of the enemy. I had not flinched. I simply found myself in a situation that did not permit me to run or fight back. I chose to survive, to stay alive to fight another day.

Ballenger and I eventually were separated from Shore, McMorrow, and Frigilano and sent back to the United States on our own air force C-135. I leaned heavily on Ballenger during that flight. I continued to babble on about my imprisonment, not quite talked out yet. His sharp sense of humor helped relieve some of my anxieties, although I'm sure he was trying to deal with his own adjustment.

In California we transferred to a C-131 and flew on to an army hospital in Denver, where we spent the night. The closer I got to home, the more anxious I became, and I had a terrible time getting to sleep in Denver. I listened to Mitch Miller music for a while and then woke Ballenger to talk to him. I would not let him go to sleep.

I was fearful and insecure about going home, and I needed him to reassure me. He was my link to everything that I had known for the past seventeen months. That black cell still had a hold on me that I could not shake.

On Friday, 24 August 1962, the Military Air Transport Service plane carrying Ballenger and me set down at Andrews Air Force Base outside Washington, D.C. A large throng of family, friends, doctors, press, well-wishers from the Pentagon, and assorted hangers-on came to greet us. I had relented on my previous request not to have anyone but Betty meet me at the airport, much to the relief of the Pentagon. Betty, her mother, and my three children were there, and Ballenger's Japanese-born wife, Miyoko, was waiting for him.

Although Ballenger and I could walk quite well, we were ordered onto stretchers. Then we were carried down the ramp as the crowd waiting on the tarmac broke into applause. Betty greeted me at the bottom of the steps, leaned over, and kissed me lightly, her dark hair brushing my face. She smelled of perfume and powder and so many of the things I had missed terribly while confined. "Gee, you're pretty," I said to her, feeling as awkward as a schoolboy on my first date.

My children were lined up next to the steps. I felt an immense sense of pride and elation when I saw them. After so many months of seeing dirty Lao kids in drab clothes, my own children looked like something out of a dream. They were all beautiful and healthy, and they were so clean and shiny they almost sparkled in the bright sun. They had not changed greatly in the twenty months since I had seen them, but there was a sense of maturity and self-assurance about them I had not seen before. They had rallied around their mother and stuck together as a family in my absence. They had held up well by doing what they had to do and going on with their lives. It made me proud to know they were my family and had been able to carry on so well without me.

Larry, my only son, then sixteen, smiled, saluted casually, and said, "Hi, Dad!" Barbara, eighteen, had become a young woman in my absence. She and Elaine, then fourteen, burst into tears when they saw me and could say nothing for a few minutes.

Ballenger and I were carried into the middle of the crowd and stretched out on the tarmac like trophies after a hunt. The day was terribly hot and bright, and the crowd pressed in on us from all sides, shutting off what little air was circulating. I felt confined and trapped there. My worst fears about the arrival were realized. There were too many people, too many cameras, and too much commotion. I would have preferred a low-key arrival.

Lieutenant General Russell L. Vittrup, deputy chief of staff for personnel, was the official Pentagon representative there to welcome us back from our ordeal. "We are mighty proud of you, not only in the army but in the whole nation," Vittrup said. "I know you are glad to see this sunlight after spending so much time in that black hole."[1]

The Pentagon's public affairs office had cranked out a two-page press release about our return. Although in its fractured syntax it referred to Ballenger and me as members of the Pathet Lao ("Army Reveals Lengthy Ordeal of Two Pathet Lao Prisoners"),[2] its purpose was to serve as our press interview. Because my voice was little more than a squeak after all the talking I had done the past ten days, I could not have said much even if permitted to do so. Nevertheless, the army wanted to make sure Ballenger and I did not say too much publicly about our captivity until we had been thoroughly debriefed by intelligence officials. "Neither will be available for press interviews until he has recovered from the effects of his imprisonment," the statement read. "At the present time their physical condition precludes interviews."[3]

There was only a small amount of truth in that statement, but it managed to deflect the horde of media that desperately wanted to tell our stories. We were still fighting the Cold War, and Ballenger and I were oddities who had survived imprisonment in Communist prison camps. There was intense public interest in what had been done to us and what we had done to survive. Those inquiries would have to wait, though.

The official welcome home ended, Ballenger was shuttled off to a plane that would take him to Womack Army Hospital at Fort Bragg, North Carolina. I was put in an ambulance and taken to Walter Reed Army Hospital for more examinations and rest.

With Ballenger gone, I was alone again. I had no one to lean on, no one to confide in, and no one who knew what I had been through and what I was feeling. Although I was surrounded by family and friends and doctors and nurses who wanted to make me comfortable and help me regain the weight I had lost, their activities and good intentions seemed almost to be directed toward someone else. I was the object of their concerns, but at times they seemed to be treating someone else, a man I did not know.

I had barely settled into my bed at Walter Reed when I was informed that President John F. Kennedy would be coming to see me on Monday, 27 August. The hospital was used to these sorts of visits, but there was a great deal of scrambling about, cleaning the room, trying to get ready, and making sure my family would be there for the ceremony.

On Monday morning one of Kennedy's advance people came into the room and began sketching on a small pad where people would stand for the ceremony and where tables and chairs should be moved. He seemed to know exactly what Kennedy wanted.

When Kennedy arrived, I was struck by how healthy he looked. He had just returned from a Florida vacation and was tanned and robust, his starched white shirt a sharp contrast to his bronzed skin. He wore a dark business suit and the famous Kennedy smile that charmed every member of my family as he shook hands with them. The room quickly filled with Kennedy aides, Secret Service men, and photographers.

"We're here to award Major Bailey the Bronze Star," Kennedy said as the photographers snapped away.

The Bronze Star medals awarded to Ballenger and me were the first given since Korea. They also were the first awarded under an executive order signed 25 August that authorized the president to give the Bronze Star and Legion of Merit medals during peacetime to American soldiers serving as trainers or advisers with friendly troops in armed conflict for "heroic or meritorious achievement against any enemy nation." Kennedy said he was awarding me the medal because what I had gone through was "in many ways more exacting" than anything I might face on the battlefield.

The official ceremony completed, Kennedy turned to the others in the room and said, "I think that will be all." The reporters and photographers tripped over one another trying to get out of the room. When Kennedy spoke, he did so with authority. Then the president turned back to me. "Did they ever tell you why they treated you like they did?" he said, anger in his voice, his eyes hard.

"No, sir," I replied, "they did not." Kennedy was upset over my physical condition and the treatment I received from the Pathet Lao. Had the situation in Laos not been overshadowed by other events, I do not doubt that any action Kennedy might have taken would have been influenced by what he learned of the inhuman treatment Ballenger, I, and the others had been subjected to, but it was not to be. Within weeks the Soviet missiles in Cuba once again relegated Laos to a foreign policy afterthought, just as the Bay of Pigs invasion had done shortly after my capture. Laos was not to emerge again in the public eye until the United States was well entangled in Vietnam.

After little more than a week in Walter Reed, I was allowed to go home on convalescent leave and begin the process of adjusting to life as a free man. I was in awe of my own home. I marveled at the simplest things: the electric lights, carpeting, soft chairs, indoor toilets, and showers. Food became an obsession. I ate as much as I could as often as I could: steak, french fries, strawberry ice cream, milk shakes.

Ballenger and I were the subject of numerous newspaper articles and editorials praising our courage in the face of Communist torture and political indoctrination. The *Indianapolis Star* wrote that the Bronze Star "said, in effect, that it is still possible for individual man to demonstrate rare courage when he believes in himself and his cause."[4]

The *Fort Lauderdale News* was even more effusive in its praise:

> The fact that Major Bailey and Sgt. Ballenger were not fighting a war to save this nation, but were engaged in a Cold War struggle against a savage ideology, makes their heroism all the more exceptional. . . . If ever two men should be elevated to the highest honors of a grateful country, Major Bailey and Sgt. Ballenger should, for theirs was exceptional heroism.[5]

Then came the letters, hundreds of them from people all around the country wanting to wish me well. "Dear Sir: Please accept the thanks and gratitude of an American for your courage, valor, honor, duty and devotion to your country."

"Dear Major Bailey: In refusing to renounce America you set an example for us all to follow if ever in similar circumstances. It would be an honor to shake your hand."

"Dear Sir: Thank you for what you've done for our country, for my four children and for my husband and myself."

And, from my father, in his own no-nonsense style: "Dear Bob: Welcome home and thank God you had the will and determination to outlast those lousy stinking Communists."

It was all quite heady stuff. I had not realized how much the POWs had touched a nerve in the American public still stinging from Korea and its humiliation. Ballenger and I and the other POWs were, in some sense, justification of the American way of life and its democratic ideals.

As the praise rolled in, however, I began to feel more and more uncomfortable. People were making me out to be something I was not. When I heard people talking about me or writing about me in this fashion, I often felt they were talking about someone else. I was not a hero, simply a survivor. I did nothing more than a thousand other soldiers would have done in my place.

The sense of unreality that accompanied all this unwanted and unwarranted attention was brought into focus by the frequent letters and telephone calls I received from family members of the crew of the downed C-47. Some had corresponded with Betty over the previous seventeen months to share their anxieties, fears, and hopes. They had coalesced around her because she was reasonably sure I was alive, and they thought the government might give her information about their sons and husbands. The mother of one of the crew members called me several times to look for some ray of light in the blackness of despair, hoping against hope that her son had not perished in the crash. "Is there any hope? Can you give me any reason to believe my son is alive?" she would ask.

The answer was always that there was no chance. He had gone down with the plane. Then she would sob into the telephone, thank me, and hang up. I would stand there with the telephone in my hand, feeling empty and alone and trying to fend off the guilt for having survived, for not dying with them.

For the first few months after I returned, I felt terribly overwhelmed by the many demands on my time. Well-meaning people wanted me to do so much that I was having difficulty keeping up. I was still trying to maintain a slower pace and savor events as they occurred, but I was having little success. On occasion, I handled public ceremonies in a less-than-admirable fashion.

One such event occurred not long after my release from Walter Reed. I was ordered to the Pentagon for a medal ceremony to be awarded the Purple Heart for my injuries. I was still gaunt and hollow-cheeked, and my uniform was baggy and ill-fitting. I was still having problems dealing with crowds or public ceremonies and felt terribly uncomfortable standing in front of several ranks of generals and colonels I did not know and who probably did not know anything more about me than what they read in the papers. A general pinned the medal on my uniform and then asked if I had anything to say.

My mind went blank. I could think of nothing. I looked out at the expectant crowd, terrified. "No sir," I stammered, "except I'll wear this medal with honor."

There was an uncomfortable silence. The officers stirred slightly in the ranks. I had been expected to say something memorable about my captivity but could think of nothing. Finally, another general stepped forward, thanked me, and complimented my family for bearing up so well during the ordeal.

Every time I turned around, it seemed that someone was after me to do something or give me something. I avoided some affairs; others I could not without embarrassing the army or my family. The town of Laurel, Maryland, held a parade and dinner in my honor. In October 1962 the Association of the U.S. Army honored Ballenger, Wolfkill, and me, and Grant was given the Medal of Freedom for assisting his fellow captives. In November I was subjected to a lengthy debriefing about my capture and imprisonment. In December I went to New York to appear on the popular television show "I've Got a Secret."

Reader's Digest approached me about doing a story and sent a writer to Washington to interview me for several days. As I waited for that story to appear, a man called and identified himself as an air force colonel. He asked me to describe in detail the cell in which I had been held, and I did so without reservation. Several months later the story I thought was intended for *Reader's Digest* appeared in *True* magazine under the title "Solitary Torment of a Tough American." It was accompanied by a drawing that showed me sitting in the cell, the names of states scratched on the wall, and a small beam of light intruding on the darkness from outside— exactly as I had described it to the so-called colonel. The army found the *True* story to be a useful tool in telling others what might happen, were they to fall into the hands of the Communists. The story was reproduced and distributed throughout the army.

Not long after the *True* story appeared, a stranger version of my imprisonment showed up in a magazine called *Man*. A drawing of my capture that went with the story depicted me with a full head of hair and dressed in an air force uniform. The story was terribly inaccurate, but the drawing made me look like a handsome devil.

I was beginning to feel used. My story was being subjected to a certain amount of commercialism that bothered me greatly. I did not want to be perceived as making money off the misfortunes of others, particularly not the crew members who had died on the C-47. I began to back away from public appearances and any hint that I might be exploiting my story for commercial gain. I attempted to disappear into the anonymity of military life to establish some control in my life, some pace, and some order, but some days I felt I was being swept along by events over which I had no control.

Physically, I was well cared for in the months after my release. Psychologically, I was left to fend for myself. Had I sought help, I am sure I would have received it, but as an American military man I was expected to survive my imprisonment without complaint and without psychological scars. I was expected to revert to a normal life as soon as I returned home and then put on the uniform, salute smartly, and be ready to march off to the next war when called to do so. The captivity, particularly the loneliness of solitary confinement, had taken a toll on me, though, that I could neither understand nor articulate to anyone who had not experienced it.

On those days when I would feel particularly stressed by demands on my time, I would go home and sit in a lawn chair in my backyard to marvel at the wondrous simplicity of the night sky and the stars I had not been permitted to see for so long. After seventeen months of being alone and seeking companionship, now I wanted to escape from people and be alone with myself. I had grown comfortable with myself during my imprisonment and I had learned to live with myself and depend on myself. I did not have to share myself with anyone. My return put me in a world where I had difficulty dealing with the demands of people and time.

During captivity I had had the luxury of time to think about things as they occurred. So little happened that I could take the time to examine each event and all the implications it might have for me. I could spend hours thinking about how to conserve my cigarettes so I would have a smoke three days from now. I could weave and reweave the cloth mules I used for my feet. There were no concerns about mortgages, car payments, my job, or the kids' grades in school. I could easily compartmentalize things and deal with them individually and on my own terms.

When I returned home, that luxury to deal with events at a slow pace was gone. I was trying to get reacquainted with my family, with my own home, with Betty, and with work, all the while I was in demand for speaking engagements, interviews, and ceremonies. I was also trying to get caught up on all that I had missed. What was the Bay of Pigs? I had had no idea what it was or what it had meant to the country. I had not grown while I was in prison, while my family and others around me had.

At times I felt like a stranger in my own house. Everything was the same as I had left it: the sofa, the drapes, the carpet, the smells of soap and perfume from the bathroom, and the laughter and chatter of children filling the house. They were all familiar, yet all strange and different. It was almost as if I were standing at a distance, watching the lives of my wife and children unfold, unsure of who I was or how I fit into their lives. Many nights I would lie in bed, unable to sleep, and peer into the blackness wondering where I was. What was this place? Was it Sam Neua? Was it home? In the dark, it was difficult to tell.

There was little doubt the captivity had changed me forever, and it had also changed my family. My children were much more aware of who they were, what they could do, and how to deal with life. They and I had few problems with the readjustment because they simply continued doing what they had been doing while I was gone. Larry would go on to become an aviator, Barbara to own an advertising agency, Elaine to be an Episcopal priest.

As so many POWs who returned from Vietnam a decade later would learn, readjusting to home life, especially to one's own wife, can be terribly difficult, even in the best of marriages. The POW wives learn to cope, learn to survive, and learn to be independent, which is just what happened to Betty. She had learned she could be in charge of her own life and did not need me around to run the family and make all the decisions. She was as changed by my POW experience as was I.

In many instances a POW's family can become prisoners of the experience as much as a POW himself, especially if they do not know if their loved one is alive or dead. They live in a world that is half hope for the best and half dread of the worst. Their lives are no longer their own because they are, by extension, captives of the same system. Betty never allowed that to happen with our family. She had learned early on through newspaper reports and the government that I had likely survived the shootdown and was in captivity. So, she sought to make as normal a life as possible under the circumstances for our children, and in doing so, she found herself.

Yet my POW experience was not entirely to blame for what became of my marriage. It only exacerbated the disaffection between Betty and me that had begun years earlier, long before I went to Laos, when I decided to stay in the army against her wishes. She had no love for the transient life of an army wife and wanted, instead, a permanent home and roots in a community. She had no desire to be picked up every two years and dragged across the country to another new post and another government-issued temporary house.

The house in Laurel, Maryland, provided Betty with a foundation in her life that she had been missing for so many years. In my absence she and the children had become a part of the community, and they were reluctant to leave it and follow me on my government-ordered changes of station. I had vowed not to be separated from my family when I returned from Laos, but the army was not particularly compassionate in that regard. After a brief stint with Second Army Headquarters at Fort Meade as operations officer in the aviation division, I was sent to the University of Southern California in Los Angeles for a four-month aviation safety course. Next I was shipped off to attend the Command and General Staff College at Fort Leavenworth, Kansas, for four months. Then I was permanently reassigned to the Joint Chiefs of Staff's Joint Task Force-2 in Albuquerque, New Mexico, as part of a program to test the low-level flight and combat capabilities of all the aircraft in the Pentagon's arsenal.

The assignment to Albuquerque was one separation too many for Betty. My absences from her and the family had become too long and too frequent, and she wanted to get on with her own life without the army or me dictating where or how she lived. In 1966, by mutual agreement, Betty and I divorced.

Through the later years of my army career in the late sixties, the focus in Southeast Asia shifted to Vietnam. Laos and the war there were hidden from public view by a shield of secrecy erected in the name of national security. The thinking was, if the public does not know there is a war in Laos, there is no war. Vietnam eventually overshadowed what had happened in Laos in 1961 and 1962. We

Americans held captive there during that time—Ballenger, Shore, McMorrow, Wolfkill, and I—were treated like remnants of an almost-war. Those who had not survived the early days of Laos— Biber, Bischoff, Moon, Duffy, and the men of the C-47—were seen as the dead of another era.

The POWs in North and South Vietnam became the focal point of national concern, frustration, and anger because of the torture and brutal treatment they received. The POWs in Laos disappeared behind a nearly impenetrable shield of secrecy, soldiers of an invisible army and casualties of a war the government denied was being fought.

16

Soldiers of the Unreturning Army

The rain drummed on the tent with an unrelenting urgency, wrapping those of us inside in a cocoon of sound that provided isolation from an outside world that could not share in what we knew or what we had been through. Bathed in the soft glow of light from chandeliers fastened to the tent poles, we ate and drank and laughed as if the memories of wartime imprisonment, torture, and pain were bad dreams from which we had just awakened.

The massive tent had been set up on the South Lawn of the White House for President Richard Nixon's party to welcome home the prisoners of war from Southeast Asia. Although I was eleven years removed from captivity and had retired from the army nearly three years earlier, my wife, Jean, and I were among the 1,260 guests of the Nixons that rainy night. It was 24 May 1973, my fiftieth birthday.

Jean and I were living in Atlanta, where I was selling real estate, when the invitation arrived for the White House dinner. Jean and I had been high school sweethearts in Waycross, Georgia, years earlier. Her first husband, a fighter pilot, had disappeared in the South Pacific while on a mission during World War II. Following my divorce in 1966, Jean and I were reunited with the help of relatives, and we married in 1967.

The White House dinner was just one of a series of events in 1973 at which returning POWs were feted. There were lavish parties, parades, banquets, speeches, free cars, free vacations, and all manner of privileges and perquisites from businesses throughout the country.

The outpouring of affection from the public at times verged on overwhelming. Typical was an incident that occurred while the returned POWs were attending a baseball game in Shea Stadium at the invitation of the New York Mets. I went to get a Coca-Cola in the middle of the game and immediately was surrounded by people seeking my autograph. People were thrusting baseballs, bats, twenty-dollar bills, and scraps of paper at me to sign. A security guard tried to rescue me, but I would have none of it. I loved it, and I was determined to sign as long as people were asking me to sign, no matter how much of the game I missed. I couldn't believe that anyone would want my autograph. I felt appreciated for what I had done for my country.

The White House dinner was Nixon's way of basking in the reflected glory of the returned POWs. The trauma of Vietnam was behind him that night, although Watergate was beginning to dog him. The president's daughters, Julie and Tricia, spoke bitterly about their father's critics when they met with the wives and mothers of the POWs before the dinner.

Nixon let nothing detract from his shining moment that night. He had ended the war and brought home the prisoners, Watergate be damned. He was on top of the world, smiling and shaking hands and raising his arms in a human victory sign as if he were campaigning. In a sense, he was campaigning, but it was not a campaign for office; it was a campaign to keep his office.

Nixon brought in many of his conservative Hollywood friends to entertain us that night. Bob Hope was the master of ceremonies. John Wayne was there, as were Jimmy Stewart and Sammy Davis Jr. Wayne sat at the table behind me. At some point I approached him for an autograph. "Mr. Wayne," I said somewhat sheepishly, "I know this isn't the right time, but may I have your autograph?"

Wayne turned slowly in his chair, looked up at me, and smiled. "I thought you'd never ask," he replied in that inimitable drawl as he scrawled his name on the program.

It was that kind of night. There were no rules or protocol to observe. I chatted for a while with Henry Kissinger about Laos. The entertainers wandered from table to table, talking to the POWs and their wives. We ate seafood salad, roast beef, and strawberry mousse, and we cheered and applauded wildly when, in response to a Nixon toast, one POW said of the 1972 Christmas bombing of Hanoi: "When we heard the B-52s dropping the big bombs I said: 'Pack your bags, boys; we're going home.'"

Everyone seemed elated. There was a sense of euphoria in the tent that I had not seen anywhere in the country since the war in Southeast Asia had started in earnest in 1965.

Despite the gaiety, there was an undercurrent of pain and doubt. I could see clearly on the gaunt faces of many of the returnees that they had not yet left Vietnam behind. When they laughed, there was something dark and painful behind their eyes: fears I no longer knew, scars that for me had healed years ago. Their pain was still there. The dress uniforms of many of the returned POWs hung loosely on them, evidence of the starvation diets many were subjected to while in captivity.

I felt strangely out of place. Because I was no longer on active duty I wore a tuxedo, and it was not readily apparent that I had been a POW. In the eleven years since my release, I had regained all of the weight I had lost and was no longer hollow-cheeked and emaciated, like many of my dinner companions.

Then there was the question of Laos. I met no other returned POWs from Laos that night, and there was little mention of Laos during the dinner or of the more than five hundred Americans still missing in action (MIA) there. The event seemed more a reunion of prisoners who had been held in North Vietnam. They talked of the Hanoi Hilton and the Rockpile and other prisons in North Vietnam that I knew nothing about. There was a sense of camaraderie among them that excluded me and my experiences so early in the war and in such an unknown place.

It was much the same wherever the POWs gathered that year. If I was with them, I was assumed to have been a captive of the North Vietnamese or Viet Cong. Not unless I mentioned Laos was the subject brought up, and those times I did mention it, there were curious stares.

"Laos?" they seemed to say. "Where is Laos?" Laos had become the black hole of the POW/MIA issue. Few who were lost in Laos were ever seen again. That country and the war there sucked in victims but rarely spit them out.

At the end of the war in Southeast Asia, the Defense Intelligence Agency reported 559 American military personnel unaccounted for in Laos. That included 233 MIA, 2 POW, 109 presumed dead, and 206 killed in action/body not recovered.[1]

Of the 591 Americans released from captivity in Southeast Asia between 12 February 1973 and 1 April 1973 during Operation Homecoming, only 9 had been captured in Laos: 2 civilians and 7 military. Moreover, all those released had been captured in areas controlled by the Vietnamese. The Pathet Lao released no American prisoners.[2] So what happened to all those men? Did they all die immediately? That answer is not likely, as U.S. officials knew the Pathet Lao held several dozen Americans who never returned home.

Most of those lost in Laos remained lost. Although rescue crews performed frequent heroic feats trying to get to downed pilots, those not rescued soon after their shootdown faced considerable difficulty surviving for any length of time. Mountains, jungles, bad water, tigers, and lack of food presented imposing barriers to survival of even the hardiest of pilots, and with most of the inhabitants of Laos concentrated in the lowlands along the Mekong River, a downed pilot was less likely to be found in Laos than in the more densely populated North Vietnam.[3]

The Pathet Lao had little regard for the lives of American pilots who fell into their hands, though. As former Ambassador William Sullivan recounted in testimony before the Senate Select Committee on POW/MIA Affairs in 1992, the fates of those shot down while flying missions against the Ho Chi Minh Trail were usually sealed by the circumstances of the shootdown. Those who survived were unlikely to live long. "In that brutal environment, anybody captured there was pretty soon disposed of with a bullet in the head," Sullivan said.[4]

In 1969 Pathet Lao spokesman Soth Phetrassy[5] told Western newsmen that more than 158 Americans were being held by the Pathet Lao, but, he said, they were considered war criminals, not POWs. "The United States and Laos have never formally declared war and therefore there will be no prisoners," he said. "They will be tried by a Laotian Peoples Court as criminals."[6]

In 1971, retired air force Col. V. J. Donahue, whose son Morgan, an air force pilot, had disappeared in Laos, was informed by Phetrassy in Vientiane that "we have over one hundred American MIAs."[7]

In 1972 Phetrassy was quoted as saying "there were many" U.S. POWs being held by the Pathet Lao. "We are willing to discuss the question of United States POW release if the American imperialists would order a total bombing halt and let alone the Laotians to solve their own internal problems," he said.[8]

During Operation Homecoming, there was surprise, anger, and then fear among members of families of men missing in Laos when so few returned from that country. The outcry from family members prompted a House Select Committee investigation in 1976. It was headed by Rep. G. V. "Sonny" Montgomery, the irascible veteran Democrat from Mississippi who for years has been a champion of military men and veterans affairs.

After studying the issue for months Montgomery's commission concluded that not only were there no easy answers for what happened in Laos but also there were no satisfactory explanations to give relatives of the missing men.

One of the most enigmatic aspects of the POW/MIA issue is the large number of MIA losses in Laos and the incredibly small number of prisoners that returned from that country. It is extremely difficult, if not impossible in many cases, for next-of-kin to accept the unexplained disappearance of so many fine Americans.[9]

Sixteen years later the Senate Select Committee on POW/MIA Affairs, headed by Sen. John Kerry, the Massachusetts Democrat and Vietnam War veteran, reached almost the same conclusion: Laos was an unfathomable black hole. There were far more questions than answers about it, in part because of the secrecy with which operations there were conducted.

Almost everyone who is familiar with the cases of the men missing in Laos or who has dealt with their families has been puzzled by the confusion and contradictions obvious in those cases. One involves me and the family of Roy Townley, an Air America employee lost in Laos in 1971.

In an effort to determine the fates of some of the missing men, the DIA put together an "album" of photographs, *Unidentified U.S. Prisoners of War in Southeast Asia*. The photographs, culled from various sources, showed unidentified Americans in captivity. Photo No. 109 was a grainy black-and-white of a round-faced man lying in what appeared to be a hospital bed, his left arm in a cast. From 1972 to 1986 the DIA distributed the photo to returning POWs and family members of missing men, hoping for an identification. None was forthcoming.

As described by the Montgomery Commission in its final report: "The individual in the picture appears to be in a small, hospital-type bed; his left arm is bandaged or in a light cast. The photograph is of poor quality, thus precluding any positive identification."[10] Townley's children were convinced it was a photo of their father.

In May 1986 the DIA contacted me, to ask if I knew anything about the photo. According to the letter attached to it, the photo

known only as "109," has remained a mystery to the Defense Intelligence Agency since August 1972. It was received from the U.S. Air Force Office of Special Investigations, which obtained it from an individual who had access to the news agencies of North Vietnam. Subsequently, no one has ever known or determined when or where it was taken, although it was believed to show an American Prisoner of War.[11]

The prisoner of war in the photo was me. It was one of those numerous photos taken shortly after I was captured and my broken arm put in a cast. I informed the DIA and the Townley family of my findings. Although I was able to set the record straight in this case, I wondered how many similar cases the DIA had been unable to resolve because of secrecy and lack of cooperation among government agencies. It had taken eleven years for the DIA to get its hands on photo No. 109, then another fourteen to identify it, simply because the agency was looking in all the wrong places and asking none of the right questions.

Of the 2.6 million American military personnel who served in Southeast Asia, 2,546 were unaccounted for at the end of the war, a figure much lower than that for any previous war in which the United States fought, but a number many Americans felt was too high for a war of dubious goals.

In the years since the end of the war, sketchy reports have filtered out of Laos regarding American POWs being held in the caves around Sam Neua and Vieng Xai. Some of those reports came from Hmong refugees fleeing persecution under the regime of their former enemies. The Hmong claim they were shown films of American POWs as late as 1978. The Americans were being held, the Hmong believed, as bargaining chips by the Lao government.[12]

These and numerous other sightings have produced something of a cottage industry of POW/MIA hunters. In the 1980s decorated Vietnam veteran James "Bo" Gritz launched several guerrilla-style operations into Laos aimed at freeing what the former Green Beret believed were American POWs. At least one mission was conducted with the complicity of U.S. government officials.[13] All failed, in part because they were too high-profile, in part because of a lack of hard evidence of where to look.

Members of Congress have even gotten involved, at one point offering a $2.5 million reward for a live American POW, but that effort seems to have done little more than add to the legion of con men and frauds in Southeast Asia who have tried to get rich off the hopes and fears of people who lost husbands or sons or brothers in Laos.

The true story of what happened to America's POWs in Laos has yet to be told, but it will not be told any time soon by the Lao government. Even though the old, hard-line Communists are dying off, replaced in many cases by more progressive, more forgiving, younger politicians, the revisionist history written at the time of the Communist takeover, the reeducation of thousands of Royal Lao soldiers, and the dominance of the Vietnamese for so many years preclude full public disclosure.

The secrecy with which the United States attempted to conduct the war in Laos has now come back to haunt its efforts to account for the missing. Too much information remains classified, and too many who were involved there are unwilling to talk about it.

There are, on the issue of American POWs in Laos, two separate but related issues: whether men were left behind at the close of the war and whether any may still be alive.

Were any American POWs left behind in Laos? I believe American military men were abandoned in Laos and Vietnam at the end of the war. There was so much pressure within the United States for the government to end the war that the negotiators were instructed to accept the first reasonable accord: Get out regardless of any differences in head count on POWs or any other problems that might prolong the negotiations. One need only read the testimonies of former Secretaries of Defense James R. Schlesinger and Melvin Laird before the Senate Select Committee on POW/MIA Affairs in 1992 to come to that conclusion.

Schlesinger said, "I have a high-probability assessment that the people were left behind in Laos and a medium-probability assessment with regard to Vietnam."[14]

Laird said, "It was my gut feeling that there were more."[15]

I was shocked when I first learned that members of the U.S. government admitted American military men were abandoned in Southeast Asia. I was stunned and angered as I watched high-ranking American officials stumbling all over themselves trying to explain under oath why they had betrayed Americans who had fought for them. I never thought I would see the day when the United States abandoned men who risked their lives for their country. A great injustice has been done not only to these men but also to their families and to the nation.

For too long and without good reason, the U.S. government has been secretive about what happened in Laos. Far more was done clandestinely than was necessary for the proper implementation of foreign policy. It was like a spider weaving a web. Eventually, the spider got caught in it.

The question then becomes, Are any Americans still alive in Laos? After much soul-searching, I can only say I have great doubts that anyone survived more than a few years after the end of the war. Based on my own experiences and my frequent brushes with death in just seventeen months of captivity, plus what I have learned from reading of Dieter Dengler and his heroic but terrifying escape from Laos,[16] survival without assistance would have been virtually impossible. Life is difficult enough for the Lao and would be ten times worse for an American thrown into that hostile environment.

Only those Americans who fell directly into the hands of the North Vietnamese had an opportunity to survive in Laos, but it was not in the political interests of the North Vietnamese to admit they held large numbers of Americans shot down in Laos because then the true extent of their involvement there would have been revealed.

There is evidence that the Pathet Lao had little regard for anyone taken prisoner. Even Lao royalty could not escape. King Savang Vatthana reportedly died of starvation in 1978 while imprisoned in the caves of Vieng Xai, as did Crown Prince Vongsavang and Queen Khamphoui.[17]

For years the area around Sam Neua and Vieng Xai has fascinated hunters of American POWs. The nucleus of the Pathet Lao leadership lived there. American and Lao prisoners were held there. It is remote, difficult to travel to, and close to Vietnam. All those factors have made it the prime focus of those who believe—and those who want to believe—that Americans are still being held against their will in Laos.

For me, the allure of Sam Neua was significantly different. The fact that I may have been the only American to survive imprisonment there was of minor importance. Sam Neua and the cell in which I was held retained a portion of my past and a part of me that I felt compelled to rescue. Unless I saw the cell again in the clear light of freedom and washed it clean of memories of me, I would never be free of it.

Epilogue

Return to Sam Neua

The lock on the door snapped shut with a chilling finality. I looked around the room, suddenly alone and frightened. The white plaster walls had gone gray with grime from years of neglect. Cobwebs and dirt were piled in the corners. The room was dark and cold and lonely. Except for the single naked lightbulb dangling from the ceiling and casting stark shadows on the walls, the hotel room reminded me of that place that was my cell so many years earlier.

As I lay in that rock-hard hotel bed in an unheated room, feverish and aching from a mild case of the flu, images of my captivity three decades earlier flashed before me. It seemed so long ago, yet on this night it seemed so close.

It was almost thirty-one years to the day that I landed in Sam Neua, blindfolded with my own shirt and trussed up in a cast, unable to walk, a prisoner of the Pathet Lao. Now, I had returned. This time, I came willingly—with my friend Bill Lnenicka; co-author, Ron Martz; two guides; and a driver—to try to rediscover parts of my past and to make peace with the present. Bill is a retired army Corps of Engineers colonel whose practicality and attention to detail provided the necessary foundation for a trip that I knew would be filled with emotional uncertainty.

I arrived in Sam Neua chilled by the cold and dampness of the mountains and this unexpected bout with the flu. As I stood in my room, I suddenly started shaking. Was it because of the flu or was it from the memories of this place? I did not know, but I could not

185

stop shaking. I took some antibiotics and lay in bed. Blankets were piled on me.

I urged Bill and Ron to go to dinner without me. Bill put another blanket on me and took a flashlight to aid his passage across the dark courtyard and through the dim hallways to the dark, austere dining room. The two hours of electricity the town receives each night is of rather low wattage and barely sufficient to light a single bulb in each room. A flashlight is essential not only for navigation at night in Sam Neua but also on occasion to see to eat.

As Bill left the room, he locked the door from the outside with a padlock. As soon as I heard the lock click shut, the memories of imprisonment, of solitary confinement, and of being shut off from everything I knew and loved came rushing back.

Returning to Sam Neua was not intended as a trip back in time to recall fond memories of a place I knew well. Instead, it was meant as a journey of discovery to try to find a place about which I knew very little and to find something of myself that I had left here.

During my imprisonment, my knowledge of Sam Neua was restricted to what I could see from the peephole in my first cell and the small, barred window in my second cell. This trip I wanted to learn what I did not know of Sam Neua and see the place that had taken seventeen months of my life without ever acknowledging I was there.

In a sense, I was trying to close the circle that first brought me here. My wife, Jean, thought this was a trip of healing, and perhaps, in a sense, it was. I felt a certain need, one last time before I died, to see the cell where I had been a prisoner. I felt that if I could see it, if I could tear down the tin that covered the windows and let the light pour in, then I could wash the darkness from the cell. With the darkness gone, so too would I be gone, no longer a prisoner of the cell or of my memories of it.

When we began planning for this trip, we did so only with the slimmest of hopes that we would be able to get to Sam Neua. There were no assurances from anyone with whom we talked, the U.S. State Department, the reluctant Lao embassy officials in Washington, or any of the travel agencies that only in recent years began offering trips to one of the last redoubts of Communism. Sam Neua remained, for most Westerners, off-limits and beyond reach, the mysterious mountain village that many believe hold the secrets to what happened to the American prisoners from the war in Southeast Asia.

During my brief tour in Laos in late 1960 and early 1961, prior to my captivity, Phong Saly and Sam Neua provinces in northeastern Laos were off-limits to Americans. They were the strongholds of the Pathet Lao. Little had changed in thirty-plus years, except that Sam Neua Province was now officially known as Hua Phan Province. The two northeastern provinces remained isolated and aloof from Vientiane, closer in thought and actions to Vietnam than to Laos. Now, as then, officials in neither place were well-versed on what the others were doing or thinking.

Getting anywhere beyond the normal tourist destinations of Vientiane and the old royal city of Luang Prabang was a chancy proposition because officials in each region had to approve special travel permits. The government in Vientiane had little say in the matter, and I had no particular diplomatic muscle to exercise.

I was intent on keeping the trip as low-key as possible, trying not to arouse the suspicions of the Lao or U.S. governments. As a former POW, I had a certain amount of clout available to me that I decided to exercise sparingly. I did not want to get the Lao government involved in my trip and had no desire to be shepherded around the country by U.S. government officials. I wanted to see what I could see and feel what I could feel on my own, without excess diplomatic baggage. So, it was not without some small measure of concern that our party set off for Laos, unsure of where we would be allowed to travel or what we would be permitted to see.

After spending several days in Bangkok to adjust to the twelve-hour time differential, we departed for Laos on 22 March 1992. As we flew over northeastern Thailand, I noticed the landscape below was tan and dusty, awaiting the first rains that would turn the rice paddies a brilliant green and the canals surrounding them a dark, dirt brown. The air was filled with haze and smoke as the farmers prepared for planting season by burning waste weeds from their fields. The Mekong River was an anemic version of what it would be in flood. Many of the mudflats and sandbars that poked above the surface of the chocolate-colored water were planted in vegetable patches by industrious Thai and Lao farmers, even though their gardens would be under thirty or forty feet of water come the rains.

A knot formed in my stomach as we prepared to touch down at Wattay International Airport. In the distance, next to the old terminal I once flew out of, I could see several An-2 Colts, the Russian biplanes in which I had been transported to and from Sam Neua. They were parked wingtip to wingtip in a fenced-off area, as if they had not been used for some time. Still, the mere sight of them caused my stomach to do flips. I had not seen one of those since my release in 1962. "Will the whole trip be like this?" I wondered. Would there be a memory waiting around every corner?

The three months I spent in Laos prior to capture in 1961 had not given me much of an opportunity to learn about Vientiane.

I knew how to get from the airport to the embassy, from the embassy to my living quarters, and back again, but not much else. So there was little for me to remember about the city. Still, on my return in 1992, it seemed far removed from what I had known thirty years earlier.

Vientiane remains a sleepy capital of a slowly emerging nation, but it was far more modern and industrious than I expected. Small businesses seemed to be sprouting everywhere in a climate where the harsh economic strictures of the past fifteen years have been relaxed in favor of a more enlightened approach to development. The fall of communism in Europe and the end of socialist largess from the Soviet Union had forced Laos into this experiment with economic independence.

The morning market in downtown Vientiane has dozens of stalls featuring Western-style clothing and appliances imported from Thailand, which are in great demand throughout the country. Dealerships for Mercedes, Toyota, and Isuzu automobiles had opened in Vientiane in the previous year, although bicycles are still the primary mode of transportation throughout the city. Hotels, some owned by industrious Thais eager to invest in the potentially lucrative Lao economy, have opened to cater to foreign tourists, although some are still rather primitive by modern standards.

The reeducation camps for political dissidents and former members of the Royal Lao Army have, by all accounts, closed, their "students" sent home. One former Royal Lao Army officer we met spent six years in a reeducation camp following the Communist takeover in 1975. "We called them political seminars," he said of the camps.

"How long do they normally last?" I naively asked him.

"Forever," he said without a smile.

Southeast of Vientiane, where the Mekong narrows and turns east before going north and then south again, the only bridge along more than fifteen hundred miles of river was being built with the aid of the Australians. The Mittaphab Bridge, or Friendship Bridge, links the Lao village of Tha Naleng with the Thai city of Nong Khai, to which I and several dozen embassy employees had escaped during the fighting in December 1960. The three-quarter-mile-long bridge, built for $30 million, is expected to speed the flow of consumer goods from Thailand to Laos. Before the bridge, Laos had to get its goods by air, by cumbersome ferries from Thailand, or by truck along tortuous roads from Vietnam.

North of Vientiane, a Japanese-built dam forming the Nam Ngum Lake is expected to bring in additional revenue through the sale of electricity to power-starved northeastern Thailand.

Curiously enough in this socialist country, religion has enjoyed a resurgence in popularity. The numerous Buddhist *wats* and shrines are an essential part of any tour of Vientiane. The government-sanctioned tourist agencies seem to be intent on convincing visitors that the country is not filled with godless Communists.

At That Luang, the Great Sacred Stupa, which is said to have been built over a shrine housing the breastbone of Buddha, we were told that Kaysone Phomvihane, the devout Marxist leader of the country until his death in November 1992, came here to pray. It seems a contradiction, as is much of the country.

"We are not Communists now," the guide said fervently, as he escorted us around the shrine. "We are a democracy. But we are only one party. We change step by step, the Lao way, very slowly." It was the same way I survived my solitary confinement for seventeen months: step by step, the Lao way, very slowly.

The guide's words were echoed by Charles Salmon, a veteran of Southeast Asia, who at the time of our visit was the chargé d'affaires for the United States in Laos. He later became the ambassador, the first since the end of the war. "Change will come, but it will come slowly. That's the Lao way," Salmon told us in a brief meeting in his office before we set out for northern Laos.

The older generation of leaders, the hard-line Pathet Lao who fought for years in the caves and jungles under terribly adverse conditions, "has questions about the second generation's revolutionary fervor," Salmon said.

Japanese and German automobiles, cellular telephones, fax machines, and American dollars are great lures for the young Lao who see their neighbors across the river in Thailand enjoying the spoils of a prosperous economy and want the same for themselves. The more distance from the revolution, the less fervent the passions for it. The new revolution is in making money and carving out a unique political, economic, and social niche for a country of fewer than five million people surrounded by 1.2 billion Chinese to the north, seventy million Vietnamese to the east, and sixty million Thai to the west and south. No longer content to be a buffer to those countries and no longer willing to allow itself to be used by any of them, the Lao in their own quiet, peaceful way seem intent on allowing past horrors of war to fade away quietly while they focus on the present and the future.

Yet Laos is filled with strange contradictions. In a country that until recently was one of the few remaining pockets of hard-line communism, there was little evidence of military presence, either Pathet Lao or Vietnamese, anywhere. Camp Chinaimo, south of town, from where Capt. Kong Le launched his coup attempt that sparked the civil war, and an antiaircraft battery north of town were the only signs of military we saw in Vientiane. There were no soldiers with weapons guarding street corners, banks, or hotel lobbies. Even the monuments to the revolution and the war dead are a curious mix of militant Pathet Lao propaganda and peaceful Buddhism.

The Pratuxi Monument, also known as the Anusawali Monument, built to honor the prerevolution war dead at the intersection of three major Vientiane thoroughfares, is one such example. Constructed with American cement originally intended for a runway at Wattay Airport, the monument resembles something of a Buddhist Arc de Triomphe.

A view from the top of the monument offers a unique perspective of Vientiane. The city, made up primarily of one- and two-story buildings, all but vanishes under the leaves of the eucalyptus trees when seen from that height. Vientiane seems strangely quiet for a city so large. The most persistent noise is the constant swish-swish-swish of the multitude of bicyclists riding along Thanon Lan Xang, Thanon That Luang, and Thanon Phone Keng. Few cars or trucks are seen or heard.

The Lao Revolutionary Museum is another study in contrasts. Formerly the Ministry of Defense building that I visited on occasion during my brief tour here, the museum glorifying the armed struggles of the Lao people is incongruously painted a subdued pink. Its photographs, paintings, and displays of captured weapons have Lao and English subtitles, although few foreign tourists are permitted to see them.

French colonialism and American intervention in the secret war are portrayed quite harshly throughout the museum, despite the strong French and American influences on the culture. General Vang Pao, who led the Hmong forces for the CIA during the war, is identified in one museum photograph as "the commander of the special forces, the key headman of the U.S. imperialists, [who] savagely murdered the Lao people." The photographs of Pathet Lao, meanwhile, invariably depict them smiling or laughing as they help people plant or harvest or build.

There is virtually no mention of American POWs or of the number of U.S. warplanes shot down in Laos. There are photos of Thai prisoners and Hmong prisoners but no photos of American prisoners, and the only photograph of a downed plane is of an F-105 supposedly shot down by a lone soldier with a rifle in Xieng Khoung Province in November 1969. There is no mention of what happened to the pilot.

On the bottom floor of the museum, near the end of the tour and almost hidden from view, is a section devoted to the history of communism. Obviously financed by the Soviets, it is decorated far more lavishly than any other display in the museum. It is also the most depressing, its heavy drapes, dark carpet, and bad lighting a remarkably fitting tribute to the dreary country that inspired the ill-fated political system.

After a few days in Vientiane, I was ready to move on. Little looked familiar after thirty years. I could not find the compound where I had lived. Even the U.S. embassy had changed significantly since I was last here. It had been expanded greatly to house the hundreds of additional personnel brought in to run the secret war, although the staff now was rather small.

The attaché's building where I had worked had become a mail room, commissary, and library. The grease pit across the street from my office, where a Royal Lao soldier crouched in fear of exploding mortars during the fighting in 1960, is gone, too. We tried to find some Lao workers at the embassy who might have remembered the layout of the buildings and offices from 1960 and 1961, but those veterans we found could not clearly recall what I remembered. Their emphasis was on the present and the future. I was trying to drag them back thirty years, and it was difficult for them to make the journey with me.

I had originally hoped on my return trip to be able to travel by road from Vientiane to Luang Prabang and the Plain of Jars. Route 13 runs north from the capital about 140 miles through the mountains and the village of Vang Vieng to the old royal city. It would be an interesting journey, I thought, and I would be able to see some of the country that I was barred from during my first tour because of bad roads and the uncertainty of the civil war.

We were told, however, that little has changed in three decades. The national highway linking two of the country's major cities is still bad, little more than a dirt track most of the way. Bus service is undependable, and attacks by anti-Communist rebels, many believed to be the remnants of Vang Pao's Hmong army, while not frequent, occur often enough to give anyone pause about making such a trip by road unless it is absolutely necessary.

The Thais have attempted in recent years to clean out the groups of resistance fighters who use Thailand as a staging area for attacks into Laos. Despite a nasty, months-long border war in 1987 and 1988, in which hundreds of Thai and Lao soldiers were killed, the Thais have been convinced that it is in their best economic interests to deal with the Lao government in its present form rather than fomenting revolution from its soil. The insurgents have been told to stop fighting or return to Laos. Some opted to leave Thailand and carry on the fight in Laos, which has resulted in attacks along Route 13.

The trip north on a Lao Air flight was as revealing as a trip by road, perhaps more so. Only from the air is it possible to see and fully appreciate the hundreds and hundreds of bomb craters around the Plain of Jars. From the ground, the craters appear to be little more than depressions in the ground, overgrown by weeds and crumbling at the edges. From the air, by contrast, the craters are clearly defined, withstanding the ravages of time and indelibly marking this region as one in which the war will not soon be forgotten.

We were awed into silence by the sheer numbers of the craters and wondered what we were flying into at Phonsavan, the old opium trading center on the Plain of Jars and the place where I was first brought after being captured. These people had lived with war for so long; we wondered if they continued to live with it.

Phonsavan seemed to be a town on the edge of nowhere, a frontier village with dusty streets, tin-roofed buildings, electricity that is available only two hours a day just after dark, and a bustling market where the detritus of war dug up from surrounding fields is brought in to be sold as scrap metal. In small, dark stalls, children sit and keep watch over brass shell casings, bits of airplanes, and aluminum containers that once held cluster bombs. Around town, the casings and cluster bomb canisters are used for flowerpots, ashtrays, and fence posts. In the ditches and fields, we occasionally saw unexploded 250-pound or 500-pound bombs, now defused, the iron left to rust away.

In Phonsavan we learned that the war is still deadly. Cluster bombs, strewn with abandon first by Americans and then by Vietnamese and Pathet Lao, are still alive and killing. Posters around town remind children not to play with the bomblets, known here as *bombis,* which can easily blow off a hand or foot. In fact, throughout the remainder of our journey in northern Laos, the posters warning of the dangers of cluster bombs were a ubiquitous reminder of the war, prominently displayed on the sides of buildings in many of even the most remote of villages.

Our guide in the north was Sousath Phetrassy, a son of the former Pathet Lao spokesman Soth Phetrassy. Like many Lao, Sousath has taken advantage of the new economic freedom in the country and opened a travel agency catering to foreigners. A sign in his Vientiane office reads "Laos Northern Expeditions. Cheaper Than You Think." Sousath also runs a construction business and a music business and seems intent on expanding his economic empire.

Although he was born in Sam Neua during the war and educated first in the caves of northern Laos and later in Vietnam and China, Sousath seemed not so much a child of the revolution as a child of economic opportunity. He was bright, charming, and witty, a young man eager to please. He was greatly amused by my feeble attempts at the Lao language and eager to hear the story of my captivity in Sam Neua.

The trip there, he informed us, was uncertain because of concerns by officials in Hua Phan Province. Americans have frequently been allowed into Sam Neua, but most have been military personnel seeking crash sites, engineers building schools or roads, or doctors and missionaries on their own journeys of mercy. No American tourists and no former POWs had visited Sam Neua.

The issue of American MIAs and POWs unsettled Sousath. He was not reluctant to discuss my captivity, but he was hesitant to talk even in generalities about the fates of the hundreds of other Americans still unaccounted for. We made several requests of Sousath to take us to his father, Soth Phetrassy, to talk about missing Americans, but Sousath said his father was now an old man, no longer in the good graces of the government, who did not like to speak about the past, especially about MIAs. It had taken one American, V. J. Donahue, three trips to Laos twenty years earlier to get an audience with Soth Phetrassy. For us to expect to be able to do it in less than ten days was somewhat unrealistic.

The farther north and east we traveled, the more identifiable the Vietnamese influence, even though virtually all combat troops have been withdrawn. Most of the soldiers who remain are advisers and engineers who wear civilian clothes and are identifiable only by their green pith helmets.

In Phonsavan and the countryside surrounding the Plain of Jars, there were a few Vietnamese engaged in public works projects. Near Muong Khome, the former Hmong capital southeast of Phonsavan, we encountered some Vietnamese troops involved in a bridge-building project. They mistook us for Russians.

"*Da svidanya,*" said one, greeting us in Russian. We smiled, waved, and walked on.

"How many Vietnamese are still in the country?" I asked one man.

"Not so many now," he replied.

"How many is that?"

"Too many."

The Vietnamese, it seems, are barely tolerated. In a Phonsavan restaurant where we took our meals, the Phonsai, run by a former Pathet Lao captain who had framed photographs of his soldiers hanging on the walls, the Vietnamese sat on one side of the room, eating and talking among themselves. The owner barely acknowledged their presence. Although we were Americans and only visiting, he hovered over us, eagerly responding to our every request for more rice, tea, or bottled water.

"The Lao don't like three things," one man in Phonsavan told us. "They don't like the Vietnamese, they don't like the Communists, and they don't like the CIA."

While in Phonsavan I also wanted to try to find the sites where Rose Bowl crashed and where the bodies of the crew members had been buried until their recent discovery and return to the United States. The U.S. embassy officials in Vientiane said they knew the crash site was within easy driving distance of Phonsavan but could not give us exact directions. My own memories of thirty years earlier were of no assistance, and all our inquiries in Phonsavan met with blank looks and negative responses. Either no one knew or no one was willing to tell us.

I had no real interest in returning to Lat Huang, where I had been held with Roger Ballenger, Grant Wolfkill, Ed Shore, John McMorrow, and Lorenzo Frigilano before my release because of the briefness of my stay there. The one other place in Phonsavan in which I had some interest—the makeshift hospital I had been taken to after the shootdown—was gone now, swallowed up by a new military base.

What I most fervently sought was not here in Phonsavan, though. It was up the road, nearly 125 difficult, mountainous miles away in the cloud-shrouded village of Sam Neua. Permission to visit it finally had been obtained, Sousath informed us, but travel would have to be by road, a two-day journey in a battered, Russian UAZ military van painted olive drab but enlivened with decals of Mickey Mouse on the windows.

The journey east through the Plain of Jars on Route 7 toward Vietnam was relatively easy on a two-lane paved road, but at the crossroads village of Ban Ban, a key road junction during the war, the road split: Route 7 continued east to Barthelemy Pass and Vietnam; Route 6 turned north into the mountains and Sam Neua.

We spent the night in a small Lao Tung village on the north bank of the Nam Neum River. The headman of the village, who spelled out his name in English as "Bualiene," was delighted to see us. With Sousath doing the interpreting, Bualiene told us the last foreign visitors to the village were some Russian engineers who built a nearby bridge.

Dinner was fresh cucumbers, boiled cabbage, and cabbage soup eaten by the light of a Coleman lantern. In honor of our visit, Bualiene broke out a jar of rice wine and insisted we participate in the ceremony. In deference to our delicate Western stomachs, he permitted us to use bottled water to filter through the fermented rice instead of the more traditional river water poured from a buffalo horn. We drank more than our share of the sweet, heady wine through bamboo reeds and retired to a bamboo-thatched eight-bed guest house for the night.

The sixty-mile trip into Sam Neua the next day took a full five hours over a one-lane, deeply rutted dirt track that forded numerous streams and climbed in and out of the clouds. The UAZ overheated on the upgrades and spit wads of differential grease on the downgrades. We wondered if it would survive the trip on a road not meant for anything more fragile than a four-wheel drive truck.

This road had been a key supply link between North Vietnam and its troops fighting on the Plain of Jars during the secret war, and convoys traveling it were frequently attacked. All along the road, we saw holes dug into the sides of the mountains—Bill referred to them as "horizontal foxholes"—that offered some protection to convoy drivers during attacks from aircraft.

It was along this route that I would have been forced to travel, had I attempted to escape from Sam Neua more than thirty years earlier. Except for the road and a few scattered villages clinging to the crests of the mountains, there was little evidence of human existence. The mountains were steep, treacherous, and inhospitable. Without a compass, without food, and without adequate clothing, escape would have been a slow dance with suicide. What I saw as we drove from the Nam Neum River to Sam Neua only reaffirmed my decision not to attempt an escape more than thirty years earlier.

It was cold and cloudy when we arrived in Sam Neua shortly after noon. I was tired and sore from the constant pounding over the bad road and was beginning to feel the first touches of the flu, but I insisted we press on to find the house where I had been imprisoned.

Nothing looked familiar except the grass airstrip east of town where I had been brought in as a POW in March 1961 and from which I departed in August 1962. The airstrip had not changed at all. It was still short, still grass, and still used for grazing by water buffalo.

Sam Neua had changed, though. It was much larger than I remembered. As I wandered the streets that day, looking for some clue of my imprisonment, trying to find someone who remembered a lone American held prisoner in the French house or the jail cell, I became increasingly frustrated. I could find nothing I remembered. The stupa I saw when I first arrived in Sam Neua was gone. The house was gone. The jail cell was gone.

We went into the lone French-style house that remotely resembled the one I had been held in, but as soon as I stepped inside I knew it was not the right house. The hallway was too wide. The soldiers had struggled with my stretcher the day I arrived. The fireplace was not in the southeast corner of the room, where the guards had warmed themselves and played cards on a cold winter night so many years ago. The room in that corner of the house was not large enough, and there were no tiles on the floor, the tiles that I had counted for so many endless hours, seventeen east to west, twenty-three north to south.

"Only one building left from the French," Sousath said, trying to console me. "The rest were broken."

Broken, apparently, by bombs that rained down on the Pathet Lao headquarters for more than four years of the secret war until U.S. intelligence officials learned American POWs were being held in nearby caves and placed Sam Neua off limits.

Accounts of what happened in Sam Neua are sketchy and difficult to obtain. Officials there remain wary of outsiders, particularly of Lao from Vientiane. They are suspicious of those with ties to the government in the capital because they find it easier to deal with their own problems at their own speed than to wait for some official in Vientiane to make a decision.

The few Americans who venture to Sam Neua provide services: schools, roads, artificial limbs for amputees, water projects, and crop substitution to wean the hill tribes from opium production. Most foreigners who come to Sam Neua deal with the present and the future. The past, particularly the war, is an ancient memory whose recounting does no good and provides no help for today or tomorrow.

One of the few Westerners to get into the province of Sam Neua during the height of the war and write about it was a French journalist named Jacques Decornoy. He went there in early 1968 and wrote a lengthy, if somewhat patronizing, piece on the Pathet Lao under siege for the Paris newspaper *Le Monde*. Portions of his series were later reprinted in the book *Laos: War and Revolution* under the title "Life in the Pathet Lao Liberated Zone."

Decornoy wrote that village officials throughout Sam Neua province reported heavy bombing between February 1965 and his arrival in March 1968. In the village of Sam Neua itself, major raids started 19 February 1965, with two particularly large raids on 17 and 19 March 1968.[1]

The town [of Sam Neua] looked like one long street, bordered with European-type houses which were built at the time of French colonial rule and with traditional Laotian dwellings of wood and bamboo. The two ends of the town were razed to the ground. The old ruins of 1965 have disappeared; those of March 1968 were still "smoking" when we visited them. Branches of trees lay all along the length of the river, and houses were totally burned out. . . .

At the other end of Sam Neua, the sight was even more painful.

Everywhere there were enormous craters, and the church and many houses were demolished.[2]

The house, the cell, and the jail were gone, victims of the war and the bombing it brought. I retired to the dingy hotel near dark. I was cold, tired, and embarrassed that I had not been able to find a single thing I remembered or a single person who remembered me. I had great expectations when I came to Sam Neua that I would find the two buildings in which I had been imprisoned. After traveling so far and holding it inside for so many years it seemed urgently important now to find them, to see them again, and wash them clean with the fresh light of day, but it was not to be.

I lay in my bed, covered with blankets, shivering, and ill with the flu, the images of the cell and my imprisonment washing over me in waves. I slept fitfully that night, trapped in a room in Sam Neua again, this time by my own memories.

The next morning, revived by the antibiotics and the warmth of the sun that had broken through the overcast, I was up early, eager to continue the search, even though by then I knew I probably would not find my past.

Nevertheless, Sousath directed our party toward Vieng Xai, thirty miles east through the mountains, near the border with Vietnam. All along the narrow paved road were limestone formations, the karst sentinels for which this part of the world is known, rising majestically from the dried brown mud of the rice paddies. In many of them we saw the yawning black maws of caves.

We stopped the van and went into several of them. The first was huge, its entrance nearly fifty feet high, with a creek flowing through it. Some of our party scrambled as far back as they could without losing the light. Spelunking equipment was needed to go farther. "Villagers say four American pilots held here," Sousath told us.

"What happened to them?" I asked.

Sousath shrugged his shoulders. "Only the government knows."

The caves we visited were deserted, littered with trash and the graffiti of war. They were especially dark and dank, not at all conducive to long-term survival by anyone held prisoner there.

Vieng Xai, formerly known as Ban Nokay Neua, became the headquarters for the Pathet Lao during those years when Sam Neua was heavily bombed. Kaysone and Prince Souphanouvong had houses here that backed up to large caves that served as bomb shelters during air raids.

There also were caves for classes, caves for cooking, caves for producing Pathet Lao propaganda, caves for storage, and caves that housed antiaircraft weapons that were virtually impossible to knock out. Most of the caves had heavy stone and concrete blast barriers that kept out fragments from exploding bombs and prevented penetration by the laser-guided munitions used later in the war.

There was more evidence of the war wherever we went. The indestructible cluster bomb canisters were used as fence posts and as spouts for waterwheels. Unexploded bombs, defused but still ominous, lay where they had fallen decades earlier.

Despite this, we were greeted warmly by villagers when they discovered that we were Americans and not Russians. In a Red T'ai village near Vieng Xai we walked into the middle of a wedding ceremony and were coerced into staying until we had participated in the rice wine ceremony and contributed to the dowry of the bride. As we were leaving, villagers stopped us long enough to honor us with a quick *baci* ceremony in which white strings are tied around the wrists of those for whom the *baci* is offered. With each string, a wish is offered: "I wish you a long life." "I wish you many children." "I wish you a safe journey."

If the ceremony is long enough and the honoree important enough, he might have strings from his wrists to his elbows. General Vang Pao and Capt. Kong Le frequently were seen with forearms covered with *baci* strings. I escaped with a half-dozen.

We returned to Sam Neua before dark for one last search through town, one last excursion into the past. It proved as fruitless as the previous efforts. I still could find nothing that even remotely resembled anything I had seen during my captivity. Reluctantly and with a great sense of disappointment, I finally resigned myself to the fact that the sites of my imprisonment are gone. We prepared to return to Phonsavan and from there to Vientiane, our mission to Sam Neua not quite a failure, but not a success either.

The return trip began at 5:00 A.M. It was an excruciating all-day ordeal over bad roads. We stopped briefly near Ban Ban to view a large cave northwest of the city. Sometime during the war, we were told, several hundred villagers crowded into the cave to escape an air attack. A rocket was fired into the cave, killing more than three hundred villagers. I asked a man if American POWs were held near here.

"Yes," he said.

"What happened to them?"

"They took them out at night and killed them so the people can't see their graves."

"Did they mark the graves?"

"Only the military knows where they are."

The question of what happened to more than five hundred Americans who disappeared in Laos during the war has been an impediment to U.S.-Lao relations for years. Lao officials say the villagers were responsible. The villagers say the Pathet Lao were responsible. Although cooperation on the POW/MIA issue has been sporadic and largely limited to investigations of crash sites, it has improved somewhat in recent years.

As we prepared to leave Phonsavan for Vientiane and our last few days in Laos, we crossed paths at the airport with members of Detachment 3 of Joint Task Force Full Accounting (JTFFA), a U.S. government operation made up primarily of military personnel who travel to Laos, Vietnam, and Cambodia to search for missing Americans and remains of the dead.

This particular eight-man detachment, comprised mainly of air force personnel, was headed by William Gadoury, a former air force enlisted man who is now an investigator for JTFFA. Although they had a Russian-made helicopter waiting for them and were in a hurry to leave, some team members seemed quite interested in my story and I had to repeat it several times as we waited for the airplane to take us back to Vientiane. They found it difficult to imagine spending seventeen months in solitary confinement. Most of the members of this detachment had not yet been born when I was a POW and were too young to have any firsthand knowledge of the war in Southeast Asia.

Gadoury also talked about his detachment's search for Walter Moon's body. They had gotten information from villagers that it was buried in a rice paddy near the old agricultural school at Lat Huang, but several days of digging had produced nothing and the group moved on.

"Spread the word about us," Gadoury said as we left. "People back in the States don't think we're doing anything out here. But we've got teams out looking for people and remains all the time."

We returned to Vientiane tired, somewhat discouraged, and more appreciative of the frustrations Detachment 3 felt in its search for answers to questions about the war. I was feeling many of the same frustrations.

Our last night in Vientiane, Bill, Ron, and I walked along the river road to the center of the city and the Nam Phou, a lighted fountain where young Lao gather to drink beer, listen to music, and be seen. It could have been downtown Bangkok, except there were neither beggars going from table to table seeking a handout nor prostitutes plying their wares. There was an infectious expectancy to the young people gathered at Nam Phou, as if they knew they were perched on the edge of a great economic and social boom. Feeling old, we retired early.

The next morning I awoke early and strolled alone along the narrow dirt road that follows the east bank of the Mekong. The sun, muted by haze and dust, was a dull orange as it rose above the low buildings to my left. It was the same color as the robes of the Buddhist monks padding quietly along the streets with their food bowls, accepting offerings from people who believe that those blessings will be returned in a future life. All around me people were stirring for the new day, sweeping leaves and dust from the steps of their houses, starting cook fires, and smiling politely as I passed.

The trip to Laos had answered only a few of my questions. I was glad I had come but terribly disappointed that I could find little of what I had come to find. My search for the crash site, for the house in which I had been held in lightless solitary confinement in Sam Neua for more than a year, and for the jail cell had been for naught. Nothing remained from my captivity more than thirty years earlier. I was ready to go home, but I knew then I would never leave Laos.

The cell is gone, but it will stay with me. Whenever I close my eyes and think of the war, I will see it there, cold and dark and ill-defined, rising out of the blackness. And time will stop and hold me there, if just for an instant, a prisoner once more, a prisoner forever.

Endnotes

Chapter 1: Rose Bowl

1. It was not until years later that I learned the names of the crew members other than Magee and Weston. I am including them here for the sake of historical accuracy. (See "Fifth Air Force in Southeast Asia Crisis of 1960–61," 42B; and *Vietnam Veterans Memorial Directory of Names* [Washington, D.C.: Vietnam Veterans Memorial Fund, Inc., 1982].)

2. Lt. Col. Butler B. Toland, U.S. Air Force Oral History Program, 34–35. (Toland, the air attaché to South Vietnam, Laos, and Cambodia during this time, says in his oral history that air crews flying over Xieng Khoung Province and the Plain of Jars were ordered to maintain a minimum altitude of 10,000 feet. After seeing the altimeter of the C-47 at 8,000 feet near Vang Vieng, I know we never climbed above that. With the Plain of Jars 3,500 to 4,000 feet above sea level, we would have been 4,000 to 4,500 feet above the ground when we reached there.)

3. H. Bruce Franklin erroneously reports in his *M.I.A. or Mythmaking in America*, 39: "In the spring of 1961, eight American soldiers and airmen were reported as missing in action in Laos; the U.S. government has never claimed that any of these were prisoners. Two U.S. Army servicemen and three civilians were actually captured in Laos in 1961; they were released within the thirty-day period stipulated in the Geneva Agreement of 1962." The actual number of Americans in Laos missing and unaccounted for in the spring of 1961 was double Franklin's figure—sixteen. (See also Defense Intelligence Agency report, "U.S. Military Personnel, Citizens and Dependents, Captured, Missing, Detained or Voluntarily Remained in SE Asia, Accounted for

or Not Accounted for from 1-1-61 through [10-11-79]," Oct. 11, 1979, for exact figures.) Those sixteen included twelve American servicemen and four civilians. Of the twelve servicemen, three were known to have been held prisoner: myself, Army Special Forces Sgt. Roger Ballenger, and Capt. Walter Moon. Moon was shot and killed in captivity. (See Grant Wolfkill, *Reported to Be Alive*, 196–97, for details of Moon's death). The other nine servicemen unaccounted for and presumed dead included the seven on the C-47 that crashed and two other army Special Forces personnel, SFC John Bischoff and Sgt. Gerald Biber. The four civilians included Air America employees Ed Shore and John McMorrow, NBC cameraman Grant Wolfkill, and Charles J. Duffy, an employee with the U.S. embassy in Vientiane. Ballenger, McMorrow, Shore, and Wolfkill were released at the same time I was. Duffy, who disappeared in January 1961 while hunting, has never been accounted for.

Chapter 2: Prisoner of War or Prisoner of Politics?

1. Rod Colvin, in his *First Heroes: The POWs Left Behind in Vietnam*, 196, erroneously reports that Eugene DeBruin, an Air America cargo kicker, and Air Force Capt. David Hrdlicka were the only Americans photographed in captivity in Laos. I was photographed repeatedly on my first day in captivity, and some of those photos were published in Communist publications. Ballenger and Moon were also photographed during their captivity. One of the photographs of me lying in my hospital bed, my left arm in a cast, later became photo No. 109 in Defense Intelligence Agency files. See my debriefing ("Debriefing Report of Lawrence R. Bailey Jr."), 11–12, and "Debriefing Report of Orville R. Ballenger," 5–6, 64, for additional information on the extent to which early POWs in Laos were photographed.

Chapter 4: Where in the World Is Laos?

1. E. Bartlett Kerr, *Flames over Tokyo*, 153.

2. Ibid., 207–8.

Chapter 5: A Very Uncivil War

1. Edward Doyle, Samuel Lipsman, Stephen Weiss, and editors of the Boston Publishing Co., *The Vietnam Experience: Passing the Torch*, 187.

2. Ibid.

3. For a more complete description of this trip, see Toland's oral history interview of 18 November 1974.

4. Although I well remember that the Soviet aircraft had markings on the wings, I am relying on Toland's official oral history for the exact nature of them.

5. "U.S. Says Soviets and Red Vietnam Aid Laos Rebels," *New York Times,* 3 January 1961, 1.

6. Arthur Schlesinger, *A Thousand Days,* 332.

7. Theodore C. Sorenson, *Kennedy,* 640.

8. Ibid.

9. Ibid.

Chapter 6: Alive But Alone

1. "Transcript of President's News Conference on World and Domestic Affairs," *New York Times,* 24 March 1961, 8.

2. Ibid.

3. "No! No! Not Lay-ohs; It's Laos, as in House," *New York Times,* 24 March 1961, 6.

4. Toland oral history interview, 35; and "Fifth Air Force in the Southeast Asia Crisis of 1960–61," 42B.

5. "U.S. Plane in Laos Downed by Reds," *New York Times,* 28 March 1961, 1.

6. "Bailey's Release Asked," *New York Times,* 31 March 1961, 3.

7. "Fifth Air Force in Southeast Asia Crisis of 1960–61," 8.

8. Schlesinger, *A Thousand Days,* 332.

9. Ibid., 338.

10. Sorenson, *Kennedy,* 644.

Chapter 11: States of Mind

1. Although I say in my official debrief that the date of this encounter was 10 November 1961, subsequent checks have led me to revise it. By 10 November stories written by the Hungarian journalist who interviewed me had reached the States and been printed in my hometown newspaper. The remoteness of Sam Neua and lack of sophisticated communications equipment lead me to believe it took the Hungarian at least a month to file his stories and have them picked up by international news wires.

2. "Red Captors Are Given Hard Time by Laurel Man Shot Down in Laos," *Washington Post,* 18 November 1961, 7.

3. "U.S. Officer Deaf to Red Brainwashing," *Arizona Republic,* 18 November 1961, 7.

4. Ibid.

5. Ibid.

Chapter 14: Free at Last

1. "Debriefing Report of Orville R. Ballenger," 193.

2. Ibid., 44–47; and Grant Wolfkill, *Reported to Be Alive*, 194–96.

3. Wolfkill, *Reported to Be Alive*, 365. Although I clearly remember the incident involving the plane and the crash helmet, I am relying here on Wolfkill's training as a journalist and his fresher memory (his book was written little more than two years after our release) for the exact wording of this conversation.

4. Ibid., 366.

5. Ibid., 368.

6. Ibid., 369–70. I am once again drawing heavily on Wolfkill's recollection of this incident. I remember the intense discussion over what should or should not be said, but Wolfkill's memory of this once again is far superior to mine.

7. Ibid., 370.

8. Ibid., 371.

9. "5 Americans Freed in Laos Call Treatment by Pro-Reds Harsh," *New York Times*, 18 August 1962, 1.

10. Wolfkill, *Reported to Be Alive*, 371.

11. "5 Americans Freed in Laos Call Treatment by Pro-Reds Harsh," *New York Times*, 18 August 1962, 1.

12. Ibid.

Chapter 15: Learning to Live with Life

1. "2 Men the Laos Reds Couldn't Crack," *New York Herald Tribune*, 25 August 1962, 1.

2. "Army Reveals Lengthy Ordeal of Two Pathet Lao Prisoners," Department of Defense, Office of Public Affairs Release No. 1388-62, 24 August 1962.

3. Ibid.

4. "Major Bailey's Courage," *Indianapolis Star*, 15 September 1962, 14.

5. "Nation Owes Grand Honors to Two American Soldiers for Loyalty under Torture," *Fort Lauderdale News*, 27 August 1962, 7-A.

Chapter 16: Soldiers of the Unreturning Army

1. "Americans Missing in Southeast Asia, Final Report," 22.

2. "Hearings before the Subcommittee on National Security Policy," 56.

3. For a particularly graphic account of the difficulties faced by pilots trying to survive in the Lao wilderness, see Dieter Dengler's *Escape*

from Laos. Dengler, a navy pilot shot down in 1966, was captured and briefly held prisoner before escaping. He was one of only two Americans who escaped Pathet Lao captivity during the war.

4. "POW/MIA's: Report of the Select Committee on POW/MIA Affairs, United States Senate," 124.

5. Although the name appears in most Western news reports of this period spelled "Petrasy" and has survived as such in U.S. government documents, conversations with a relative of the Pathet Lao spokesman during our 1992 trip to Laos revealed that the preferred English spelling of the family name is "Phetrassy" and thus it appears as such in this work.

6. United Press International news item of 11 November 1969 as quoted in "Hearings before the House Select Committee on Missing Persons in Southeast Asia," Part 3, 217.

7. "Hearings before the House Select Committee on Missing Persons in Southeast Asia," Part 3, 90; and author's interview with V. J. Donahue, March 1988, Cocoa Beach, Florida.

8. United Press International news item of 22 April 1972, as quoted in "Hearings before the House Select Committee on Missing Persons in Southeast Asia," Part 3, 216.

9. "Americans Missing in Southeast Asia, Final Report," 13.

10. Ibid., 84.

11. Letter of 5 May 1986 from D. Warren Gray, Defense Intelligence Agency, to Colonel Bailey, in authors' personal files.

12. Jane Hamilton-Merritt, *Tragic Mountains: The Hmong, the Americans and the Secret Wars for Laos, 1942–1992*, 407.

13. "Mercenaries Sent to Laos Seeking MIAs," *Washington Post*, 21 May 1981, 1.

14. Testimony of former Director of the Central Intelligence Agency (1973) and Secretary of Defense (1973–1975) James R. Schlesinger before the Senate Select Committee on POW/MIA Affairs, 21 September 1992, as quoted in "POW/MIA's: Report of the Select Committee on POW/MIA Affairs, United States Senate," 123; and "Excerpts from Remarks by 2 Ex-Defense Chiefs on M.I.A.'s," *New York Times*, 22 September 1992, A6.

15. Testimony of former Secretary of Defense (1969–1973) Melvin R. Laird before the Senate Select Committee on POW/MIA Affairs, 21 September 1992, as quoted in "POW/MIA's: Report of the Select Committee on POW/MIA Affairs, United States Senate," 123; and "Excerpts from Remarks by 2 Ex-Defense Chiefs on M.I.A.'s," *New York Times*, 22 September 1992, A6.

16. Dengler, *Escape from Laos.*

17. Hamilton-Merritt, *Tragic Mountains: The Hmong, the Americans and the Secret Wars for Laos, 1942–1992*, 405.

Epilogue: Return to Sam Neua

1. Nina S. Adams and Alfred W. McCoy, eds., *Laos: War and Revolution*, 414.

2. Ibid., 414–15.

Bibliography

Books

Adams, Nina S., and Alfred W. McCoy, eds. *Laos: War and Revolution.* New York: Harper & Row, 1970.

Champassak, Sisouk Na. *Storm over Laos: A Contemporary History.* New York: Frederick A. Praeger, 1961.

Colby, William, with James McCargar. *Lost Victory.* Chicago: Contemporary Books, 1989.

Colvin, Rod. *First Heroes: The POWs Left Behind in Vietnam.* New York: Irvington Publishers, 1987.

Dengler, Dieter. *Escape from Laos.* Novato, Calif.: Presidio Press, 1979.

Dommen, Arthur J. *Conflict in Laos: The Politics of Neutralization.* Rev. ed. New York: Praeger, 1971.

Dooley, Dr. Thomas A. *The Edge of Tomorrow.* New York: Farrar, Straus and Cudahy, 1958.

———. *The Night They Burned the Mountain.* New York: Farrar, Straus & Giroux, 1960.

Doyle, Edward, Samuel Lipsman, Stephen Weiss, and editors of the Boston Publishing Co. *The Vietnam Experience: Passing the Torch.* Boston: Boston Publishing Co., 1981.

Eden, Anthony. *Memoirs: Full Circle.* Boston: Houghton Mifflin, 1960.

Fall, Bernard B. *Anatomy of a Crisis.* Garden City, N.Y.: Doubleday, 1969.

Franklin, H. Bruce. *M.I.A., or Mythmaking in America.* New York: Lawrence Hill Books, 1992.

Hamilton-Merritt, Jane. *Tragic Mountains: The Hmong, the Americans and the Secret Wars for Laos, 1942–1992.* Bloomington: Indiana University Press, 1993.

Hanley, Fiske. *History of the 504th Bomb Group in World War II.* Enfield, Conn.: 504th Bomb Group Assn., 1992.

Hannah, Norman B. *The Key to Failure: Laos and the Vietnam War.* New York: Madison Books, 1987.

Hersh, Seymour M. *The Price of Power: Kissinger in the Nixon White House.* New York: Summit Books, 1983.

Hilsman, Roger. *To Move a Nation.* Garden City, N.Y.: Doubleday, 1967.

Kerr, E. Bartlett. *Flames over Tokyo.* New York: Donald I. Fine, 1991.

Lloyd, Alwyn T. *B-29 Superfortress.* Blue Ridge Summit, Pa.: Tab Books, 1983.

McCoy, Alfred W. *The Politics of Heroin in Southeast Asia.* Singapore: Harper & Row, 1972.

Plumb, Charlie, and Glen DeWerff. *I'm No Hero: A POW Story.* Independence, Mo.: Independence Press, 1973.

Prouty, Fletcher L. *JFK: The CIA, Vietnam and the Plot to Assassinate John F. Kennedy.* New York: Birch Lane Press, 1992.

Robbins, Christopher. *Air America.* New York: Avon Books, 1979.

———. *The Ravens: Pilots of the Secret War in Laos.* London: Corgi Books, 1989.

Rowe, James N. *Five Years to Freedom.* Boston: Little Brown and Company, 1971.

Schlesinger, Arthur. *A Thousand Days.* Boston: Houghton Mifflin Company, 1965.

Simpson, Charles M. III. *Inside the Green Berets: The First Thirty Years.* Novato, Calif.: Presidio Press, 1983.

Sorenson, Theodore C. *Kennedy.* New York: Harper & Row, 1965.

Tilford, Earl H. Jr. *Setup: What the Air Force Did in Vietnam and Why.* Maxwell Air Force Base, Ala.: Air University Press, 1991.

Toye, Hugh. *Laos: Buffer State or Battleground.* London: Oxford University Press, 1968.

Waters, Andrew W. *All the U.S. Air Force Airplanes, 1907–1983.* New York: Hippocrene Books, 1983.

Vietnam Veterans Memorial Directory of Names. Washington, D.C.: Vietnam Veterans Memorial Fund, Inc., 1982.

Wolfkill, Grant, with Jerry A. Rose. *Reported to Be Alive.* New York: Simon and Schuster, 1965.

Government Documents

"Americans Missing in Southeast Asia," Final Report, Together with Additional and Separate Views of the Select Committee on Missing Persons in Southeast Asia, House Report No. 94-1764 (Washington, D.C.: Government Printing Office, 1976).

"An Examination of U.S. Policy toward POW/MIAs," U.S. Senate Committee on Foreign Relations Republican Staff, 23 May 1991.

"Army Reveals Lengthy Ordeal of Two Pathet Lao Prisoners," Department of Defense, Office of Public Affairs Release No. 1388-62, 24 August 1962.

"Debriefing Report of Lawrence R. Bailey Jr.," Headquarters, 902nd Intelligence Corps Group, Washington, D.C., 30 November 1962.

"Debriefing Report of Orville R. Ballenger," Headquarters, 902nd Intelligence Corps Group, Washington, D.C., 2 September 1962.

"Fifth Air Force in the Southeast Asia Crisis of 1960–61," Fifth Air Force History, prepared by Arthur C. O'Neill, Chief, Historical Division, Office of Information, Fifth Air Force, 8 June 1961.

"Hearings before the House Select Committee on Missing Persons in Southeast Asia," Feb. 4, Feb. 18, Feb. 25, March 3, March 17, March 25, and March 31, Part 3 (Washington, D.C.: U.S. Government Printing Office, 1976).

"Hearings before the House Select Committee on Missing Persons in Southeast Asia," April 7, May 12, May 26, and June 2, Part 4 (Washington, D.C.: U.S. Government Printing Office, 1976).

"Hearings before the Subcommittee on National Security Policy and Scientific Developments of the Committee on Foreign Affairs, House of Representatives," May 23, 30, and 31, Part 4 (Washington, D.C.: U.S. Government Printing Office, 1973).

Keefer, Edward C., ed., *Laos Crisis: Foreign Relations of the United States, 1961–1963* (Washington, D.C.: U.S. Government Printing Office, 1994).

"POW/MIA's: Report of the Select Committee on POW/MIA Affairs, United States Senate" (Washington, D.C.: U.S. Government Printing Office, 1993).

"Summary of CINCPAC Participation in Events in Laos through 1961," Camp H. M. Smith, Hawaii, Commander in Chief, U.S. Pacific Command, 1961.

"U.S. military personnel, civilians and dependents captured, missing, detained or voluntarily remained in SE Asia, accounted for or unaccounted for from 1-1-61 through (Oct. 11, 1979)," Defense Intelligence Agency POW/MIA Branch master list, 11 October 1979.

Oral Histories

Boyle, Lt. Gen. Andrew J. (U.S. Army, retired), Senior Officers Debriefing Program, U.S. Military History Institute, March 1971.

Toland, Lt. Col. Butler B., U.S. Air Force Oral History Program, Albert F. Simpson Historical Research Center, Air University, Maxwell AFB, Montgomery, Ala., 18 November 1974.

Miscellaneous Articles

Arizona Republic, 18 November 1961.

Dommen, Arthur J., and George W. Dalley. "The OSS in Laos: The 1945 Raven Mission and American Policy." *Journal of Southeast Asian Studies* 22 (1991): 326–46.

Fort Lauderdale News, 27 August 1962.

Garrett, W. E. "The Hmong of Laos: No Place to Go." *National Geographic* 145 (1974): 78–111.

Indianapolis Star, 15 September 1962.

New York Herald Tribune, 25 August 1961, 1.

New York Times, 3 January 1961–22 September 1992.

Sesser, Stan. "A Reporter at Large: Forgotten Country." *New Yorker,* 20 August 1990, pp. 39–68.

White, Peter T. "Laos." *National Geographic* 171 (1987): 772–95.

Index

About the Authors

LAWRENCE R. "BOB" BAILEY, JR., a native of Waycross, Georgia, entered military service in December 1942 and was commissioned a second lieutenant with a pilot's rating in the U.S. Army Air Forces upon graduation from the Flying Cadet Program in March 1944. During World War II he served as a B-29 pilot with the Twentieth Air Force, flying fifteen combat missions over Japan in 1945.

Following the war he left active duty but retained his reserve commission in the U.S. Army. He worked in commercial aviation as an aircraft flight instructor, charter pilot, and ground school instructor. He also was a security inspector with the Sandia Corp. in Albuquerque, New Mexico, until recalled to active duty in April 1951.

During the Korean War he served as the aviation staff officer and pilot with Headquarters, 25th Infantry Division artillery, flying spotting missions in North Korean territory in an 01-G Bird Dog.

Assigned as an assistant attaché to the U.S. embassy in Vientiane, Laos, in December 1960, he was shot down over central Laos in March 1961 and held as a prisoner of war in solitary confinement for seventeen months. He retired from active duty as a colonel in 1970.

Bailey is a graduate of the U.S. Army Command and General Staff College, the U.S. Army Aviation Safety School at the University of Southern California, and the U.S. Army Attaché Course.

His military awards and decorations include the Bronze Star Medal with one Oak Leaf Cluster, Air Medal with six Oak Leaf Clusters, Ex-Prisoner of War Medal, Purple Heart Medal, World

War II Victory Medal, United Nations Service Medal, Korean Service Medal, American Campaign Medal, Joint Services Commendation Medal, and Asiatic Pacific Theater Ribbon.

Bailey is a member of numerous veterans' and civic organizations and has served on the Cobb County Jury Commission, the Cobb County Board of Elections and Voter Registration, and the Cobb County Clean Commission. He has three children. He and his wife, Jean, live in Atlanta.

RON MARTZ writes on military affairs and national security issues for the *Atlanta Journal-Constitution*. A veteran of the U.S. Marine Corps (1965–68), he is a 1979 graduate in mass communications from the University of South Florida. He is the coauthor with Jack Terrell of *Disposable Patriot: Revelations of a Soldier in America's Secret Wars,* and with Col. Ben Malcom of *White Tigers: My Secret War in Korea.*

A native of Elizabethtown, Pennsylvania, he now lives in Roswell, Georgia, with his wife, Cindy, and their three children.